A CENTENNIAL BOOK

One hundred books
published between 1990 and 1995
bear this special imprint of
the University of California Press.
We have chosen each Centennial Book
as an example of the Press's finest
publishing and bookmaking traditions
as we celebrate the beginning of
our second century.

UNIVERSITY OF CALIFORNIA PRESS

Founded in 1893

ST. TERESA
OF AVILA

ST. TERESA OF AVILA

AUTHOR OF A HEROIC LIFE

CAROLE SLADE

UNIVERSITY OF CALIFORNIA PRESS

BERKELEY / LOS ANGELES / LONDON

Permission to reprint portions of chapters 2 and 7 granted
by the University of Notre Dame, Notre Dame, Indiana,
and *Religion and Literature.*

University of California Press
Berkeley and Los Angeles, California

University of California Press
London, England

Copyright © 1995 by Carole Slade

Library of Congress Cataloging-in-Publication Data

Slade, Carole.
    St. Teresa of Avila: author of a heroic life / Carole Slade.
       p.   cm.
    Includes bibliographical references and index.
    ISBN 0-520-08802-6 (alk. paper)
    1. Teresa, of Avila, Saint, 1515–1582. Libro de la vida.
    2. Christian women saints—Biography—History and criti-
cism.   I. Title. II. Title: Saint Teresa of Avila.
BX4700.T4S63   1995
282'.092—dc20   94-28476
[B]   CIP

Printed in the United States of America

1 2 3 4 5 6 7 8 9

The paper used in this publication meets the minimum re-
quirements of American National Standard for Information
Sciences—Permanence of Paper for Printed Library Materials,
ANSI Z39.48–1984 ∞

In memory of
my mother and my father

Others were women, and they have done heroic things for love of You.

St. Teresa of Avila, *Book of Her Life*

CONTENTS

PREFACE

This book began with my realization that I had no good answer to the most basic question a reader of autobiographical narrative brings to a text, why the writer chooses to say what she says. Why, for example, would Teresa have begun her *Life* with this sentence: "To have had virtuous and God-fearing parents along with the graces the Lord granted me should have been enough for me to have led a good life, if I had not been so wretched [*El tener padres virtuosos y temerosos de Dios me bastara, si yo no fuera tan ruin, con lo que el Señor me favoreciá para ser buena*]"? If the sentence were intended as a formulaic assertion of exaggerated sinfulness, why would she have used a weak epithet such as *ruin*, which refers generally to the fallen condition of humanity, rather than actually naming herself a sinner? If Teresa meant to recommend her parents' extraordinary piety, why the suggestion that it did not suffice for her? The original Spanish resists interpretation even more strenuously than the translations. The sentence virtually writhes away from self-accusation: the two most important segments of the sentence, the first and last, contain the positive information, her parents' virtue and her own potential for goodness, leaving the negative turn to the middle. While such imprecision was long attributed to carelessness or ignorance, recent criticism shows that Teresa was a deliberate writer and a skillful rhetorician. Some background reading in Inquisition studies gave me the embryo of an explanation of her motives. Inquisitional interrogations, I learned, required an autobiographical narrative designed to elicit information about genealogy and parental instruction in Christian worship. This genre, judicial confession, shared linguistic features with several other first-person genres, including penitential confession and spiritual testimony. In short, I realized that I had been trying to read Teresa's texts in the wrong genre.

Defining Teresa's writings as a project of self-interpretation provoked largely by actual and imagined accusations of heresy, I demonstrate that she transformed judicial confession, a genre that presumed the guilt of the narrator, into a vehicle for self-defense. I bring to Teresa's texts the methods of literary criticism, specifically, close reading informed by theory of autobiography, feminist theory, scriptural hermeneutics, hagiography, and Inquisition studies. Rather than concentrating on whether the events Teresa narrates actually happened, information that the hagiographical approach to her life has rendered largely unrecoverable, I concentrate on the interpretation of self that emerges in her account of them. Whatever the actuality of her life, we know it, particularly the years of adolescence and early adulthood, principally through her representation of it in writing. During her lifetime Teresa's writings helped to generate ecclesiastical authorization for the life she projected, and since her death they have been the foundation of her reputation: in these senses she was author of her life of heroic sainthood.

In chapter 1, I describe the horizon of expectations her contemporary readers brought to the work now known as the *Life*. Using manuals for Inquisitors and Inquisitional readings of the *Life*, I reconstruct the characteristics of judicial confession, the principal genre in which she was ordered to write, and I consider the dangers it held for her. She avoided writing judicial confession, I argue, by shifting the generic resonance of the words she used and by introducing the self-interpretative aspect of Christian autobiography in the Augustinian tradition. To illustrate Teresa's use of that genre, I introduce the comparative reference to Augustine that continues throughout my book. Teresa relates that she read the *Confessions* and that Augustine's story moved her deeply. At the same time, her adaptations of his concepts indicate that she found them inapplicable to her own experience, to female experience in general.

As a prelude to bringing Teresa's figural reading of her life into relief, I devote chapter 2 to defining her concept of Scripture and her feminist hermeneutic for reading it. Like Augustine, Teresa interprets Scripture typologically, but the disparity between their interpretations of the Exodus, the most important scriptural figure of Christian redemption, demonstrates Teresa's differing assumptions about the fulfillment of divine prophecy in human life. For Teresa, the event of the Exodus, while it gives her spiritual salvation, has not liberated her from temporal bondage, which she identifies as the Church's constriction of her active role in Christian history. Teresa's interpretation of the Song of Songs argues that the Church denies women historical experience, limiting them to spiritual experience alone, and in her construction of the figure of Mary Magdalene, Teresa shows that a woman requires direct communication with God, or mystical experience, for complete fulfillment of the Exodus. Her treatment of the Exodus thus shares with the Judaic concept of Scripture an emphasis on the incompletion, hence the continuing relevance, of Old Testament prophecy.

In chapters 3, 4, and 5, I divide the life Teresa narrates into three phases: the old life, narrated in chapters 1 through 10 of the *Life*; the mystical experience, in chapters 11 through 22 of the *Life* and the *Interior Castle*; the new life, in chapters 32 through 36 of the *Life* and the *Foundations*. (Because the *Road to Perfection* is the least autobiographical work, I do not devote a separate discussion to it. Neither do I consider the letters, where she frames some of her most intimate thoughts in code to thwart Inquisitional interception, as these comprise a different project of self-representation, private rather than public.) Teresa's thinking developed and her experience multiplied over time, of course, so that the later works do not simply repeat but rather amplify the previously related material. The full progression of her life can be sketched as follows: the old life; conversion; a new life of conviction and dedication frustrated by the obstacles to her activity; the last two stages of this first cycle repeated on a higher plane as mystical experience and a new life as a religious reformer. Because she often associates her conversion with her mystical experience and because she considers her first foundation of a convent in Avila a precursor of her later campaign for monastic reform throughout Spain, the pattern she imposes on her life remains essentially tripartite.

Developing my contention that Teresa exploited the nuances

of genre to create a textual "I" independent of the "I" of judicial confession, I analyze the texts with an emphasis on the genres she evokes in them. To explain Teresa's principle of selection in chapters 1 through 10 of the *Life,* I devote chapter 3 to showing that she juxtaposes a response to the standard Inquisitional questionnaire with first-person hagiography. Rejecting the generic designation of allegory for her descriptions of mystical experience in the *Life* and the *Interior Castle,* I treat them in chapter 4 as treatises on mystical theology in the form of anatomies of her own soul. Teresa employs the Augustinian vocabulary of memory, intellect, and will for the faculties, or functions, of the soul, but rather than applying them to Augustine's purpose of knowing God, she adapts them to self-interpretation. While considering the *Foundations* principally as memoir, I show in chapter 5 that Teresa represents herself in heroic terms by evoking the genre of New World chronicle. And in making the *Foundations* an unlettered version of a book of the city of ladies, an allegory of female authority, she represents herself as a writer. The mutual contestation of these genres in the arena of gender illustrates the contradictions in Teresa's life project of valorizing women within a patriarchal society. In chapter 6, I describe the defining role that Teresa's books played in the proceedings for her canonization, and in chapter 7, I use some psychoanalytic interpretations of Teresa's mystical experience—those of Jacques Lacan, Julia Kristeva, and Luce Irigaray—to raise questions about the nature of that experience.

The notes do not fully convey my indebtedness to several recent books. Alison Weber's *Teresa of Avila and the Rhetoric of Femininity* effectively establishes the centrality of gender issues to Teresa's thought and the ambiguity of her prose, relieving subsequent critics of making those arguments. Victoria Lincoln's *Teresa, A Woman,* though very problematic, also makes a contribution to Teresian studies. Taking a subjective, novelistic approach to her biography of Teresa, Lincoln makes many extravagant claims and, unfortunately, leaves them undocumented. Still, her book provides detail not elsewhere available in English, and when I have been able to discern her source, I have sometimes seen a possible basis for her conclusions. To avoid the risk of circulating misinformation, however, I generally refrain from repeating them here. Two historical studies, Jodi Bilinkoff's *The Avila of St. Teresa* and Mary Elizabeth Perry's *Gender and Disorder in Early Modern Seville,* demonstrate the importance of the sociocultural context for deciphering Teresa's texts. Víctor García de la Concha's *El arte literario de Santa Teresa* provides valuable technical information about the grammar, rhetoric, and aesthetics of Teresa's prose and poetry. All these studies confirm the necessity for skeptical reading of Teresa's texts: often she does not mean what she seems to be saying.

For important financial support of my research, I thank the Columbia University Council in the Humanities and the American Philosophical Association. I also wish to thank librarians in the Columbia University Libraries, the Biblioteca Nacional in Madrid, the Hispanic Society of America, and the New York Public Library for their generous assistance.

I have accumulated many debts of gratitude in writing this book, and I am happy to acknowledge them. Joseph A. Mazzeo, whose work on hermeneutics and allegory influences the method of my study, shared his profound knowledge of Christianity with me. Howard T. Young, in whose Pomona College classroom I first read Teresa, gave me many leads to sources in Spanish. Many colleagues at Columbia University assisted my work in various ways, including their own scholarly work in fields adjacent to mine: Kathy Eden, Joan Ferrante, Wayne Proudfoot, Edward Tayler, Priscilla Wald, and the late Ward Dennis. Deborah Palmer, a graduate student in English literature there, proofread the manuscript and page proofs. Readers for the University of California Press, Catherine Connor of the University of Wisconsin at Madison and Thomas C. Werge of the University of Notre Dame, generously gave expert and wise comments. If I have made errors despite their help, I must claim them as my own. For emotional and intellectual sustenance, I am deeply grateful to Laura Brown, Marsha and Herman Cummins, Michiyo Ishii, Warren Johnson, Ann Van Sant, Carmen Virgili, and especially my husband, George Harlow.

NOTE ON EDITIONS,
TRANSLATIONS, ABBREVIATIONS,
TERMINOLOGY

For the Spanish version of Teresa's works I rely on the edition by Efrén de la Madre de Dios and Otger Steggink, *Santa Teresa de Jesús: Obras completas* (Madrid: Biblioteca de Autores Cristianos, 1986). This edition preserves many of the idiosyncrasies and inconsistencies of Teresa's style; readers of modern Spanish should find the language recognizable, however.

I use the English translation by Kieran Kavanaugh and Otilio Rodríguez, *The Collected Works of St. Teresa of Avila*, 3 vols. (Washington, D.C.: Institute of Carmelite Studies, 1976–1985). Very occasionally and where noted, I supplement that translation with my own or with E. Allison Peers's version: *The Complete Works of Teresa of Avila*, 3 vols. (London: Sheed and Ward, 1944–1946). Unless otherwise identified, all translations of secondary literature are mine.

I include the Spanish original in endnotes for most quotations of more than a sentence and of shorter passages essential to my argument. A disparity between the numbering of chapter or paragraph in the English translation and the Spanish version indicates that the respective editors have paragraphed the text differently.

For the *Road to Perfection*, Kavanaugh and Rodríguez combine two manuscripts, the so-called Valladolid and the Escorial, while Efrén and Steggink print them separately; thus English translations of the *Road* refer to Kavanaugh's composite version while Spanish passages are identified by manuscript.

For passages from Scripture I quote the *New English Bible, with the Apocrypha*, edited by Samuel Sandmel (New York: Oxford University Press, 1976), except for the Song of Songs, where I use the translation by Marvin H. Pope in *Song of Songs: A New Translation with Introduction and Commentary*, Anchor Bible (London: Sheed and Ward, 1946). For Augustine's *Confessions* I use the translation by R. S. Pine-Coffin (Harmondsworth, England: Penguin, 1961).

I preserve the Spanish original for names of most persons and places, with the exception of those that have an established English version: Ferdinand and Isabella, Philip II, John of the Cross, Seville, Castile. Otherwise I have not Anglicized names, preferring Luis de León to the nearly unrecognizable Anglicized version, Louis of León, for example. Religious names, such as Ana de Jesús are shortened in subsequent reference and alphabetized by the first name, Ana in this case, or Efrén for Efrén de la Madre de Dios. Family names, such as Alonso de la Fuente, are shortened to the last name, in this case Fuente, and alphabetized by it. Teresa refused to use her family name, Teresa de Ahumada y Cepeda, insistently preferring her religious name, Teresa de Jesús, which I shorten to Teresa. Because her name acquired the description "of Avila" only at canonization, I refer to her either as St. Teresa of Avila or as Teresa (de Jesús).

Abbreviations Used in Text and Notes

BAC   Biblioteca de Autores Cristianos

CSIC   Consejo Superior de Investigaciones Científicas

CIT   Teófanes Egido Martínez, Víctor García de la Concha, and Olegario González de Cardenal, eds., *Congreso internacional teresiano, 4–7 octubre 1982,* 2 vols. (Salamanca: Universidad de Salamanca, 1983).

Conf.   Augustine, *Confessions*

ICS   Institute of Carmelite Studies

STLMH   Manuel Criado de Val, ed., *Santa Teresa y la literatura mística hispánica,* Actas del I congreso internacional sobre Santa Teresa y la mística hispánica (Madrid: EDI, 1984).

TVST   Efrén de la Madre de Dios and Otger Steggink, *Tiempo y vida de Santa Teresa*, 2d ed. (Madrid: BAC, 1977).

Numbering for Works in Parenthetical Documentation

Life 22.1   *Book of Her Life*, chapter 22, section 1

Road 3.1   *Road to Perfection*, chapter 3, section 1

Meditations 4.1   *Meditations on the Song of Songs*, chapter 4, section 1

Castle 4.1.2   *Interior Castle*, fourth dwelling place, chapter 1, section 2

Foundations 3.1   *Book of Her Foundations*, chapter 3, section 1

Testimony 2.1   second *Spiritual Testimony*, section 1

Soliloquy 4.1   fourth *Soliloquy*, section 1

Confessions 8.2   Augustine of Hippo, *Confessions*, book 8, chapter 2

Constitutions 8   item no. 8

Poetry 3.14–17   poem no. 3 (Kavanaugh translation), lines 14–17

CHRONOLOGY

INTRODUCTION

In 1576, at the age of sixty-one, Teresa posed for Juan de la Miseria, a young Italian painter who had been commissioned to make portraits of the nuns for the recently founded Barefoot Carmelite convent in Seville. Jerónimo Gracián, one of Teresa's protégés and closest associates, relates that on seeing the finished portrait Teresa complained that Juan had made her "old and bleary eyed."[1] It is not known whether Teresa found the likeness too faithful, considering that up to about this time she was often remarked to look much younger than she was, or not faithful enough, given that Juan was not especially gifted. Either way she would have been concerned. Teresa had an acute appreciation of the power of one's image to affect the reception of words and actions, as she explains in the *Foundations*: "We are in a world in which it is necessary to consider the opinions others have of us in order that our words take effect" (8.7). She had already portrayed herself as she wished to be regarded by her contemporaries and remembered by posterity, not with pigment but with words. Taken together her writings comprise an elaborate project of self-representation and self-interpretation.

Rather than representing themselves, women in Renaissance Europe were most often represented by men. Representation, whether narrative or pictorial, is a technology of gender, as Teresa de Lauretis demonstrates in the instance of cinema. Representation thus serves to define the relative value of male and female, or gender relationship. He who represents, then, controls the social construction of gender, which reciprocally derives from and translates into political and economic relationships. Individuals construct their own gender principally by absorbing societal representations. While some critics consider that in patriarchal society woman's attempt at self-representation can only reproduce her subjugation, de Lauretis allows for a reciprocal process of societal and individual gender definition: "the subjective representation of gender—or self-representation—affects its social construction." Making this assertion, de Lauretis continues, "leaves open a possibility of agency and self-determination at the subjective and even individual level of micropolitical and everyday practices."[2] An attribution of such power to feminine self-representation explains the lengths to which the Spanish Church and state went to deny Teresa's authorship of her own life. Juan added a dove to the upper left-hand corner of his portrait of Teresa, and after her death others painted in a banner inscribed with the words, in Latin, "Eternally I will sing God's mercies." The dove and banner became standard elements in the iconography of Teresa because, the brief for her canonization declares, with circular causality, the fact that "she has been and shall be painted with a dove over her head" signifies that the doctrine in her books was "not acquired or taught by human industry but infused by God."[3] With very few exceptions, then, women did not represent their own lives textually before the twentieth century.

Teresa of Avila's *Book of Her Life* seems to loom as the only peak in the relatively featureless landscape of women's self-representation in the form of autobiography. (The term "autobiography," although anachronistic for texts written before the nineteenth century, serves well as a general description of a first-person discursive representation of a particular life.) Several founders of the study of autobiography see the *Life* as one of the few works by women that evince the sense of an individualized self, which influential critics such as Georges Gusdorf identify as a prerequisite for writing autobiography. Karl Joachim Weintraub, for example, includes Teresa as one of only two women in his history of the assertion of individuality from Augustine to Goethe, *The Value of the Individual*. Yet Weintraub does not succeed in locating any expression of individuality in Teresa's *Life*. While claiming that she "test[ed] her experience against the established norms of an old tradition," he concludes that "her self-conception stayed within the tradition of the model [Christian] life."[4] What Weintraub leaves as a contradiction actually implies the paradox that while following a Christian model, Teresa reveals something of a private, unique self. The reasons for this illustrate Michel Foucault's idea that by forcing interiorized surveillance, modern innovations in methods of punishment created a new subjectivity.[5]

What is known of Teresa's confrontations with the Inquisition indicates that all of her writings, in particular the *Life* but to some extent the other works as well, are Inquisitional documents. As Antonio Márquez puts it in *Literature and Inquisition in Spain*, "The works of St. Teresa cannot be explained genetically without the action of the Inquisition."[6] Writing with officers of the Inquisition as her most significant audience, Teresa faced a double bind:[7] she could not stray outside the lines of a standard female script of subservience and subordination, yet in limiting her capacity to explain her experience, this script placed her in danger. Essentially a medieval rather than a modern autobiographer in the sense that she viewed her life as conforming to a universal pattern rather than developing in a unique design, Teresa replaced the model by subtly transmuting the female script of nun to another Christian script, that of apostle. In the interstices of these standard plots, Teresa shows something of her face.

The rules according to which Teresa wrote both demanded and precluded absolute autobiographical truth. Manuals for Inquisitors describe the genre in which she was commanded to write as judicial confession; ignoring the inevitable distance between the subject in life and the subject in language, they specify its principal generic requirement as the literal transcription of a life into language, or in linguistic terms, the unmediated referentiality of signifier to signified. The last thing Teresa wanted was to represent her life literally, even to the extent that language does allow. Too many facts of her life, even though known to most of her readers, had to remain unspoken and unwritten, in particular Jewish heritage on her paternal side, which had it been stated would have excluded her from any religious order, to mention only the penalty that now seems most inconceivable. And Teresa's unusual spiritual experiences, including visions similar to those that had condemned other women to burn at the stake for heresy, required not straightforward presentation but carefully crafted proof that their origin was divine rather than demoniacal. To conduct her self-defense while appearing to meet the Inquisitional demand for literal representation, Teresa extended the inevitable gap between her "I" in life and the "I" in her text into a chasm.

Teresa's principal tool for creating an innocent textual self was the manipulation of genre. In Mikhail M. Bakhtin's terminology, she uses dialogized heteroglossia to exploit the different valences a single word has when used in different genres. Teresa mingles the mandated "I" of judicial confession with the "I" of many other first-person genres circulating in the culture, most important of them for her project of self-interpretation, Christian spiritual autobiography, or conversion narrative in the tradition of Augustine's *Confessions*. Because by definition conversion divides the self into an old and a new, the old self that sinned and the new self that from the vantage point gained in the gyration of conversion understands the sinfulness of the previous life, Christian autobiography foregrounds the distinction between the "I" of the narrator and the "I" of the protagonist. In addition to disguising her exaggeration of the ficticity of the textual self, Teresa's displacement of the "I" of judicial confession into the "I" of conversion narrative or Christian autobiography permitted her to introduce its aspect of self-interpretation. In the *Confessions*, Augustine interprets his life with the tools of scriptural typology, a theory of the systematic analogy between historical events. While this typological method constitutes Augustine's theology and epistemology, typological self-representation persisted in the genre apart from his original purpose. Teresa puts her self-interpretation to polemical use, in the early works principally to self-defense and later to something like self-promotion.

Typological self-interpretation necessarily rests on scriptural exegesis. Forbidden to interpret Scripture and eventually even to read a Bible, Teresa joined the long line of women working without knowledge of each other who nevertheless created a tradition of feminine scriptural interpretation. In Gerda Lerner's words, "Each woman reason[ed] out, as best she could, alternative interpretations to the patriarchal interpretations she had been taught."[8] Teresa adopted several of the "predictable patterns" of alternative interpretation that Lerner discovers: juxtaposition of contradictory passages, redefinition of the central texts and figures, appeals to common sense, and divine revelation. To create the figure of Mary Magdalene, with whom she identifies typologically, Teresa combines several New Testament women, including Mary of Bethany and her sister Martha, the Samaritan woman, and the Canaanite woman, who have in common their encounters with the incarnate Christ. And like many other female interpreters of Scripture, Teresa rejects the standard identification of woman with sin: she never even mentions Eve. Although in both popular and learned opinion Mary Magdalene was a repentant prostitute, Teresa's interpretation of her life rejects her sexual sin, giving alternative explanations of the Pharisees' criticism and of her conversion. Taking an aspect of the life of Mary Magdalene from the Gospel of John, Teresa defines her as an apostle.

If Teresa, rejecting the patriarchal design, nevertheless describes her life as conforming to a pattern, what of herself can she be said to have revealed? Assuming, as Elizabeth Bruss does, that the relationship with the audience reveals something of the personality of the writer,[9] I surmise that she was charismatic, manipulative, eloquent, and very funny. I say funny rather than witty because I see her humor deriving not so much from wordplay as from a lively appreciation of the ludicrous contradictions in everyday life, particularly the arbitrary conventions for assigning societal status. Her inductive construction of the basic principles of the sciences of her time, such as crystal structure and circulation of atmospheric moisture, suggests an extraordinary intelligence. In the insecurity that continuously verges into paranoia, she evinces a Nietzschean *ressentiment*, which Angela Selke considers typical of even the completely assimilated *converso*, the label used for Jews converted to Christianity and their descendants.[10] And in her frequent tone of anguish, I sense a great deal of perplexity over the operations of her soul, particularly a weak memory, inability to control her mental activity, and unidentifiable desires and griefs. In the narratives of her subsequent life of action, I find an energetic, effective administrator, with special gifts for diplomacy and timing. While she expresses some awareness of exercising these particular talents, she also suggests her discomfort with individual qualities. Teresa's identification with Mary Magdalene probably served more than rhetorical and polemical purposes: she seems literally to have considered herself Mary Magdalene's successor. In one of several locutions on the subject, God told her that His substitution of her for Mary Magdalene required her to perform great works.

> On the feast of St. Mary Magdalene while I was reflecting on the friendship with our Lord I'm obliged to maintain and also on the words He spoke to me about this saint, and having insistent desires to imitate her, the Lord granted me a great favor and told me that from now on I should try hard, that I was going to have to serve Him more than I did up to this point. (*Spiritual Testimony* 37)

Even when the rhetorical element in Teresa's transcription of such locutions is discounted, she can be seen to desire an imposed identity.

In treating Teresa principally as a writer, I give her a role she would not have wanted for herself. It is easy for a literary critic to exaggerate the importance of writing as a means of expression, but Teresa considered words inferior to deeds: "I'm not good for anything but talk, and so You don't desire, my God, to put me to work; everything adds up to just words and desires about how much I must serve" (*Life* 21.5). Florence Nightingale states this same preference with similar force: "I had so much rather live than write—writing is only a substitute for living. . . . I think one's feelings waste themselves in words, they ought all to be distilled into actions, and into actions which bring results."[11] Yet it is Teresa's texts that remain for analysis (along with her legacy to the Carmelite order and the Roman Catholic church), and at this moment when feminist scholarship is reconstructing women's history, they provide an important early account of the entire course of a woman's life, one that includes an appraisal of the ways it differed disadvantageously from a man's life.

Teresa's writings also provide a means of evaluating the role of religion in women's lives. In their focus on doctrinal misogyny, many feminist critics have dismissed religion altogether as a source of autonomy for women. Lerner writes of learning the significance of religion as a result of research for *The Rise of Patriarchy*, the first volume of her recent *The Creation of Feminist Consciousness*: "The insight that religion was the primary arena on which women fought for hundreds of years for feminist consciousness was not one I had previously had."[12] The emphasis Christianity places on individual history as a divine instrument of salvation gave Teresa particularly convincing grounds for protesting the constraints on women's lives in the world. Teresa argues that the Church artificially truncates her own history in the world, confining her to spiritual history alone. Teresa's conviction, essentially feminist but based almost entirely on religious grounds, that the standard female life script did not coincide with the Christian life forced her to a self-consciousness that while grounded in medieval concepts, sometimes startles with its modernity.

1

THE GENRES OF
THE *BOOK OF HER LIFE*

In the *Book of Her Life,* Teresa repeatedly asserts that she writes not of her own will but at the command of her confessors. She does not explain, however, not in any consistent or plausible way at least, the reason these confessors commanded her to write. Evidence in the *Life* and in the Inquisition's records on Teresa indicates that in addition to the various motives she does attribute to her confessors, such as their need to base pastoral guidance in thorough knowledge of her spiritual life and their wish to chronicle the founding of her reformed Carmelite order, the suspicion of unorthodox beliefs and practices, even of heresy, also prompted her commands to write. In the words of Enrique Llamas Martínez, the historian who first presented the record of Teresa's numerous encounters with the Inquisition, "The book of the *Life* of Mother Teresa was born under the Inquisitorial sign." This origin, he continues, "gives us the guide to determining its true structure, in its accurate dimension, and its architectural lines."[1] The potential charge of heresy affects nearly all the authorial choices Teresa made in the *Life,* most important among them for understanding her mode of self-interpretation, the genre.

The *Directorium Inquisitorum,* the most authoritative manual for Inquisitors during the fifteenth and sixteenth centuries, traces heresy etymologically to the verb *to elect* (*eligo*); the heretic, then, is one who "refuses the true doctrine and chooses as true a false and perverse doctrine."[2] This definition, implying deliberate choice of an erroneous doctrine, applied to male heretics only, however: women were not considered to possess the faculty of reason. While the heretical man was considered to have chosen his belief, the heretical woman was thought to be deluded by the devil. Defining possession by the devil in terms of sexual intercourse, medieval theologians held that the inordinate sexual appetite attributed to women made them particularly susceptible to heresy.[3] In Teresa's case, these theories translated into a fear that feminine irrationality might have caused her to ascribe her spiritual experience to God when actually it came from the devil and that thus her teachings on mental prayer and her plans for new Carmelite convents under reformed rule were diabolically instigated.

With its delineation of the consequences of heresy, the *Directorium* associates heresy with dissidence, social and political as well as religious, and with civil, political, and economic disorder.[4] The implied link between heresy and national weakness generated particularly intense fear in Spain, which had spent nearly eight centuries pushing Moorish invaders south from the Pyrenees before defeating them at Granada in 1492. In the belief that heresy threatened not only the authority of the Church but also the integrity of the state, Ferdinand of Aragón and Isabella of Castile, whose marriage in 1469 led to reunification of Spain, founded the modern Inquisition as a branch of state government in 1480.[5] While the Catholic kings intended the Inquisition principally as a mechanism for converting Jews and Moriscos, their grandson, Philip II, who inherited the throne in 1555, defined its mission as eliminating all heresy, which he blamed for the rebellions against Spanish imperial rule in the Netherlands and elsewhere. Determining that he must step up the punishment of heresy, he ordered increasingly spectacular public trials (known as *autos-de-fé* from the Portuguese *autos-da-fé*, meaning acts of faith) for increasingly slight offenses.[6] Even the suspicion that Teresa might be a heretic, then, aroused enormous alarm among her confessors, who would themselves feel the force of both Church and state if they mistakenly encouraged her, and it represented mortal danger for her.

That the Inquisitional origin of her commands to write the *Life* has only recently been remarked can be attributed in part to the dexterity with which Teresa directed attention away from the issue of heresy while satisfying her confessors' demands for a text they could use to measure the orthodoxy of her religious experience and practice. In so doing, she created an eclectic work that defies easy identification with respect to genre. The *Life* passed her confessors' scrutiny, but a few sixteenth-century readers did understand that her confessors probably did not have a work like the *Book of Her Life* in mind when they ordered her to write. In denouncing the *Life* for heresy in 1589, the year following its posthumous publication, one Inquisitor, Alonso de la Fuente, charges Teresa with exceeding the scope of her confessors' commands: "The author of this book writes a long history of her life, conversation, virtues, using the very slight pretext that she was ordered to do so by her confessors."[7] Fuente, an extremely acute if unsympathetic reader of Teresa, correctly perceives that Teresa manipulated her confessors' commands in the matter of genre.[8]

Twentieth-century critics have given numerous generic definitions of the *Life*, many of them subgenres of autobiography. E. Allison Peers established the trend of postwar Anglo-American criticism by defining the *Life* as a spiritual autobiography defined generally as an account of religious experience: "For the profundity and detail of its psychological analysis and for the sublimity of the spiritual mysteries which it unfolds, it is worthy of a place beside the *Confessions* of St. Augustine."[9] Américo Castro considers the *Life* an autobiography more nearly secular than religious. Distinguishing the *Life* from Augustine's *Confessions* and from the letters of Abelard and Heloise, Castro defines it as a biography as well as an autobiography, and he names the *Life* a precursor of Cervantes's *Don Quijote* and of the novel in general.[10]

Many critics writing in the past two decades have jettisoned the designation of autobiography for the *Life*, taking some version of the position that Ricardo Senabre states very strikingly: "The original thing about the *Book of Her Life* is that it is not the book of the life of St. Teresa."[11] These critics can be divided into those who have given the Inquisition a determining role with respect to genre and those who have not. Those in the latter group have related the *Life* to works in a number of other genres popular in sixteenth-century Spain. Emphasizing the exemplarity of the *Life*, Senabre labels it a treatise on humility in the tradition of Luis de Granada's collection of sermons, *Guía de pecadores;* Fernando Lázaro Carreter considers the *Life* a manual of spirituality with links to genres of penitential confession, the picaresque novel, self-portraiture, and Augustinian confession; Antonio Carreño likens the *Life* to the Renaissance personal letter and the picaresque novel.[12] Most of those who have considered the Inquisition a compositional constraint on the *Life* define it as one variety or another of self-defense: Francisco Márquez Villanueva identifies the *Life* as a spiritual *apologia pro vita sua*; Alison Weber discusses the *Life* as "a psychological as well as a theological *apologia*," a personal self-defense and a defense of women; Sol Villacèque defines the *Life* as a "chronicle of the fundamental antagonism between grace and sin, God and the Devil," made in the form of a confession to Church and Inquisition.[13]

These generic descriptions of the *Life* do not necessarily have to be considered mutually exclusive or contradictory, however. The *Life* can fruitfully be considered within many of the traditions these critics have named, both the religious—spiritual autobiography, confession, devotional manual, mystical treatise—and the secular—novel, biography, letter. Teresa drew on a range of the existing first-person genres, creating a discourse that can be described as dialogized heteroglossia, a Bakhtinian term for a discourse that puts the voices of more than one order of thought into dialogue.[14] Teresa gives these voices expression, not with characters as the novelist does but with an interplay of genres. In addition to wielding the rhetorical weapons that have been ably explored by Concha and Weber, Teresa orchestrates the intonations of several genres as a means of defending herself against charges of heresy.

Bakhtin's work on language, which he defines as responsive to other linguistic acts or dialogical rather than as referential to objects, serves well for explaining Teresa's approach to genre. For Bakhtin, the life of every word develops through its transfer "from one mouth to another, from one context to another context," and it carries the history of all these exchanges. Thus, Bakhtin considers that "when a member of the speaking collective comes upon a word, it is not as a neutral word of language, not as a word free from the aspirations and evaluations of others, uninhabited by others' voices."[15] Similarly, each genre, which Bakhtin defines as a "stratification of language" or a "sphere in which language is used" and without which it cannot be used, carries with it an ideology or belief system developed through its entire history. "Even the archaic elements preserved in a genre are not dead but eternally alive; . . . A genre lives in the present, but always *remembers* its past, its beginning."[16] As a result, the same word, when used in a different genre, or accentual system, has a different meaning, and every word carries semantic pulls from the genres in which it has been used, as does also every syntactic structure and thematic content.[17] For this reason, any totalitarian institution, whether in his own Stalinist Russia or in Spain of the Inquisition, that attempts to dictate the meaning of words or genres must inevitably fail. By calling on the multiple intonations of the words she uses, then, Teresa undermines the Inquisition's hegemonic claim to them.[18]

Teresa's confessors, concerned that her unusual spiritual experience and her convictions concerning prayer might be diabolical in origin, commanded her to write a work that can be defined as a judicial confession. Judicial confession per se was by the sixteenth century a highly conventionalized sphere of written language. The formal judicial confession was written to or taken down by an officer of the Inquisition in the hearings, which according to Jean Pierre Dedieu, "always included (at least after 1565) a questionnaire on the suspect's identity, followed by a recitation of his genealogy (*genealogía*), an autobiography (*discurso de su vida*) and an interrogation of the accused on Christian doctrine (*doctrina cristiana*)."[19] Almost anything an accused had ever written (or said) could serve as a judicial confession, however. In connection with administering the sacrament of penance or with pastoral counseling, priests sometimes requested confessions in writing. These ecclesiastical confessions might take the form of a penitential confession (*confesión general*), a confession of sin or of faith put in writing for the purpose of recalling previous events with sorrow sufficient to merit forgiveness, and a spiritual testimony (*relación espiritual* or *cuenta de conciencia*), an account of spiritual experience. Once in writing, the penitential confession and the spiritual testimony frequently served as a prelude or as an adjunct to formal judicial confession.[20]

Writing in the genre of judicial confession, whether formal or informal, held the certainty of self-incrimination. Manuals of Inquisitional procedure define that genre as a sphere of language in which the writer inevitably condemns himself or herself. The *Repertorium*, a dictionary of Inquisitional concepts first published in Valencia in 1494, directs that although the penitential or pastoral confession and the judicial confession might in practice coincide in every respect, the audience must take different stances toward them.

> In the penitential forum, the penitent should always be believed, whether he speaks for himself or against himself, whether he affirms or denies, especially if he swears to what he confesses. In the judicial forum it is completely otherwise: here, the witness is believed only if he speaks against himself, never if he speaks on his own behalf.[21]

In Bakhtin's terminology, the genre of judicial confession gave to the words used in it an "accent" or self-condemnation. Once employed in the "accentual system" of "stratification" of judicial confession, no word could exonerate the writer. To have the possibility of clearing herself of the suspicion of heresy while appearing to obey her commands, Teresa gives the words she uses the accents of several other genres.

To counter the response mandated for a reader of judicial confession, Teresa draws from the several first-person genres that also have a semantic pull on the words she uses. The prologue to the *Life* illustrates Teresa's use of dialogized heteroglossia particularly well, as she substitutes words with the inflection of the various first-person genres in which she would have a chance of defending herself for those of a genre in which she could only confirm her guilt. With her opening complaint that she has not been permitted to narrate her sins, she immediately places the genre of penitential confession in competition with judicial confession.

> Since my confessors commanded me and gave me plenty of leeway to write about the favors and the kind of prayer the Lord has granted me, I wish they would also have allowed me to tell very clearly and minutely about my great sins and wretched life. This would be a consolation. But they didn't want me to. In fact I was very much restricted [tied down] in those matters. (*Life*, prologue 1)[22]

Teresa's assertion here that she has been given "plenty of leeway," if only with regard to her spiritual favors and methods of prayer, and her subsequent depiction of herself as restricted, for which she uses an image of physical constraint not fully communicated in the English translation, contradict one another, not alone in substance but in significance for identifying the genre of the *Life*. In giving an account of "great sins and wretched life" in penitential confession, the confessant was encouraged to search through the events of his or her own life and to probe thoughts and feelings for evidence of sin. If confessors used a schema, such as the seven deadly sins or the Ten Commandments, it served more as a heuristic device than as a questionnaire.[23] In judicial confession, however, the confessor controlled the subject matter with a standard list of questions and, failing voluntary confession, with a rigorous and deliberately devious interrogation designed to elicit specific information or with physical torture. By opposing the relative freedom of penitential confession to the rigid requirements of judicial confession, then, Teresa suggests the possibility of reading the text of the *Life* in a genre other than judicial confession.[24]

In the remainder of the prologue, Teresa sounds the notes of several different genres, with judicial confession the faintest of them, in such a way as to reduce considerably the possibility that her readers will hear it alone, or even hear it at all.

> And so I ask, for the love of God, whoever reads this account to bear in mind that my life has been so wretched that I have not found a saint among those who were converted to God in whom I can find comfort. For I note that after the Lord called them, they did not turn back and offend Him. As for me, not only did I turn back and become worse, but it seems I made a study out of resisting the favors His Majesty was granting me. I was like someone who sees that she is obliged to serve more, yet understands that she can't pay the smallest part of her debt.
>
> May God be blessed forever, He who waited for me so long! I beseech Him with all my heart to give me the grace to present with complete clarity and truthfulness this account of my life which my confessors ordered me to write. And I know, too, that even the Lord has for some time wanted me to do this, although I have not dared. May this account render Him glory and praise. And from now on may my confessors knowing me better through this narration help me in my weakness to give the Lord something of the service I owe Him, whom all things praise forever. Amen. (*Life*, prologue 1, 2)[25]

Here Teresa continues her effort to subdue the self-condemnatory voice of judicial confession by imploring readers to construct for themselves the penitential confession she was not permitted to write, the story of her "great sins and wretched life." And while claiming not to have written such a narrative and to have been denied the consolation of doing so, Teresa suggests that the *Life* might allow her confessors to fulfill the disciplinary and instructional functions associated with penitential confession: "From now on may my confessors knowing me better through this narration help me in my weakness." She also introduces a complex of other genres, including the multiple genres Augustine uses in his *Confessions*, especially the conversion narrative and the soliloquy with God, as well as hagiography in the first-person variant that has been called autohagiography,[26] which she begins here by protesting that she should not be compared to the saints "who were converted to God" and "did not turn back." Finally, in transferring the origin of the intention to write away from her confessors and to God with her statement, "The Lord has for some time wanted me to do this, although I have not dared," she suggests divine sponsorship of the *Life* more suitable to the treatise on mystical theology than to any of the confessional genres. The conclusion "Amen" evokes the discourse of both the prayer and the sermon.

With this heteroglot of the first-person genres adjacent to judicial confession, Teresa conducts what Bakhtin calls a "hidden polemic" with the assumptions of judicial confession. "In a hidden polemic," Bakhtin explains in *Problems of Dostoyevsky's Poetics*,

> the author's discourse is directed towards its own referential object, as in any other discourse, but at the same time every statement about the object is constructed in such a way that, apart from its referential meaning, a polemical blow is struck at the other's discourse on the same theme, at the other's statement about the same object.[27]

Bakhtin distinguishes the hidden polemic from the open polemic, in which the author presents the other discourse to discredit it (with a quoted passage, as in academic prose, or in the mouth of a character, as in fiction) or in which the writer obviously parodies or stylizes another discourse. In the hidden polemic the other discourse exercises its influence from *outside* the text. Even though absent, the other discourse governs the meaning of the text: "Alongside its referential meaning there appears a second meaning—an intentional orientation toward someone else's words. Such discourse cannot be fundamentally or fully understood if one takes into consideration only its direct referential meaning."[28] The polemic Teresa constructed with dialogized heteroglossia disputes the condemnation inherent in judicial confession.

Teresa does not restrict the *Life* to the defensive operation of the hidden polemic, however; she takes the offensive by centering the work in the genre of spiritual autobiography, specifically, the Christian version inaugurated by Augustine in the *Confessions.* Christian spiritual autobiography, Linda H. Peterson explains in *Victorian Autobiography,* is essentially a hermeneutic genre for two interrelated reasons: it emphasizes self-interpretation rather than self-expression, and it relies on the system of biblical hermeneutics known as typology.[29] While Augustine employs typological interpretation of his life principally to assert the theological proposition that individual and scriptural history comprise a single system of divine revelation, Teresa applies the genre to the problem of self-interpretation. With the dual purpose of explaining her past life and shaping her future, Teresa portrays herself as a figure of several New Testament women who met the incarnate Christ in this life.

Readings of the *Life* as Judicial Confession

The Inquisition never brought Teresa to trial, but potentially serious charges were made against her numerous times, and in response it conducted several formal investigations of her activities and those of the nuns in the Barefoot Carmelite convents she founded. Llamas Martínez judges that some of these encounters with the Inquisition had potentially serious consequences: "Without the mediation of certain particular circumstances and the interest of some influential persons, Teresa of Avila would have been a victim of the severity of the Inquisition."[30] For the proceedings of 1575, Domingo Báñez, one of the confessors who had commanded her to write some of the *Life,* wrote an analysis of the work for the Inquisition. This document provides a look at an Inquisitional reader reading the *Life* as judicial confession.

Teresa's name first appears in Inquisition records in connection with the 1574 trial of Dr. Bernardino Carleval by the tribunal of Córdoba for the heresy of Illuminism. Teresa had a long-standing and well-known friendship with Carleval, rector of the University of Baeza, whom she had appointed confessor for her new convent at Malagón in 1568. Both Carleval and Teresa counted themselves followers of Juan de Avila (1500–1569), a priest who gave spiritual education and guidance to large numbers of laity and clergy in Andalucía.[31] From 1572 to 1574, the Inquisition conducted an intensive investigation of Carleval's work in spiritual advisement, in part because the small groups he organized for prayer meetings usurped the organizational prerogative of the Church, in part because he was thought to have encouraged Illuminist practices among his followers.

The term "Illuminism" (*alumbradismo*) encompassed a wide range of approaches to spirituality, all emphasizing a personal relationship between God and the soul, or interior enlightenment.[32] Far from being heretical in origin, Illuminism can be traced to Franciscan affective spirituality.[33] The Church initially adopted some of these spiritual practices, such as meditation on the Passion and the imaginative imitation of the life of Christ, for the purpose of strengthening piety among its congregations. By the mid-sixteenth century, however, Illuminism had become synonymous with Lutheranism, a term used in Spain to refer not specifically to Protestantism but generally to any religious belief or practice perceived to undermine the authority of the Roman Catholic church, including various forms of Erasmian humanism, mysticism, and charismatic movements.[34]

The Illuminists' concentration on the interior life, while not in itself heretical, challenged both the doctrine and the authority of the Church. The emphasis on individual contact with God tended to diminish the importance of works as a requisite for salvation, thus, when pressed to extremes, to approximate the Lutheran doctrine of justification by faith alone.[35] And Illuminists extended recollection or concentration on God in prayer (*recogimiento*) into an entirely passive state of absorption in God (*dejamiento*), which they considered to render them incapable of sin. They considered this impeccability to allow them antinomian license in conduct as well as to exempt them from the mandate to do charitable works. Also, many Illuminists actively opposed the rituals of the Church, including vocal prayer, reverence of images of Christ and the Virgin, adoration of the cross, and intercession of the saints. Perhaps most important, as

Melchor Cano, a powerful Dominican ecclesiastic and theologian, fulminates, the Illuminists arrogated to themselves the authority for scriptural interpretation that the Church claimed for itself: "Without learning, human erudition, academic degrees, but guided by the Holy Spirit, they [Illuminists] betrothed themselves to the light of understanding, as if God opened to them, as to the apostles, the meaning of the Holy Scripture."[36] Put into practice, these beliefs not only undermined ecclesiastical authority but also threatened many of its means of raising revenue.

While Teresa's beliefs merge with those of the Illuminists in their emphasis on a personal relationship with God, her version of Christian doctrine departs from the Illuminist in significant ways. Teresa accepts the notion of the innate sinfulness of humankind, which the Illuminists repudiated; Teresa places Christ at the center of her devotional practice, while the Illuminists reduced the significance of Christ for human salvation. At some points she quite explicitly distinguishes the phenomena she experiences from those described by the Illuminists. In the *Foundations*, for example, she explains that while observers might perceive rapture (*arrobamiento*), a stage in her own spiritual progress, and absorption (*dejamiento*), a state the Illuminists cultivated, as identical, they would be "right as regards appearance but not as regards reality" (*Foundations* 6.4); rapture, she continues, effects an alteration in the faculties of the soul (memory, understanding, and will), while absorption leaves them unaffected: "A rapture leaves great effects in the soul; this other [absorption] leaves no more effects than if it had not occurred, but tiredness in the body" (*Foundations* 6.14).[37] On the issue of mental prayer, the term for silent meditation or contemplation, however, Teresa's experience and conviction did not allow her to avoid being linked with the Illuminists. The Church responded to the Illuminist rejection of vocal prayer, the oral recitation of standard prayers, by making it the sole type of prayer permitted to any but "learned men" (*letrados*). While Teresa never opposed vocal prayer, she herself did not find it beneficial. From the outset, the greatest obstacle to her spiritual development was concentrating her attention on prayer. She discovered that she kept better focused if she had a book with her, a practice often forbidden by her confessors: "When I was without a book, . . . my soul was thrown into confusion and my thoughts ran wild" (*Life* 4.9). Similarly, without a mental exercise to accompany vocal prayers, Teresa found them meaningless. Weber observes that Teresa's second book, the *Road to Perfection*, encourages her nuns to engage in mental prayer even as they mouth the words of the *Pater Noster* or the *Ave Maria*.

> Realize, daughters, that the nature of mental prayer isn't determined by whether or not the mouth is closed. If while speaking I thoroughly understand and know that I am speaking with God and I have greater awareness of this than I do of the words I'm saying, mental and vocal prayer are joined. (*Road* 22.1)[38]

Unlike the Illuminists, Teresa never rejected the institutional Church even though she differed with some of its policies. Indeed, by founding seventeen convents and monasteries that embraced many persons, including women without dowries and conversos, who otherwise would have remained on the margins of the Church, she may be said to have extended its authority.

In the search for scapegoats that developed with the economic and political setbacks to Spain during the late sixteenth century, the anti-Semitism that had caused Spain to expel those Jews on whom it could not force conversion reemerged. This racism took the official form of the "purity of blood" (*limpieza de sangre*) statutes that through the century restricted more and more narrowly the economic opportunities and personal freedoms of the conversos. Unofficially, it surfaced as fear that the conversos were heretics, if not through reverting to Jewish traditions, then by subverting the Spanish state and the Catholic church in some other way. Philip II expressed, and undoubtedly helped to shape, the national sentiment when in a 1556 letter he attributed all heresies, in effect all his political problems in consolidating the Spanish empire, to conversos: "All the heresies which have occurred in Germany and France have been sown by the descendants of Jews, as we have seen and still see daily in Spain."[39] Accordingly, the Inquisition often automatically suspected a converso of heresy, and those religious movements that attracted large numbers of conversos, Illuminism the most important of them, were investigated continually.[40]

Carleval, like his mentor, Juan of Avila, and most of his own followers, had a family lineage that included conversos. This heritage almost certainly contributed to the initial suspicion that he was a heretic, and for the zealous Inquisitor who requested permission to detain him when he entered the region, it increased the likelihood of leading to other dissidents.[41] While it would not have been usual practice to have entered as formal evidence his family's genealogy, it probably influenced both the course and the outcome of the proceeding. Angel Alcalá has observed with regard to the proceedings against Luis de León for his translation of the Song of Songs from Hebrew into the vernacular that his Jewish lineage did not cause him to be brought to trial, but it "explains the rancor with which the trials were conducted."[42]

Teresa first came to the attention of the Córdoba tribunal when María Mejías, one of the women Carleval advised on the spiritual life, told the Inquisition that he had validated her propensity to make prophecies by referring to the *Life*. On this information, the Inquisition initiated another investigation, one of Teresa herself, and in interviewing everyone who had known her when she had been in the region in 1568 to found a convent at Malagón, the Inquisition received a report that described her as follows: "She [Teresa] was a great servant of God, and she had a book of revelations higher than those of Catherine of Siena, and among them was a vision that there would be many martyrs from her Order [the Barefoot Carmelites]."[43] (Carleval probably referred to the vision in which a saint appears before Teresa and reads a prophecy: "'In the time to come this order will flourish; it will have many martyrs'" [*Life* 40.13].)[44] This characterization of Teresa as a prophet would seem complimentary, and indeed after her death it was adduced as evidence for her canonization. Yet in mentioning prophecy, which from those not already designated as saintly the Inquisition defined as a form of blasphemy, it accused Teresa of heresy. Even Saints Catherine of Siena and Bridget of Sweden had for their prophecies been named in Inquisitional trials as sources of heretical ideas.[45] In the margin beside this reference to the *Life*, an officer of the Inquisition wrote, "Have it sent to the Holy Office immediately." The Inquisition concluded its investigation of Carleval and Mejías by bringing them to trial, where they were convicted of Illuminism and sentenced to burn at the stake. Unable to turn up a copy of the *Life*, the Córdoba tribunal sent the accusation against Teresa to the Holy Office in Madrid on 12 March 1575.[46]

When this charge against Teresa arrived in Madrid, the Holy Office had just received another report linking Teresa to someone else suspected of teaching Illuminist beliefs, Ignatius of

Loyola. Melchor Cano had denounced Ignatius's *Spiritual Exercises* as heretical for their emphasis on techniques of meditation through which the individual might acquire knowledge of God's will and for their apparent reliance on Ignatius's own spiritual experience rather than on Church doctrine.[47] To a request from the Holy Office in Madrid for information that could be used as evidence against Ignatius and others suspected of Illuminism, an officer of the Valladolid tribunal replied that he would proceed by obtaining what he described as "the book by Teresa de Jesús."[48] On instructions from Madrid, Valladolid Inquisitors located the manuscript of the *Life* in Avila and in preparation for bringing formal charges against Teresa, commissioned at least two reviews of it.[49]

In one of those reviews, a document entitled *Censure* (Censura), Domingo Báñez (1528–1604), the Dominican confessor who is thought to have commanded Teresa to write the section on her visions and favors from God (chaps. 37–40 of the *Life*), represents himself as a reader of judicial confession (my translation of the *Censure* appears in Appendix A). Even though he identifies the *Life* as a spiritual testimony, asserting that she originally wrote "for the purpose of being taught and guided by her confessors," he declares that he has always maintained the judicial reader's predisposition to find her guilty rather than innocent, particularly where heresy might be concerned: "I have always proceeded cautiously in the examination of this account of prayer and the life of this religious woman. No one has been more skeptical than I in regard to her visions and revelations, though not in regard to her virtues and good desires." Ecclesiastical authority, not the state of Teresa's soul, occupies Báñez's full attention in the *Censure*. On the one hand, he worries that she might be one of the "mockers who paint themselves virtuous," and, on the other, he hesitates to condemn her since that punishment, should it prove misplaced, could reduce the authority of the Church by calling its judgment into question: "It is curious how much weak and worldly people amuse themselves by seeing people with this kind of virtue deprived of authority [*desautorizados*]." As evidence against her having previously arrogated authority, Báñez cites her consultation with authorities in the Church, praising "her humility and discretion in always choosing enlightenment and learning in her confessors," himself presumably among them. Nevertheless, he argues, the suspicion of heresy should be maintained, not because she has visions, for he is able to cite scriptural and historical evidence that visions have provided important guidance for the Church, not even because these visions although once certified as divine might change and become demonic, since he admits that the devil meddles in the lives of even the most pious, but because as a woman she would be incapable of judging the source of her experience. On Báñez's recommendation, the Inquisition impounded the *Life* and held it until 1586.[50]

Báñez bases his conclusion that the author of the *Life* is not a heretic on a stylistic property he calls plainness (*llaneza*). He makes a causal relationship between the plainness of the *Life* and his decision that she does not represent a threat to ecclesiastical authority.

> Although she is deceived in some things, this woman, as far as can be seen in this account, is not a deceiver, *because she speaks plainly* [*llanamente*], both the good and the bad things, and with such a desire to express them accurately that she leaves no doubt about her good intentions. (My emphasis)[51]

Báñez gives no particular stylistic requirements for plainness, except to say that the detail should be exhaustive and the information accurate. Instead he specifies that he requires sincerity, which he defines as a manifestation of an author's submission to the authority of the Church: "I have looked, with great attention, at this book in which Teresa de Jesús, a Carmelite nun and founder of the Barefoot Carmelites, gives a sincere report [*relación llana*] of all her spiritual experiences, for the purpose of being taught and guided by her confessors." As a reader of judicial confession, Báñez easily dismisses her sins, which he euphemistically calls "the bad things," as a sign she belongs to that spiritual elite with especially intense inclinations to both sin and virtue, but he reads carefully for any violation of stylistic plainness, which he counts as a challenge to the authority of the Church, that is, as evidence of heresy.

Teresa frequently indicates that she understands the requirements of her writing assignment. She concludes the *Life*, as she opens it (*Life*, prologue 2, quoted above), by offering its plainness as evidence of her sincerity: "I have put down what happened with plainness and truth" (*Life* 40.25). Yet Teresa also implies that such plainness represents a risk to her. Her plain response to several priests investigating charges against her around 1559 permitted them to interpret her visions as demonic: "They asked me some things; I responded plainly [con llaneza] and carelessly. . . . Since I spoke carelessly about some things, they interpreted my intention differently and thought that what I said, without my being careful, as I say, showed little humility" (Life 28.17).[52] Plainness, she elsewhere explains, is the appropriate style for confessing to God: "Here there is no demand for reasoning but for knowing what as a matter of fact [con llaneza] we are and for placing ourselves [with simplicity] in God's presence" (Life 15.8). Because God, as Teresa explains in Life 10.9, already knows who she is and what she intends, there is no possibility for misunderstanding. With a human audience, however, plainness amounts to the carelessness of permitting herself to be misinterpreted.

The sixteenth-century Spanish plain style resembled other variations of the plain style, from the Ciceronian to the English Puritan. The common goal of all the versions is clarity, and the prescriptions for achieving it are similar: avoidance of rhetorical embellishment, of calculated stylistic effects, and of figurative language.[53] In Spanish debates about the most appropriate style for sermons, the word *plainness* sometimes refers to a stylistic choice an author might make to communicate with an uneducated audience.[54] While this use of the word implies that it is a human linguistic or rhetorical skill, other instances define plainness, particularly when used to express divine truths, as a sign of spiritual perfection or a supernatural gift.[55] When Báñez attests to the plainness of Teresa's *Life*, he does not mean that it is an effective means for teaching or that it constitutes proof of spiritual purity, however. When applied to the language of the confessant, plainness meant submission to the authority of the Church.

The definition of *llano* in Sebastián de Covarrubias Horozco's *Tesoro de la lengua castellana o española*, the first Spanish-language dictionary (1611), demonstrates that in everyday usage the word had connotations of the subservience that Báñez required in judicial confession: "The castrated steer is plain [llano], unlike the bull with balls. To become plain is to reduce oneself and to adjust oneself to the will of the other."[56] While the *Tesoro* does not consider plainness as a prose style, the qualities the *Te-*

soro forbids in the plain thing or the plain person can be considered as qualities of language.

> Metaphorically, plain describes the thing that has no impediments [*estropieço ninguno*], only plainness [*llaneza*] and truth. The plain man is not haughty [*no tiene altivezes*] nor cunning [*ni cautelas*]. To confess openly [*plano*], which is the same as plainly [*llano*], means to tell everything that happens.[57]

Estropieço, which I translate as "impediment(s)" to show its connotation of the pitfalls a foot-traveler might encounter, also refers, through the *Tesoro's* definition of *estropieço* as *trampa*, to verbal strategies of deception in jokes and stories, whether lies or misleading plot lines. The qualities a plain person should avoid can also be translated into stylistic qualities: *altivez*, which in addition to arrogance or insolence means having "elevated thoughts or ideas" and when used to describe architecture, has connotations of excessive grandeur; and *cautelas*, or cunning, which the *Tesoro* defines in verbal terms as "the ingenious deception of one by another, using ambiguous terms and equivocal, indeterminate words." What these qualities described as antithetical to plainness—cunning, deceptiveness, arrogance, and secretiveness—share in common is the exercise of authorial power over the audience, whether with a display of rhetorical or linguistic wealth, with exploitation of the ambiguity of language to deceive, or with manipulation and evasion.

The demand for plainness in the sense of "tell[ing] everything that happens" in judicial confession exceeded that for penitential confession, where, Henry C. Lea explains, "forgotten sins are charitably held to be included."[58] Completeness in penitential confession required a thorough examination of conscience but not an account of every incidence of sin. Jean Gerson, the fifteenth-century French theologian who wrote a tract on confession, exhorted penitents to avoid "irrelevancies," apparently preferring the risk of incompleteness to that of superfluity, which might lead to boredom on his part or bragging by the confessant.[59] With the judicial confession, however, completeness required a detailed listing of every incidence of wrongdoing, without exception. Any omission, Lea explains, renders the confession "nugatory, *ficta* and *diminuta*, and an aggravated guilt."

While Teresa evaded the requirement for plainness in various ways, she certainly cannot be said to have used an elevated style; to the contrary, her style has been labeled rustic, uncultivated, conversational, spontaneous, feminine. For example, Robert Ricard describes her as "a spontaneous spirit, intuitive, who usually proceeds by association of ideas, whose vocabulary has no consistency or stability and whose works abound in parentheses, repetitions, and logical leaps forward and backward."[60] It is true that Teresa's prose gives the reader and translator many difficulties: the sentences often run together; the syntax is sometimes convoluted to the point of unintelligibility; many words appear in corrupted or misspelled forms; pronoun reference is frequently ambiguous; the organization often appears to be associational.

For the colloquial and haphazard effect, Teresa's style has often been judged natural and sincere. Many early twentieth-century commentators regarded her prose as transparent. In 1914, Blanca de los Ríos wrote, "The prose of St. Teresa is inseparable from her spirit; it is the esthetic of her sanctity"; Peers continues the tradition of considering Teresa's texts as a window into her self: "In studying her style, therefore, we shall be studying herself, and it is that, above all, which makes the task worthwhile."[61] More recently, critics have better appreciated the subtlety and intricacy of Teresa's writing and begun to regard her as a resourceful writer who made deliberate compositional choices: Ramón Menéndez Pidal attributes the rusticity of her style to "ascetic mortification" and "eremetic humility" and judges that "departing from the correct forms undoubtedly cost her more work than following them"; Felicidad Bernabéu Barrachina proposes that Teresa chose an uncultivated style to distance herself from the conversos, who were known for emphasis on education, and to affiliate herself with the Old Christian peasantry; Elías Rivers proposes that she "refuses to accept the analytical or linear sequence of linguistic discourse, and she strives for simultaneity, for saying everything at once"; Weber argues that "Teresa wrote as she believed women were *perceived* to speak."[62] While any of these theories might have value for analyzing a particular passage, it must also be said that Teresa's style is not low in every respect. Concha and Weber demonstrate that she wields a number of sophisticated rhetorical devices, chief among them ambiguity and irony, and she employs figurative language, the tropes of doubleness forbidden by the mandate of Inquisitional plainness.

Some aspects of a high style, such as ornamentation and correctness, would not have served Teresa's purpose of interpreting her experience as divine, but she did need figurative language, metaphor in particular. Experience with God can be communicated only with metaphoric or symbolic language, Thomas Aquinas explains in the *Summa Theologiae*.

> *Reply to Objection 1*. There are some names which signify these perfections flowing from God to creatures in such a way that the imperfect way in which creatures receive the divine perfection is part of the very signification of the name itself as *stone* signifies a material being, and names of this kind can be applied to God only in a metaphorical sense.[63]

In Paul Tillich's words, "Nothing else [apart from the abstract statement 'that God is being-itself or the absolute'] can be said about God as God which is not symbolic."[64] Despite the theological necessity for metaphor, Teresa invariably introduces her metaphors with invitations to ridicule her skimpy imaginative resources, as in her introduction of the section of the *Life* known as Four Ways of Watering the Garden.

> I shall have to make use of some comparison, although I should like to excuse myself from this since I am a woman and write simply what they ordered me to write. But these spiritual matters for anyone who like myself has not gone through studies are so difficult to explain. I shall have to find some mode of explaining myself, and it may be less often that I hit upon a good comparison. Seeing so much stupidity will provide some recreation for your Reverence. (*Life* 11.6)[65]

Teresa contrasts metaphor and "spiritual language," by which she probably means rational argument and abstraction, but in fact metaphor is spiritual language, the only linguistic means of attempting to make visible the invisible.

Because, as Terence Hawkes explains, metaphor "interferes with the system of literal usage by its assumption that terms literally connected with one object can be transferred to another object," the plainness Báñez commanded would preclude its use.[66] In common usage, the word *metaphor* had negative connotations. Defining *metaphor* as "inappropriate words," the

Tesoro illustrates its meaning with an anecdote that emphasizes the potential of metaphor for deception through the potentially ambiguous substitution of meaning.[67] The *Directorium* warns Inquisitors about deceptive techniques based on verbal ambiguity, such as the confusion of an indeterminate pronoun reference.

> Questioned on the true body of Christ, they [the accused] respond with regard to the mystical body. Thus, if one says to them, "Do you believe that that is the body of Christ?" they respond, "Yes, I believe that that is the body of Christ" (meaning a stone that they see, or their own body in the sense that all bodies are of Christ, because they are of God, who is Christ).[68]

Also, the *Directorium* explains, a conditional clause can be used to negate or alter the meaning of an assertion: "If you ask the accused, 'Do you believe that marriage is a sacrament?' he responds, 'If God wills it, of course I believe it' (the subtext is that God does not will that he believe it)."[69] The *Directorium* instructs Inquisitors that they should be the ones to take advantage of ambiguity, advising them in methods of trapping the accused into admission of guilt, by, for example, asking the same question several ways or constructing a line of misleading questions to conceal the exact nature of the charge.

The distrust of metaphor cast suspicion also on allegory, one of its extended forms. A contemporary dictionary of rhetorical figures defines allegory as a kind of ambiguity: "It is effected when the meaning of the words and the meaning the orator gives them are different."[70] And the related forms to which it directs readers—catachresis, enigma, and parable—all violate the Inquisitional requirement for plainness. The prohibition on allegory, like that on metaphor, had consequences for Teresa more serious than the mere limitation of stylistic resources: it precluded the writing of Christian spiritual autobiography. John Freccero explains that Christian autobiography, which he calls confession here, requires the allegorical reading of one's own life: "Christian allegory . . . is identical with the phenomenology of confession, for both involve a comprehension of the self in history within a retrospective literary structure."[71] The writer of Christian autobiography employs allegory, in the sense of the interpretation of one story in reference to another story, to locate his or her individual history in relation to universal history, the personal in relation to the divine.

If judicial confession may be said to require a naive narrator, Christian autobiography requires a narrator with a perspective on the events narrated, what I will call a converted narrator. In Freccero's words, "Biblical allegory, conversion, and narrative all share the same linguistic structure."[72] While the narrator of penitential confession takes essentially the same stance as the protagonist, Robert Bell explains that "spiritual autobiography, as Augustine presents it, posits a crucial disparity between the narrator and the protagonist, which involves more than the usual autobiographical time lag."[73] In Augustine's *Confessions*, the prototypical Christian autobiography, conversion entails directing his desire away from the material world, that is, the sensual pleasures and professional accolades he chronicles in books 1 through 7. In practical terms, as Robert Durling explains, he must "resolve the split in his own will that holds back his commitment to Christian abstinence and a monastic way of life."[74] His conversion takes place when he interprets Paul's epistles to Romans 13:13–14, a verse that concludes with the injunction to "spend no more thought on nature and nature's appetites" (*Conf.* 8.12), as counsel for his own life, specifically, as instructions to retire from the world to the priesthood. Augustine thus locates his life in relation to sacred history, and to communicate the connection between the two, he must draw on Christian allegory.

In the *Life*, Teresa conceals her use of metaphor and allegory with a style so apparently plain that most Inquisitors were satisfied that she had entirely surrendered authority for interpretation to the reader. Although several readers saw heresy and blasphemy in her writings, Fuente, a posthumous Inquisitional reader, was one of a very few who charged her with the stylistic violations of deception (*engaño*) and contrivance (*artificio*).[75] And he notices that her narrative operates on two levels.

> She mixes falsehood with truth and water with oil. . . . And the water, which is heresy, remains on the bottom, covered with the oil of truth. It will be necessary to stir these two liquids many times to uncover the concealed water, to discover the poisonous meaning that lies underneath sweet words and spiritual language.[76]

In particular, he finds her self-referential language to mean something other than it seems to mean: "Among many words that have a humble meaning, she speaks a million vanities."[77] Fuente's exasperation demonstrates the extraordinary subtlety with which Teresa forges her self-interpretation in the *Life*. Appreciating the artfulness requires a look back at Teresa's first autobiographical essays.

Teresa's Development as a Writer of Christian Autobiography

Teresa's earliest autobiographical writing did not serve her nearly as well as the *Life* did, in spite of the fact that by underscoring passages in Bernardino de Laredo's *Ascent of Mount Sion* to indicate those that best described her spiritual experience, she aligned her narrative with a text the Inquisition had already certified as orthodox.[78] Teresa made this first written confession at the request of Francisco de Salcedo (d. 1580), a distant relative in whom she began to confide when priests offered her no advice but to discontinue prayer and when gossip that she could trace to them began to circulate.[79] The talk held considerable danger for Teresa because, as she puts it, "at that time other women had fallen into serious illusions and deceptions caused by the devil" (*Life* 23.2). Most editors consider "other women" a reference to Magdalena de la Cruz, an abbess in Córdoba who was respected throughout Spain for her visions. As Teresa would also, Magdalena de la Cruz even enjoyed favor with the royal family: the infant Prince Philip was wrapped in her vestments as a protection against the devil.[80] When some of her nuns also began to have visions, including a vision of black goats at the head of Magdalena's bed, the Inquisition investigated the convent and, as Perry puts it, "convinced sor Magdalena to confess that for forty years she had been a servant of the devil."[81] In a dramatic, widely publicized auto-de-fé, Magdalena was sentenced to banishment from the convent and lifelong isolation.

Salcedo comforted Teresa at first, but after a time he also began to doubt the divinity of her experiences. Speculating that "her sins were not compatible with her gifts from God" (*Life* 23.11), he asked her to submit a written report to himself and Gaspar Daza, a parish priest in Avila whose previous advocacy of religious reforms might have inclined him to support Teresa.[82] In complying, Teresa submitted what she calls a "general account of her life and sins" (*Life* 23.14) and, in place of a spiritual testimony, her underlined copy of Laredo's *Ascent*. For some reason, which Teresa does not give, Salcedo and Daza traced her experiences not to God but to the devil: "At length they gave me the reply I had awaited with such dread. . . . [W]hen this gentleman [Salcedo] came to me, it was to tell me with great distress that to the best of their belief my trouble came from the devil" (*Life* 23.14; Peers's translation). Unable to help her further, they suggested she seek counsel in the new Jesuit convent in Avila, where she found a more sympathetic audience in Diego de Cetina, a young intern.[83]

Apart from a brief business letter arranging payment for a delivery of wheat, Teresa's first extant writing is an autobiographical narrative known as *Spiritual Testimony* 1, dated October–December 1560.[84] Teresa again wrote in threatening circumstances. Opposition to her plans for a new convent in Avila had arisen on every side, from her Jesuit confessor (Baltasar Alvarez), influential members of the clergy, citizens of Avila, and nuns in the convent of the Incarnation, where she was prioress at the time (*Life* 33.1). Teresa appealed to Pedro Ibáñez, a Dominican priest and theologian who had spoken in favor of the project, to receive a written confession, specifically, to decide whether anything in her spiritual experience contradicted Holy Scripture (*Life* 33.5). Ibáñez wrote an evaluation of this testimony, a statement known as *Judgment* (Dictamen), for a group of Avilan priests and citizens who were concerned about Teresa's project.[85] (My translation of the *Judgment* appears in Appendix B.)

This first spiritual testimony, although written little more than a year before she began writing the *Life*, demonstrates Teresa taking the role of the naive narrator required by judicial confession. Apparently adhering strictly to Ibáñez's request, she narrates her experiences as isolated events in the present, without interpreting their significance for either personal or salvation history.

> My present procedure in prayer is as follows: I am seldom able while in prayer to use my intellect in a discursive way, for my soul immediately begins to grow recollected; and it remains in quiet or rapture to the extent that I cannot make any use of the senses. This recollection reaches such a point that if it were not for hearing—and this hearing does not include understanding— none of the senses would be of any avail. (*Testimony* 1.1)[86]

In the most vigorous passages, Teresa simply asserts her certainty that her inspiration is divine, here, for example, insisting that she would not waver even before the kind of torture that was associated with the Inquisition.

> If when I'm in prayer or on the days in which I am quiet and my thoughts are on God, all the learned men and saints in the world were to join together and torture me with all the torments imaginable, and I wanted to believe them, I wouldn't be able to make myself believe that these things come from the devil; for I cannot. (*Testimony* 1.26)[87]

While she persuades with sheer strength of conviction, she does not, as she will in the *Life*, employ the genre of Christian autobiography to make her conclusion inevitable for readers.

Ibáñez's *Judgment* gives none of the indications found in Báñez's *Censure* that either Teresa or her text causes him to worry about ecclesiastical authority. His repetition of her claims in nearly the same words can be counted an unstated acknowledgment of the plainness of the testimony (his paragraph 4 echoes *Testimony* 1.2 and paragraph 27 rephrases *Testimony* 1.26, for example). Further, it is Ibáñez, not Teresa, who undertakes her defense against specific charges, that as a woman and a converso she probably followed the devil's dictates and that her prior relationship with the Jesuits indicates that she might collaborate with them. By attributing virtue and chastity to her, Ibáñez clears her of feminine sexual weakness: "She is above the frivolity and childishness of women, who are very much without scruples; she is extraordinarily virtuous." In using the word *clean* to describe Teresa's soul, Ibáñez implies that she comes from an Old Christian, rather than converso, heritage.[88] Finally, Ibáñez goes to great lengths to emphasize Teresa's independence from the Jesuits, possibly because their spiritual exercises, like Teresa's mental prayer, were associated with Illuminism: "She has told me that if she were to know that perfection does not include conversing with the Jesuits, she never would see or speak to them again, even though they are the ones who calmed her and led her to these visions." In her later works Teresa does not leave the answering of these kinds of charges, actual or potential, to her readers.

In this testimony Teresa expresses a desire to write a more complete report of her experience: "When I meet any person who knows something about me, I want to explain my life to him" (*Testimony* 1.25). Exactly why she eventually received such a command and what had happened in the interim to permit her to take the stance of a converted narrator are not entirely known. Teresa gives conflicting versions of the source of the commands that provided her that opportunity. In a spiritual testimony written for the Inquisition in Sevilla during the 1576 investigation of her convent there, she attributes the suggestion to an Inquisitor, Francisco de Soto.

> It was about thirteen years ago, a little more or less, that the Bishop of Salamanca [Soto] went there [to Avila], for he was the Inquisitor, I believe, in Toledo and had been here [in Seville]. For the sake of greater assurance she [Teresa] arranged to speak with him and gave him an account of everything. He told her this whole matter was something that didn't belong to his office because all that she saw and understood strengthened her ever [*sic*] more in the Catholic faith. . . . Since he saw she was so concerned, he told her that she should write to Master Avila—who was alive—a long account of everything, for he was a man who understood much about prayer; and that with what he would write her, she could be at peace. (*Testimony* 58.6)[89]

It seems unlikely that an Inquisitor, particularly when visiting the convent to investigate it, as Soto was, would have asked her to write outside the judicial context, and it seems improbable as well that he suggested that she send the *Life* to Juan de Avila, whose works the Inquisition had placed on the 1559 Index. When Teresa did send Juan the *Life* in 1568, she did so against Báñez's expressed orders, stealing the manuscript and urgently charging her emissaries with getting it back to her before Báñez returned from a trip.[90] In the 1577 prologue to the *Foundations*, Teresa ascribes her commands to García de Toledo, the confessor to whom she presented at least a portion of the *Life* with the June 1562 letter that is usually printed with it.[91] In the canonization hearing, Báñez described another scenario, assigning the original command to Ibáñez and the commands for additional material, probably the chapters on the mystical way (10–22) and on the founding of St. Joseph (32–36), to García de Toledo and asserting that he asked her to add chapters on her subsequent spiritual favors (37–40). While all these explanations may have some basis in fact, they come closest to the truth when taken as a composite: her confessors commanded her to write, in part because her activities continually attracted Inquisitional scrutiny, in part because her accomplishments were remarkable.

For the purpose of explaining her life, Teresa takes the stance of a converted narrator, a narrator separated from the protagonist by an experience of conversion. Religious conversion, in the definition of Arthur Darby Nock, is "the reorientation of the soul of an individual, a turning which implies a consciousness that a great change is involved, that the old was wrong, and the new is right."[92] Or, in William James's more psychologically oriented definition, conversion is "the process, gradual or sudden, by which a self hitherto divided, and consciously wrong, inferior and unhappy, becomes unified and right, superior and happy."[93] Jean Starobinski proposes that all autobiographical writing requires some kind of radical change in the writer: "It is the internal transformation of the individual—and the exemplary character of this transformation—that furnishes a subject for a narrative discourse in which 'I' is both subject and object."[94] For Christians, conversion provides this transformation of perspective, as Freccero explains: "The literature of confession needs a point outside of itself from which its truth can be measured, a point that is at once a beginning and an end. . . . 'Conversion' was the name that Christians applied to such a moment in history and in the soul."[95] In keeping with the requirements of the genre of Christian autobiography (which Freccero calls confession here), the *Life* includes a testimony of the events that provided her this new perspective.

Chapter 9 contains narratives of two events, both placed by biographers in 1554, that have often been interpreted as Teresa's conversion, the first relating Teresa's emotional reaction to an image of Christ in passion, the second what might now be called her reader's response to book 8 of Augustine's *Confessions*. Critics generally designate these narratives either as a two-part conversion or as a primary conversion, which has variously been taken to be either of the two, consolidated by a secondary experience. Alberto de la Virgen del Carmen asserts that her reading of Augustine produced "marvelous effects" and a "consequent conversion"; Efrén and Steggink judge that her conversion consists in a resolve first made before the painting and then confirmed in the reading of Augustine; Concha writes that the reading of the *Confessions* provided an authentic revelation but that the contemplation of the wounded Christ "moved her to conversion."[96] Contrary to the tradition of comparing some part of Teresa's chapter 9 to Augustine's book 8, Freccero does not find a conversion scene in the *Life* at all.

> The contribution of narrative form to the phenomenology of conversion or maturation becomes apparent when we contrast St. Teresa's observation of her conflicting moments of sin and sanctity with the strict linearity of Augustine's crisis. . . . There is probably no escape from these conflicts in real life, but in literature there does seem to be a way to transform discontinuous moments into linear trajectory.[97]

Measured against Augustine's conversion, Teresa's does lack narrative condensation, but not because the *Life* is less literary than the *Confessions*. The *Life* does have linear trajectory, albeit partly submerged, but it traces a conversion that differs experientially from the Augustinian. Caroline Walker Bynum explains that because of lack of control over their own lives, medieval women wrote spiritual autobiographies that avoid the sharp turns and definitive conversions characteristic of men's accounts.

> Men were inclined to tell stories with turning points, to use symbols of reversal and inversion. . . . Women more often used their ordinary experiences (of powerlessness, of service and nurturing, of disease, etc.) as symbols into which they poured ever deeper and more paradoxical meanings.[98]

Teresa's conversion in the *Life*, which embraces both the narratives in chapter 9 but is not resolved in either of them, evinces the intensification of prior experience that Bynum designates as feminine and articulates a resistance to the widely held belief that Augustine's religious experience was paradigmatic for all Christians.

The form a conversion takes, James explains in *The Varieties of Religious Experience*, "is the result of suggestion and imitation."[99] Erich Auerbach considers the mimetic aspect of conversion particularly significant for Christianity, which the New Testament demonstrates to gain historical momentum by describing "time and time again the impact of Jesus' teaching, personality, and fate upon this and that individual."[100] Teresa's allusion to Augustine's conversion might suggest that she imitates

Augustine. Augustine himself enters a series of mimetic conversions with his reading of Romans 13 in the garden: he imitates the two Roman agents, who were converted by reading the
Life of St. Antony, while Antony had been converted by reading
the Gospel, which narrates the prototypical Christian conversion experience, Paul's confrontation with Christ on the road to
Damascus (*Conf.* 8.6, 12). In schematic outline, Augustine's conversion corresponds to Paul's: he journeys away from God; he
responds to a call from God; he accepts a vocation in the Church.
As I will show in subsequent chapters, Teresa does not understand her life as following this pattern. She considers her lack
of vocation not a result of her refusal to serve but rather of the
Church's rejection of her efforts. Not surprisingly, then, she con-
strues her conversion differently, taking a female object for imitation, not Augustine but Mary Magdalene.

Teresa's narrative of her reaction to an image of Christ, which
nuns identified in the canonization hearings as a painting that
included the figure of Mary Magdalene rather than as the statue
Teresa mentions here, represents a decisive experience, though
not one with the closure of Augustine's conversion.

> Well, my soul now was tired; and, in spite of its desire, my
> wretched habits would not allow it rest. It happened to me that
> one day entering the oratory I saw a statue they had borrowed for
> a certain feast to be celebrated in the house. It represented the
> much wounded Christ and was very devotional so that beholding
> it I was utterly distressed in seeing Him that way, for it well rep-
> resented what He suffered for us. I felt so keenly aware of how
> poorly I thanked Him for those wounds that, it seems to me, my
> heart broke. Beseeching Him to strengthen me once and for all
> that I might not offend Him, I threw myself down before Him with
> the greatest outpouring of tears.
>
> I was very devoted to the glorious Magdalene and frequently
> thought about her conversion, especially when I received Com-
> munion. For since I knew the Lord was certainly present there
> within me, I, thinking that He would not despise my tears,
> placed myself at His feet. And I didn't know what I was saying
> (He did a great deal who allowed me to shed them for Him, since
> I so quickly forgot that sentiment); and I commended myself to
> this glorious saint that she might obtain pardon for me.
>
> But in this latter instance with this statue I am speaking of, it
> seems to me I profited more, for I was very distrustful of myself
> and placed all my trust in God. I think I then said that I would

not rise from there until He granted what I was begging Him for. I believe certainly this was beneficial to me, because from that time I went on improving. (*Life* 9.1–3)[101]

The episode relates the kind of deepening of prior experience that Bynum considers typically feminine. Through repeated use of the imperfect tense, which indicates habitual action in the past, Teresa emphasizes that she had repeatedly taken the same postures: she used to think of the Magdalene's conversion; she often knelt before Christ; she frequently commended herself to Mary Magdalene. On previous occasions she had not been able fully to identify with Mary Magdalene, however, because the "hardness of her heart" prevented her from weeping along with the Magdalene. Contrary to Freccero's estimate that she has not transformed her experience into linear trajectory, she does give singular importance to the events of this particular day, distinguishing them with verbs in the preterite tense to indicate a single action in the past. This time, she felt sympathy with His suffering, and taking the posture of Mary Magdalene, she threw herself at His feet. This breakthrough of emotion moves her to make an unprecedented request to Christ for help, the action to which she traces the beginning of her spiritual renewal: "from that time I went on improving." Still, as the imperfect tense in this sentence implies, she does not consider that her conversion has reached closure.

With the first episode of chapter 9 read as an initiatory gesture toward conversion, the second, her reading of Augustine's *Confessions*, can be seen as a premature attempt to conclude the experience of conversion. Although Teresa expresses the desire to imitate Augustine's conversion and Paul's, her experience differs from theirs in crucial ways.

> At this time they gave me the *Confessions of St. Augustine*. It seems the Lord ordained this, because I had not tried to procure a copy, nor had I ever seen one. . . .
>
> As I began to read the *Confessions*, it seemed to me I saw myself in them. I began to commend myself very much to this glorious saint. When I came to the passage where he speaks about his conversion and read how he heard that voice in the garden, it only seemed to me, according to what I felt in my heart, that it was I the Lord called. I remained for a long time totally dissolved in tears and feeling within myself utter distress and weariness. (*Life* 9.7, 8)[102]

While Paul and Augustine are portrayed as hearing sounds from external sources, Paul's words from Christ audible to his traveling companions in one account (Acts 9:4–7) and Augustine's voices of children calling "*Tolle, lege*" presumably also heard by others, Teresa hears interior words spoken by God to her alone, and then she asserts only that she *seemed* to hear them, not that she actually heard them.[103] Further, Teresa closes the passage by describing this event as exacerbating rather than alleviating the sensations of fatigue and affliction that conversion typically resolves.

Teresa's account of reading Augustine does adumbrate the experience that eventually culminates the prior experience. In straining to hear interior words from God, Teresa indicates that her conversion awaits a reply to her request. Teresa relates that the first words God spoke to her in rapture, "No longer do I want you to converse with men but with angels" (*Life* 24.5), made a definitive change in her life: "From that day on I was very courageous in abandoning all for God, as one who had wanted from that moment—for it doesn't seem to me that it was otherwise—to change completely" (*Life* 24.7).[104] The next locution from God, which Teresa also discusses in terms of Christian renewal, echoes Christ's words to Mary Magdalene after His Resurrection: "'Do not fear, daughter; for I am, and I will not abandon you'" (*Life* 25.18).[105] Efrén and Steggink label the first locution experience her mystical betrothal,[106] and although I would reserve this term for later stages of her mystical experience, as Teresa herself does, they correctly point out the mystical quality of Teresa's conversion, which centers on communication with God, first her request to Him from the stance of Mary Magdalene and then, probably about two years later, His response.

To explain the significance Teresa gives to Mary Magdalene and the other New Testament women she uses as prototypical figures for herself, in chapter 2 I define the hermeneutic Teresa applied to Scripture and describe some of the interpretations she derived.

2

TERESA'S FEMINIST FIGURAL
READINGS OF SCRIPTURE

When Teresa explains at the end of the *Book of Her Life* that she
has given order to her disorderly life (*Life* 40.24), in effect she
announces that she has read her own life figurally. The figural
reading of a life rests on scriptural typology, an essentially allegorical hermeneutic that, as Auerbach defines it in "Figura,"
"establishes a connection between two events or persons, the
first of which signifies not only itself but also the second, while
the second encompasses or fulfills the first."[1] The first part of
the typological equation, which Auerbach designates as the figure, both contains and prophesies another event, which is its fulfillment. The Old Testament, according to this mode of interpretation, not only refers to the history of the Jewish people but
also forecasts the history of the Christian people narrated in
the New Testament; similarly, the New Testament anticipates
the eternal salvation to be afforded by God's grace at the Last
Judgment; and in that all events narrated promise deliverance
from sin for every Christian, they signify individual history.
Scholastic theologians labeled these layers of salvation history
according to the mode of reading that produces knowledge of
them: the literal, which narrates historical events; the allegorical, which refers to the Christian Church or defines its doctrine;
the tropological, which promises individual salvation; the anagogical, which prophesies the events of the Last Judgment and
the fate of souls after death.[2]

In these standard hermeneutic terms, Teresa's figural ordering of her life required making an analogy between salvation
history as a whole, which the allegorical and anagogical senses
provide, and her individual history, which the tropological sense
of Scripture designates. The impasse Teresa encountered in making this analogy with the Scholastics' tools of Scriptural typology, that is, the disjuncture between the allegorical sense as
interpreted by her Church and the tropological sense as she
understood it, caused her to revise that hermeneutic. Teresa's
readings of the Song of Songs and the New Testament imply a
hermeneutic that may be considered feminine and feminist. She
deployed this hermeneutic to buttress her argument that the
Church's confinement of a woman's history in this life to spiritual experience alone denies her the possibility of fulfilling her
moral obligation to perfect human society in preparation for the
Last Judgment. The restoration of wholeness to her artificially
truncated life, she maintains, depends on divine intervention,
or mystical experience.

Teresa's Feminist Hermeneutic: The Divided Tropological Sense

Augustine's *Confessions* demonstrates that Christian conversion, hence the writing of Christian spiritual autobiography, depends on typological interpretation of Scripture, specifically, on
tropological reading. As a young man, Augustine could not read
Scripture at all. Measured against the classical criterion of beauty,
Scripture seemed rustic, even barbaric, to Augustine: "To me
[the Scriptures] seemed quite unworthy of comparison with the
stately prose of Cicero" (*Conf.* 3.5). Augustine does more than
express an aesthetic preference here: he rejects the Incarnation,
the event that produced the incongruity of testaments that requires different readings for each, the letter of the Old Testament and the spirit of the New Testament.[3] Ambrose, the bishop
of Milan who explains Christian truth with eloquence, is the
first to make scriptural typology plausible to Augustine.

> I was glad that at last I had been shown how to interpret the
> ancient Scriptures of the law and the prophets in a different light
> from that which had previously made them seem absurd, when I
> used to criticize your saints for holding beliefs which they had
> never really held at all. I was pleased to hear that in his sermons

> to the people Ambrose often repeated the text: "The written law inflicts death, whereas the spiritual law brings life" [2 Cor. 3:6], as though this were a rule upon which he wished to insist most carefully. And when he lifted the veil of mystery and disclosed the spiritual meaning of texts which, taken literally, appeared to contain the most unlikely doctrines, I was not aggrieved by what he said. (*Conf.* 6.4)

Augustine finally comprehends that typology is the appropriate hermeneutic for Scripture, but still he does not read it typologically himself. When he admits soon afterward, "I did not yet know whether it was true" (*Conf.* 6.4), in effect he states that he does not read the allegory, the interpretation that according to a medieval mnemonic device tells "what to believe," or more narrowly construed, that coincides with the doctrine of the Church.[4] And when Augustine continues, "I refused to allow myself to accept any of it in my heart" (*Conf.* 6.4), he asserts a resistance to reading the tropological sense, in effect rejecting Christ's gift of redemption. Augustine takes the first step toward knowing "what to believe" when he accepts on faith even the parts of Roman Catholic doctrine he finds improbable (*Conf.* 6.5), but he still does not know, in the medieval shorthand for the tropological meaning, "what to do."

Augustine reads tropologically for the first time when he picks up Paul's epistles in the garden. The impact this reading makes on Augustine illustrates the difference between the simple moral sense, which is closely related to the literal, and the tropological sense. Augustine's reading of the verses that end with the injunction, "spend no more thought on nature and nature's appetites," provides more than an understanding of the value of continence, which he might have gleaned from a literal reading of Romans. Rather, in this verse that addresses his most immediate concern, the struggle for chastity, Augustine for the first time recognizes that his life is inscribed in Scripture. As Lawrence Rothfield puts it, "In the sentence [Augustine] reads, he finds himself interpreted. The scattered self finds itself resumed within the Christian text."[5] Augustine acknowledges that the promises of Scripture implicate him personally, and as a result, he adjusts his life in accord with the Christian text, which he reads as a direction to take up a monastic life.

The dual movement of Augustine's soul here, his spiritual assent to redemption accompanied by moral resolve, illustrates the reason that some theologians designated the tropological as a double sense, one sense relating to the redemption promised to every Christian soul and the other to the responsibilities this gift entails. Honorius of Autun (fl. 1106–1135) defines the parts of the tropological level as two different types of union: one of these joins two parts of the soul, with the effect of generating good works, while the other unites the soul with Christ, thus perfecting the capacity for spiritual love.[6] Developing the same idea of the soul's double movements in tropological reading, A. C. Charity explains in *Events and Their Afterlife* that in accepting redemption through Christ, the individual not only inserts himself in Christian history but also acquires an obligation to advance that history.

> [Typology] is applied . . . not only *to* the hearer and his existential understanding, but *in* the actual response of the hearer to God's acts. The hearer's right response means that there is initiated a self-conforming with the act of God. . . . In the New Testament, the central concept of the imitation of Christ itself contains both the idea of eschatological self-alignment and the idea of alignment with the past. For God's future is already contained in Christ's history and the individual's relation to the one involves him in the same relation to the other. (Original emphases)[7]

In the terms Charity uses here, tropological reading of Scripture involves both accepting Christ's sacrifice and contributing to the future fulfillment of salvation history. Referring principally to Dante's *Divine Comedy*, which he considers the consummate expression of the individual's tropological reading of Scripture, Charity designates this contribution as the ethical "subfulfillment" of Scripture.[8]

Teresa's interpretations of Scripture imply that she also thinks of the tropological sense as double, but unlike the Scholastics, who drew heavily on Augustine's formulations of exegesis and experience, Teresa does not consider both facets of tropology to have been fulfilled, not for a woman. Teresa never questions that Christ's sacrifice won her salvation, but she despairs of being allowed to carry out the corresponding imperative for works. Thus she divides the tropological sense into two distinct parts, separating the promise of her redemption, which she considers to have been fulfilled, from her ethical subfulfillment of that promise, for which she requires additional divine intervention. Because, as Northrop Frye observes, scriptural typology is essentially a "theory of historical process,"[9] Teresa's applications of her divided tropological sense make a statement about history, in particular, the history of a female life. Her theory of the divided tropological sense thus reflects the disjuncture she finds between the spiritual and material reality of her own life, and of women's lives in general, and it comments on the Church's failure to incorporate women into the Christian community.

Teresa cannot be said to have read Scripture in the same sense that Augustine did: Joel Sangnieux explains that Teresa lived in "a culture of things heard and seen rather than of things read."[10] Her works suggest that while scriptural allusion came readily to her, most of her store of knowledge came from oral sources, such as sermons, confession, and the Daily Office. Her frequent use of paraphrase rather than quotation and when she does quote directly, her misspelling of the Latin and misquotation of the Spanish suggest that she most often drew scriptural references from memory rather than from a text.[11] Even though numerous Spanish translations of the Scriptures existed, she could not easily have secured a copy. When Spain's leaders began to construe political unity as religious homogeneity, they feared that these translations, drawn mainly from the Hebrew, might perpetuate Judaic tradition. Beginning around 1492, the Catholic kings made several decrees prohibiting the possession and use of vernacular translations, and these restrictions tightened until the Spanish Church, having failed to convince the Council of Trent to adopt its motions to ban Scripture in the vernacular, did so unilaterally with its 1551 Index.[12] Formal education in Latin was so strictly forbidden to women that Teresa felt constrained to attribute the understanding she did have to a transitory divine gift: "While in this quietude, and understanding hardly anything of the Latin prayers, especially of the psalter, I have not only understood how to render the Latin verse in the vernacular but have gone beyond to rejoicing in the meaning of the verse" (*Life* 15.8).[13] If for various reasons Teresa did not attend closely to the letter of Scripture, however, she did comprehend its spiritual sense.

Teresa's conversion, like Augustine's, pivots on tropological reading, but rather than a text of Scripture she reads an image of Christ, as we have seen. In a later locution, God designated the equivalence of Christ and Scripture as means of His revelation

when, after the 1559 Index added short translated passages of
Scripture in devotional books to the 1551 ban on complete texts,
He gave her the consolation of a vision of Christ, calling it a
"living book."

> When they forbade the reading of many books in the vernacular, I
> felt that prohibition very much because reading some of them
> was an enjoyment for me, and I could no longer do so since only
> the Latin editions were allowed. The Lord said to me: "Don't be
> sad, for I shall give you a living book." . . . His Majesty had be-
> come the true book in which I saw the truths. (*Life* 26.5)[14]

Teresa relates her response to seeing this vision of Christ in
terms that recall both parts of the tropological sense.

> Blessed be such a book that leaves *what must be read and done*
> so impressed that you cannot forget! Who is it that sees the Lord
> covered with wounds and afflicted with persecutions that does
> not *embrace them and love them and desire them?* (*Life* 26.5;
> my emphases)[15]

Teresa thus specifies that the individual's reading of revelation,
whether Scripture or a vision of Christ, entails two spiritual
movements, "love" and "desire" for Christ and acceptance of
the obligation to do "what we should."

Teresa most often describes her debt in general terms, as a responsibility to serve God, but her later works define the service
she desires more specifically as bringing souls to God, or contributing to the evangelical mission of the Church. Yet while
those to whom Augustine reports his new dedication, his mother,
Monica, and his friend, Alypius, applaud and promote his plans
for converting others to Christianity, Teresa confronts only im-
pediments when she attempts to follow the dictates of her tropological reading of revelation: "There is nothing that comes to
mind that [the soul] thinks would be of service to Him that it
wouldn't venture to do. . . . The trouble is that for persons as
useless as myself there are few opportunities to do something"
(*Life* 21.5). Here she disguises the required deference as humility, attributing inaction to her own failings, but the succeeding sentences begin to render the argument, which continues
throughout all of her works, that men have excluded women
from Christian history despite their considerable abilities. Teresa most often expresses this grievance indirectly, but in a pas-

sage from *Road to Perfection* that, not surprisingly, was blotted out by censors, she accuses "the [male] sons of Adam" of preventing women from doing "anything worthwhile" for God.

> It is not enough, Lord, that the world has intimidated us [women] . . . so that we may not do anything worthwhile for You in public or dare speak some truths that we lament over in secret, without Your also failing to hear so just a petition? I do not believe, Lord, that this could be true of Your goodness and justice, for You are a just judge and not like those of the world. Since the world's judges are sons of Adam and all of them men, there is no virtue in women that they do not hold suspect. (*Road* 3.7)[16]

The inversion of values she diagnoses, that virtues are considered faults and truth must be spoken in secret, illustrates the deterioration of worldly society. She continues by warning God that males' responsibility for this disrepair makes them unreliable instruments for the fulfillment of scriptural promise: "These are times in which it would be wrong to undervalue virtuous and strong souls, even though they are women."

The extent to which these obstacles to her ethical subfulfillment of Scripture influenced Teresa's theory of scriptural typology can be seen most clearly in her allusions to the Exodus, the most important Old Testament figure of Christian redemption. Augustine's typological reading of the Exodus, which he develops in his sermon on Psalm 114, emphasizes the completion of its promise. Literally, according to Augustine, the psalm tells a "well-known truth" about Israel's miraculous crossing of the River Jordan. Allegorically, Augustine asserts with a paraphrase of Paul's definition of the Church as the "Israel of God" (Gal. 6:16), the verse refers to the salvation dispensed by the Church through the sacraments. In the tropological sense, Augustine explains, the Exodus promises the divine grace, bestowed with the Incarnation, necessary for each individual's conversion: "As they did not depart until freed by divine help, so no man is turned away in heart from this world unless aided by the gift of divine mercy." Anagogically, Augustine takes the Exodus as a reference to "the end of the world," or eternal salvation. In Augustine's analysis, the reparation of the world necessary for the Second Coming requires no additional divine intervention: "All these things which were done in figure, are now fulfilled in our salvation; because then the future was predicted, now the past is read, and the present observed."[17] In the meantime, for Augustine the Church suffices for mediation between humankind and God.

Teresa's references to the Exodus more closely resemble its use in the rhetoric of political change than the Scholastic justification of the role of the Church or the projection into eschatology. In *Exodus and Revolution*, Michael Walzer demonstrates that the Exodus can be understood as a political as well as a religious event.[18] While most reformers citing the Exodus have used it to inspire human effort to re-create the escape from bondage, often through revolution, Teresa calls on God to intervene in her personal history. For Teresa, the Exodus signifies an example of God's exercise of power in human affairs, one that gives her hope that He might again "extend His powerful arm" to remove her chains but not one that contains permission to carry out the ethical subfulfillment of Scripture.

> [After the experience of union with God, the soul] would want to enter into the midst of the world to try to play a part in getting even one soul to praise God more. And if it is a woman, she is afflicted by the bondage of her nature because she cannot do this, and she has great envy of those who have the liberty to cry out and proclaim who is this great God of Chivalry.
>
> Oh, poor little butterfly, tied with so many chains that do not let it fly where You would like! Have pity on it, my Lord, ordain that she might fulfill something of her desires for Your honor and glory; do not keep in mind its scant merit and weak nature; You, Lord, are powerful enough to make the great sea and the large river Jordan roll back and allow the children of Israel to pass. Do not have pity on her, because with the help of your strength, she can suffer many trials; she is determined to do so and desires to suffer them. Extend your powerful arm, Lord, that she might not spend her life on lowly things. (*Castle* 6.6.3–4; my translation)[19]

Teresa does not question that Christ secured her spiritual redemption, that is, that the first part of the tropological sense is fulfilled for her. Mystical union, which approximates the bliss of heaven, gives her this assurance, and indeed it often tempts her to proceed immediately to her place in eternity, which as Augustine states is the anagogical promise of the Exodus. Teresa gives relatively little attention to eschatological matters, however, preferring to concentrate on the imperative of the second part of the tropological sense. Although she wants, as she puts it here, "to play a part in getting even one soul to praise God more," she cannot do so.

The conflict Teresa describes represents a clash between the allegorical and tropological readings of Scripture, or between Church doctrine and personal salvation for women. James Samuel Preus explains that "when the promise to the Church is made the primary one," as it is in Roman Catholicism, "the way is clear for the claim that all other biblical promises (such as that of the Spirit or of eternal life) are subject to the Church's interpretation of them."[20] Teresa's Church drew its interpretation of the promise to women from Paul's prohibitions against their participation, like 1 Corinthians 14:34: "As in all congregations of God's people, women should not address the meeting. They have no licence to speak, but should keep their place as the law directs." In his introduction to the 1588 edition of her works, Luis de León remarks that Teresa circumvented this Pauline proscription on an active role for women in the Church: "What a miracle it is that a woman, and a woman on her own, could have brought orders of men and women to perfection. . . . Women not being those who teach but those who are taught, as St. Paul writes."[21] One of Teresa's locutions from God illustrates the grounds on which she contradicted ecclesiastical readings of these Pauline instructions. When detractors used Titus 2:5, where Paul specifies that women's activity should be confined to the home, against her proposed foundations, God told her, "'Tell them that they should not follow only one part of Scripture, that they should look at other parts'" (*Spiritual Testimony* 16).[22] Rather than admit to contradictory texts of Scripture, the locution suggests that humanity's flawed wisdom requires occasional divine correction. What Luis de León calls the "miracle" that permitted Teresa to privilege her reading of the tropological sense over the ecclesiastical or allegorical sense was such personal communication with God, or mystical experience.

Accordingly, Teresa often gives the vocabulary of figural fulfillment private rather than collective significance, using the words *promise* (*promesa*) and *fulfillment* (*cumplimiento*) to mean not promises to all of humanity to be executed by the Church but rather God's personal assurances to her. Teresa used fulfillment as a touchstone for distinguishing a divine locution from a diabolical one: "When it is from God I have had much experience in many things that were said to me and were fulfilled after two or three years" (*Life* 25.2). Further, Teresa promises God to help Him fulfill His promises: "I remained with the greatest fortitude and strongest intention to fulfill with all my strength the smallest part of the divine Scripture" (*Life* 40.2).

The view of Scripture revealed in Teresa's theory of typology can be correlated in some of its aspects with the Judaic perspective, though it does not coincide with it. Teresa's sense of temporal bondage, and her call for additional divine revelation, resembles the emphasis in Jewish discourse of the period of the wait for the Messiah; Sanford Shepard relates that in sixteenth-century Spain, "to be a Jew" meant "to await stubbornly the coming of the savior."[23] While the *Repertorium*, a 1494 Inquisitor's manual, provides that in some cases ignorance may be an excuse for sin, it specifies that "the ignorance of the Jews who continue to believe that the Messiah has not yet come is entirely inexcusable."[24] Also, Teresa's attitude toward the Old Testament more nearly resem-bles the Judaic than contemporary Spanish theological opinion, which tended to dismiss the Old Testament as merely an invitation to renewal of Jewish practices. As early as 1484, Hernando de Talavera, a confessor to Queen Isabella and humanist theologian of converso origin, conceded reluctantly that the Church could dispense with the Old Testament.

> The New Testament makes mention of [the Old Testament] as a thing and gives it authority and is figured in it. . . . But we could exist without the Old Testament, even though it is mentioned many times in the New, as we exist with the new [civil] decrees, each of which refers to old ones that we do not have.[25]

The *Repertorium* completely diminishes the significance of the Old Testament, even as prophecy: "[The old laws] did not prefigure anything accomplished by the new law, except accidentally, in that the state of that people represented the images of the people under the New Testament."[26] While Christian typological interpretation tended to blanche the Old Testament of historical significance, few versions of the theory went so far toward annulling its meaning.

Teresa's works suggest that, in contrast with the official Christian view, she did give historical significance to the persons and events of the Old Testament. One of her locutions from God echoes Jesus' words in Matthew 5:17–18 ("not a letter, not a stroke, will disappear from the Law until all that must happen has happened"), an assertion of the continuing validity of Judaic law.[27]

> Within this majesty I was given knowledge of a truth that is the fulfillment of all truths. . . . I clearly understood that it was Truth itself telling me: "This is no small thing I do for you, because it is one of the things for which you owe Me a great deal; for all the harm that comes to the world comes from its not knowing the truths of Scripture in clarity and truth; not one iota of Scripture will fall short." (*Life* 40.1)[28]

Teresa finds her own experience prefigured in the Old Testament. She considers, for example, that her own distinction between imaginative and intellectual visions allows her to evaluate the nature of Jacob's vision of the ladder in Genesis 28:12.

> By means of the ladder Jacob must have understood other secrets that he didn't know how to explain, for by seeing a ladder on which angels descended and ascended he would not have understood such great mysteries if there had not been interior enlightenment. (*Castle* 6.4.6)[29]

And she argues from her own mystical experience that because Moses' vision of the burning bush in Exodus 3:2 does not suffice to explain his subsequent actions, he must also have had what she calls a locution (*Castle* 6.4.7). This attention to the Old Testament verged on heresy by the Inquisition's standard.

Teresa does not move into anti-Christian territory, however. Christ remains firmly at the center of her theology, and she considers Him her personal recourse against the misogynistic provisions of Church doctrine.

Teresa's Tropological Commentary on the Song of Songs

Teresa's most extended application of her feminist hermeneutic appears in her *Meditations on the Song of Songs*, a commentary written between 1566 and 1571 on several verses of the Song. Teresa's division of the tropological sense serves to demonstrate that the Church confines women's experience to the spiritual realm, denying them a history in any other sphere, and that her own fulfillment of the moral imperative of Scripture depends on an additional promise from God in mystical experience.

Of all Teresa's works, the *Meditations on the Song of Songs* provoked the most hostile reaction from the Inquisition. Although Domingo Báñez signed one of the manuscripts of the *Meditations* to indicate his approval on 10 June 1575, in 1580, Diego de Yanguas, another of Teresa's confessors and a theologian of the Inquisition, ordered her to destroy the manuscript and all copies. Jerónimo Gracián, who published the first edition of the work in 1611 in Brussels, maintains in the introduction that Yanguas condemned the work because reading Scripture defied the limitations Paul had placed on women's participation in the Church, not because he found any heretical statements.

> But one of her confessors, thinking it a new and dangerous thing that a woman should write on the Song, ordered this book to be burned, moved with zeal for Saint Paul's instruction that women should keep silence in the Church of God. This meant that they should not preach in churches, nor give lectures nor print books. And because at the time she wrote the Lutheran heresy was doing great damage, opening the door for women and the ignorant to read and explicate the divine Word . . . it seemed to him that the work should be burnt.[30]

Teresa is said to have burned the manuscript in his presence, but some of the numerous copies already made by her nuns survived in convent libraries. Luis de León left the *Meditations* out of his 1588 edition of her works, possibly because having spent nearly five years (1572–1577) in prison for translating the Song of Songs from the Hebrew, he did not wish to risk his truce with the Inquisition.[31] Gracián divided the work into chapters and supplied the chapter descriptions and epigraphs, and he gave the work a title, *Conceptions of the Love of God* (Conceptos del amor de Dios). Within the text, Teresa refers to the work as her "meditations," a label used to create the modern title, *Meditations on the Song of Songs* (Meditaciones sobre los Cantares).

The tradition of mystical commentary on the Song of Songs, in which Teresa's *Meditations* belongs, begins with Origen's *Commentary and Homilies on the Song of Songs* (In Canticum Canticorum), circa 240–244. Origen elaborated three senses of the Song, which, in accordance with his view of Scripture as an Incarnation constructed according to the Platonic tripartite image of the human being, he denominated *body, soul,* and *spirit,* or in the standard exegetical terms, the literal, allegorical, and tropological. For Origen, the body represents the historical meaning, which he considers a marriage song in dramatic form; the soul, the nuptials of Christ and the Church; and the spirit, the union of God and the individual soul.[32] The numerous mystical exegetes of the twelfth century devote attention principally to Origen's tropological sense. In his *Sermons on the Song of Songs* (Sermones supra Cantica Canticorum, 1135–1153), Bernard of Clairvaux encourages his audience of Cistercian monks to identify imaginatively, first, with the sensual experience of the male Bridegroom, then, in the feminine role of Bride, with the spiritual passions.[33] Bernard's equation of the affective movements of the soul with tropological reading serves to reconcretize the literal level, which had previously been spiritualized with allegorical interpretation. In mystical commentaries such as Bernard's, Ann W. Astell explains in *The Song of Songs in the Middle Ages,* "the allegory is literalized, joined again to the letter from which it was derived, and ascent turns into descent."[34] While Origen's commentaries have principally an exegetical purpose, then, Bernard's sermons also serve the rhetorical end of guiding his monks to cultivate the ascetic life.

An Inquisitor's judgment notwithstanding, Teresa's *Meditations* resembles biblical exegesis only in superficial ways.[35] Teresa takes her translations of the Song from the Daily Office of the Virgin, which Carmelite nuns recited daily except on feast days, rather than from a text of the Bible.[36] The exegetical format, with quotation of and commentary on five verses from the Song (1.1, 1.2, 2.3, 2.4, 2.5) as well as brief reference to several other verses (2.16, 4.7, 6.3, 6.10, 8.5), was imposed on the work by Gracián. Teresa does acknowledge the existence of an exegetical tradition, but she places her work outside it by pleading a weak memory and citing God as her only source: "His Majesty knows well that even though at times—and these were few— I have heard explanations of some of these words and have been told their meaning when I asked, I don't remember the explanations at all, for I have a very poor memory. Thus, I shall be able to say only what the Lord teaches me and what serves my purpose" (*Meditations* 1.9).[37] Besides, she complains, the explications by "doctors of the Church," probably a reference to Bernard, have not satisfied her desire for the true meaning of the Song (*Meditations* 1.8).[38] Teresa remarks two philological problems that had been addressed by many commentators (the shift in person of the possessive pronoun in Song 1:1 from third person to second person, a characteristic of Hebrew poetry sometimes construed as the presence of a third speaker,[39] and the repetition of the word *kiss* and the apparent redundancy of the word *mouth* in the first line), but she declines to solve these issues by rational means: "I don't understand why this [use of pronouns in two different persons] is; and that I don't understand gives me great delight" (*Meditations* 1.1).[40] Rather than for explication of the Song of Songs, Teresa uses her *Meditations* principally for self-interpretation.

Like Bernard, Teresa reliteralizes the tropological sense of the Song—but to the end of narrating her spiritual history. Teresa's tropological reading of the Song establishes a connection between two events she describes as concrete, if not historical in the ordinary sense: the marriage of the Bride in the Song of Songs and her own mystical marriage with God. She states this allegorical equation straightforwardly: "a soul in love with its Spouse" can "experience all these favors, swoons, deaths, afflictions, delights, and joys [narrated in the Song] in relation to Him" (*Meditations* 1.6).[41] With this literalized tropological sense, Teresa shows that the only history allowed her by the Church is spiritual, the first part of the tropological meaning, and she argues that she be allowed to undertake the ethical subfulfillment that a full tropological reading of Scripture mandates.

As a corollary to her concretization of the tropological sense, Teresa values the purely verbal aspect of the literal level of the Song more than either Origen or Bernard. Probably because the Song so aroused his sexual desire Origen prohibited reading it to all but the most spiritually advanced: "I advise and counsel everyone who is not yet rid of the vexations of flesh and book and has not ceased to feel the passion of his bodily nature, to refrain completely from reading this little book."[42] Teresa seems to know the tradition of restricting readership of the Song, but possibly because for her the Song releases passions more various than specifically libidinal, she gives the words of the Song a role in creating her spiritual interpretation of it:

People will say that I am a fool, that the words [of the first line of the Song] don't mean this, that they have many meanings, that obviously we must not speak such words to God, that for this reason it is good that simple people do not read these things. I confess that the passage has many meanings. But the soul that is enkindled with a love that makes it mad desires nothing else than to say these words. Indeed, the Lord does not forbid her to say them. (*Meditations* 1.10)[43]

The Song itself has a materiality for her, as she implies by comparing it to a king's brocade robe.

And I interpret the passage in my own way, even though my understanding of it may not be in accord with what is meant. . . . I hold it as certain that we do not offend Him when we find delight and consolation in His words and works. A king would be happy and pleased if he saw a little shepherd he loved looking spellbound at the royal brocade and wondering what it is and how it was made. (*Meditations* 1.8)[44]

Like the king's gown, the words of the Song cloak profound mysteries (*Meditations* 7.1) and tremendous secrets (*Meditations* 4.1), the allegorical or spiritual senses. Against those who argue that the Song "could have been said in another style," presumably without the similitude of human love, Teresa defends God's choice of medium as well as message: "What more was necessary than this language in order to enkindle us in His love and make us realize that not without good reason did He choose this style" (*Meditations* 1.4).[45] Reading the text of the Song, in which Teresa considers that God "humbled" Himself as in the Incarnation, provides her a sensory pleasure equivalent to meditating on the body of Christ.

Teresa leaps over the allegorical or ecclesiastical sense, which traditionally intervenes between the literal sense and the spiritual senses, to the tropological.[46] The ideal reader of Teresa's tropological sense, in both of its aspects, is the Virgin Mary. Rather than reason or curiosity, the approaches Teresa finds characteristic of male interpreters, Mary uses feeling as an instrument of reading. Employing the double meaning of the word *sentir*, which signifies both *to mean* and *to feel*, Teresa equates feeling with reading and vice versa: "What deep secrets there are in these words! May the Lord give us experience of them, for they are very difficult to explain" (*Meditations* 4.1; also see 3.1).[47]

Accordingly, the Virgin refrained from conducting rational inquiry into the mystery that the angel Gabriel announced to her.

> She did not act as do some learned men (whom the Lord does not lead by this mode of prayer and who haven't begun a life of prayer), for they want to be so rational about things and so precise in their understanding that it doesn't seem anyone else but they with their learning can understand the grandeurs of God. (*Meditations* 6.7)[48]

In still more exemplary fashion, the Virgin accepted her role in the Incarnation, improbable though it initially seemed. While she followed her first instinct and asked Gabriel, "How can this be?" after he answered, "The Holy Spirit will come upon you; the power of the Most High will overshadow you" (Luke 1:34–35), she did not pursue her inquiry: "As one who had such great faith and wisdom, she understood at once that if these two intervened, there was nothing more to know or doubt" (*Meditations* 6.7).[49] In agreeing to become mother of Christ, the Virgin undertakes the ethical subfulfillment of her tropological reading.

Teresa begins the sections on Song 1:1 by phrasing the request for His kiss, which she interprets as a sign of His friendship and peace, with a direct command ("'Kiss me with the kiss of your mouth'" [*Meditations* 1.10]) rather than with the indirect command ("Let Him kiss me . . .") that more literally translates the verse. The boldness of the request startles her into a realization of her unworthiness for this reading of the Song, and she vows to undertake spiritual development, which coincides with refinement and enlargement of the capacity to feel, that is, to read. Her path begins with the purgative process, which she defines as learning to feel spiritual pain. Using third-person narrative, she tells her history of learning to read the Song tropologically. The first step is rejecting the sins she calls the "kiss of Judas," or the kinds of false peace that anesthetize and atrophy the soul. In the sense that Dante's sins in the *Inferno* can be said to converge in treachery, Teresa's catalog of sins centers on failure of feeling: insensitivity to one's own sinfulness, indicated by relaxation of discipline and disobedience of superiors; fascination with worldly rewards such as material wealth, honor, and praise; indulgence in the pleasures of the flesh, including eating well, sleeping long, and seeking entertainment. Teresa then turns to the positive feelings the soul must develop to merit the true kiss: developing contempt for earthly things; spending time only with those who love God; and desiring to give one's life in martyrdom (*Meditations* 3.3; 3.4, 5; 3.8). When the soul at last desires this kind of sacrifice, it has earned the right to request God's kiss, as Teresa herself does in a passionate restatement of the verse that merges her own voice with that of the Bride: "I repeat, my God, and beg You through the blood of your Son that You grant me this favor: 'Let Him kiss me with the kiss of His mouth,' for without You, what am I, Lord?" (*Meditations* 4.8).[50]

Teresa devotes her discussion of the next several verses of the Song to explaining the stages leading toward mystical union, the point at which she must begin to carry out the ethical subfulfillment. (See chap. 4 for a discussion of all the terms Teresa uses to describe the progression toward mystical union.) Drawing on a tradition of describing God with maternal imagery that was prominent in the affective spirituality of the late Middle Ages, Teresa portrays God as mother, sole source of joy and nourishment to the infant soul. Suckling the divine breast, the soul experiences enjoyment equivalent to all earthly pleasures combined as well as understanding of this verse of the Song through enjoyment: "May our Lord give us understanding or, to put it better, a taste—for there is no other way of being able to understand—of what the soul's joy is in this state" (*Meditations* 4.7).[51] Once having understood God's gift, Teresa returns to her plea for a way to acknowledge the moral imperative inherent in Christ's suffering: "'What can I do for my Spouse?' . . . Truly, sisters, I know not how to resolve this difficulty" (*Meditations* 4.10, 11; Peers's translation).

In her commentary on Song 2.3, 4, Teresa takes the maturing soul through its increasing enjoyment of God's pleasures to mystical union. God now prepares a kind of baby food for the weaned soul: "The Lord gives from the apple tree, . . . the fruit already cut, cooked, and even chewed. So that she says 'His fruit is sweet to her taste'" (*Meditations* 5.4). To the more developed soul God becomes a vintner with a fully stocked cellar of fine wines, each supplying devotion, fortitude, or virtue as the individual soul requires. In mystical union, where following the Latin translation of Song 2.4, which emphasizes the humanitarian over the erotic aspects of the Hebrew word for love, Teresa relates with the Bride that "'He set charity (*caridad*) in order within me.'" Yet Teresa goes on to specify that the Bride actually means love (*amor*): "How well ordered love [*amor*] is in this soul!" (*Meditations* 6.11). To the soul, for whom mystical experience has worked its metal and adorned it with jewels and pearls, God speaks the words of Song 4:7: "'You are all beautiful, my love'" (*Meditations* 6.9).

Ordered in both charity and love and armed with their opposite, disregard (*desamor*) for the rewards and comforts of this world, the soul now desires acts of charity and courage. Teresa interprets the flowers requested by the Bride in Song 2:5 as charitable works for God and the apples as persecutions for Christ: "I understand by these words ['Stay me with flowers and surround me with apples'] that the soul is asking to perform great works in the service of our Lord and of its neighbor. For this purpose it is happy to lose that delight and satisfaction" (*Meditations* 7.3).[52] When a woman attempts to undertake such heroic deeds, however, she finds herself thwarted by the prohibitions on women's activity in the Church. Hindered by these obstacles, she comes to the end of an unfolding history in the world.

Teresa projects an imaginary historical trajectory for the Bride by linking her figurally to the Samaritan woman of John 4:7–42 who talked with Christ at the well. Christ's words to the Samaritan woman produce both the desire and the capacity for heroic works on His behalf. As in most of His dialogues in the Johannine Gospel, Christ attempts to lead the Samaritan woman to a spiritual understanding of physical phenomena, beginning with water and leading to Himself. He presents the possibility that well water she has drawn could give her insight into God's gift of eternal life: "Everyone who drinks this water will be thirsty again, but whoever drinks the water that I shall give him will never suffer thirst any more" (John 4:14). When she continues to understand the water in material terms, He proves His prophetic power by telling her that contrary to the impression she gives when she says that she has no husband, she has been married five times and lives with yet another man. Now ready to listen, she concurs with his statement that "those who are real worshippers will worship the Father in spirit and in truth" and affirms her belief in the coming Messiah. Christ then gives her a revelation that Teresa considers analogous to her own vision of Christ, the "living book": "I am he, I who am speaking with you" (John 4:26). Using imagery she often applies to the mystical encounter, piercing of the heart and wounding by a celestial herb, Teresa describes the Samaritan woman as transformed by these words from Christ.

> I recall now what I have often thought concerning that holy Samaritan woman, for she must have been wounded by this herb. How well she must have taken into her heart the words of the Lord, since she left the Lord for the gain and profit of the people of her village. This explains well what I am saying. And in payment for her great charity, she merited to be believed and to see the wonderful good our Lord did in that village. . . . This holy woman, in that divine intoxication, went shouting through the streets. What amazes me is to see how the people believed her—a woman. And she must not have been well-off since she went to draw water. Indeed she was very humble because when the Lord told her faults to her she didn't become offended . . . but she told Him that He must be a prophet. In sum, the people believed her; and a large crowd, on her word alone, went out of the city to meet the Lord. (*Meditations* 7.6)[53]

The imagery of intoxication here makes the analogy between the Samaritan woman and the Bride, whose mystical communication with God Teresa considers to give her also the capacity for heroic works. After this meeting with Christ, the Samaritan woman undertook the mission of preaching the arrival of the Messiah: "Many Samaritans of that town came to believe in him because of the woman's testimony: 'He told me everything I ever did'" (John 4:39). Teresa takes the words of Song 8:5, "'Under the apple tree I raised you up'" (*Meditations* 7.8), as God's promise that He will intervene in the world to permit His mystical Bride to undertake the works appropriate for her ethical subfulfillment of the tropological sense.

Fulfilled Tropology in the Lives of New Testament Women: Mary Magdalene and the Samaritan Woman

In a late work entitled *Satirical Critique*, Teresa makes explicit the significance she gives to the New Testament women, like the Samaritan woman and Mary Magdalene, who encountered Christ incarnate. When in 1576 she heard God tell her, "Seek yourself within Me" ("Búscate en Mí"), she related His words to her brother Lorenzo, who gathered some friends for a contest in which each offered an interpretation. Their letter to Teresa, probably written toward the end of 1576, has not survived, but her response can be found in the *Satirical Critique* (Vejamen, meaning taunt or lampoon).[54] In tones ranging from bemused tolerance to disdain, she criticizes the interpretations of four male correspondents and the bishop of Avila, who had requested her reply. Responding to John of the Cross's explication, Teresa writes, "Seeking God would cost very dear if we could only do it when we were dead to the world. The Magdalene was not dead to the world when she found him, nor was the Samaritan woman or the Canaanite woman [Matt. 15:21–28; Mark 7:24–30]."[55] With this rejection of John's explanation, which apparently divorced spiritual experience from the physical world, Teresa emphasizes the importance of the encounter with Christ for the subsequent lives of the New Testament women. Teresa ascribes to the words Christ spoke to these women not simply prophetic power but what J. L. Austin calls "performative" power, the power to accomplish what they assert.[56] Teresa considers that the words Christ spoke to Mary Magdalene, "Your faith has saved you; go in peace" (Luke 7:50), actually produced peace within her: "This greeting of the Lord [referring to 1 Cor. 6:17] must have amounted to much more than is apparent from its sound. So, too, with the Lord's words to the glorious Magdalene that she go in peace. Since His words are effected in us as deeds" (*Castle* 7.2.7).[57] Thus Teresa regards the New Testament women as having been transformed by the words Christ spoke to them.

Based on her analogy between the words Christ spoke to the New Testament women in this life and the words God speaks to the soul in mystical experience, Teresa makes the lives of these New Testament women scriptural paradigms for her own life. Like the words Christ spoke to the Samaritan woman, the Canaanite woman, and Mary Magdalene, God's words to the soul are performative: "Words composed by the intellect do not produce any effect. Those the Lord speaks are both words and works" (*Life* 25.3; also see *Life* 25.18). These divine words, Teresa demonstrates, should permit the ethical subfulfillment of

Scripture, or, as she puts it in the *Meditations*, spiritual marriage with God should produce regal actions.

> If a peasant girl should marry the king and have children, don't the children have royal blood? Well, if our Lord grants so much favor to our soul that He joins Himself to it in this inseparable way, what desire, what effects, what heroic deeds will be born from it as offspring, if the soul be not at fault! (*Meditations* 3.9)[58]

For Teresa, then, the lives of the New Testament women represent the completed fulfillment of both phases of the tropological sense of Scripture, and they promise similar fulfillment for those who achieve mystical union: "What He did in a short time for the Magdalene His Majesty does for other persons in conformity with what they themselves do in order to allow Him to work" (*Life* 22.15).[59]

Of the lives of these New Testament women, Teresa develops only that of Mary Magdalene. While any single allusion to Mary Magdalene seems random and obscure, and Teresa changes her interpretation slightly over time, the isolated references can be fitted together into a coherent construction of her life. For her version of Mary Magdalene's life, Teresa draws principally on the *Flos Sanctorum*, the Spanish translation of Jacobus de Voragine's *Golden Legend* (Legenda aurea, ca. 1260).[60] Jacobus combined scriptural story, patristic commentaries, and hagiographical legend with fanciful etymological derivation of names to create the most widely known medieval lives of the saints. Although the *Golden Legend* had been condemned not just by Protestants but by Catholic thinkers as divergent as Juan Luis Vives, humanist scholar, and Melchor Cano, scholastic theologian, for its historical inaccuracy, Teresa writes of reading it at home with her brothers (*Life* 1.5), and she lists it as a book that prioresses should make available in the convents (*Constitutions* 8). Parallel with the *Golden Legend*, Teresa's concept of Mary Magdalene conflates the fisherwoman who bathed Christ's feet with fragrant oil and her tears in the home of Simon the Pharisee (Luke 7:36–50), Mary of Bethany, the sister of Martha and Lazarus (John 11), and Mary Magdalene.[61] In a move of what Alicia Ostriker calls "mythic revisionism," however, Teresa alters the significance of Mary Magdalene.[62] Adding Martha of Bethany to the cluster of scriptural figures comprising the Mary Magdalene of the *Golden Legend*, Teresa discards her traditional identity as a prostitute, and in showing her Mary and Martha working simultaneously in their respective vocations, the contemplative and the active life, Teresa illustrates the fulfillment of both phases of the tropological sense.

Teresa's integration of Martha into her figure of Mary Magdalene allows her to alter the significance of the Pharisees' designation of her as a "sinner." Mary Magdalene was so thoroughly identified with prostitution that priests visited the brothels on her feast day to urge the women's repentance. Those who accepted were paraded through the streets to have their conversions officially recognized. Through this ritual, Perry observes, "a woman could thus exchange her formal label of prostitute for that of penitent."[63] The life of Teresa's Mary Magdalene before the meeting consists instead in performing the domestic labors associated with Martha (Luke 10:38–42), such as showing Christ hospitality and preparing His meals. Wishing for suspension of the faculties in ecstasy before having fully exercised the soul in the rigors of meditation is like "wanting to be Mary before having worked with Martha" (*Life* 22.9), Teresa warns.

Before assuming the privileged role of contemplative, Teresa explains, Mary "had already performed the task of Martha, pleasing the Lord by washing His feet and drying them with her hair" (*Castle* 7.4.13). Mary's performance of these humble works demonstrates the injustice of the gossip, which Teresa attributes to envy of her nobility and wealth, a biographical detail probably drawn from the *Golden Legend*.[64]

> And do you think it would be a trifling mortification to a woman in her position to go through those streets—perhaps alone, for her fervour was such that she cared nothing how she went—to enter a house that she had never entered before and then to have to put up with uncharitable talk from the Pharisee and from very many other people, all of which she was forced to endure? (*Castle* 7.4.13; Peers's translation)[65]

After her meeting with Christ, Teresa speculates, Mary Magdalene would have aroused still more hostility. In one of very few explicit references to the Jewish people, Teresa represents them taunting the Magdalene in the streets for her new relationship with Christ, which Teresa considers to have been signaled in sartorial terms.

What a sight it must have been in the town to see such a woman as she had been making this change in her life! Such wicked people as we know the Jews to have been would only need to see that she was friendly with the Lord, Whom they so bitterly hated, to call to mind the life which she had lived and to realize that she now wanted to become holy, for she would of course at once have changed her style of dress and everything else. Think how we gossip about people far less notorious than she and then imagine what she must have suffered. (*Castle* 7.4.13; Peers's translation)[66]

Teresa's Magdalene draws strength for withstanding such undeserved torment in the knowledge that God will defend her, as Christ did when the Pharisees rebuked her and when Martha complained about the apparent inequities in their work: "Observe how the Lord answered for the Magdalene both in the house of the Pharisee and when her sister accused her" (*Road* 15.7).[67] Teresa's Magdalene enjoys Christ's constant advocacy.

While medieval legend invariably considered Mary Magdalene's turn away from prostitution to be her conversion, Teresa locates it in her expression of love for Christ in the house of the Pharisee. Of the various ways in which John's fisherwoman demonstrates her love—kissing Christ's feet, washing His feet with her tears, drying them with her hair, anointing Him with oil—Teresa privileges the tears as the most important sign of her piety. Teresa recalls that it was Mary of Bethany's weeping that moved Christ to raise Lazarus from the dead (*Road* 23.7; *Soliloquies* 10.2, 3), and she relates, here in a third-person autobiographical passage, that she reexperiences Mary Magdalene's tears every time she takes communion: "She [Teresa] considered she was at His feet and wept with the Magdalene, no more nor less than if she were seeing Him with her bodily eyes in the house of the Pharisee" (*Road* 34.7).[68] Christ's reward to Mary Magdalene, the words "Go in peace," perform a conversion swifter even than Paul's: "Look at St. Paul, or the Magdalene. Within three days the one began to realize that he was sick with love; that was St. Paul. The Magdalene knew from the first day; and how well she knew!" (*Road* 40.3).[69] These words to Mary Magdalene correspond to Christ's revelation of his divinity to the Samaritan woman: "How many times do I recall the living water that the Lord told the Samaritan woman about!" (*Life* 30.19)[70] As the Samaritan woman exhibited great charity (*Meditations* 7.6), the

Magdalene also, according to Teresa's representation of her life, immediately committed herself to serving God.

Teresa's portrayal of the life of Mary Magdalene after the Crucifixion contains traces of several of the roles she takes in medieval legends—hermit, martyr, preacher—but the inclusion of Martha in the figure permits Teresa to emphasize the role least developed in prior tradition, that of the apostle.[71] One of the paths on which Teresa places her follows that of the Mary Magdalene portrayed by the *Golden Legend*, who after several adventures at sea becomes a hermit in southern France, and of another Mary associated with the Magdalene in medieval legend, St. Mary of Egypt, a converted prostitute who spent forty-seven years in the desert with only her long hair as clothing and three loaves of bread as sustenance:[72] "Let [the soul] remain [at the feet of Christ] as it desires; let it imitate the Magdalene, for if it is strong, God will lead it into the desert" (*Life* 22.12).[73] Yet while Teresa recognizes the desert as a ground of sainthood, she more often considers it an escape from the greater challenges found in the world. Teresa acknowledges that "many saints have gone to the desert to protect themselves from gossip and criticism," but she considers remaining with people an act of greater humility: "It is a kind of humility not to trust in oneself but to believe that through those with whom one converses God will help and increase charity while it is being shared" (*Life* 7.22). For her Magdalene as for herself, Teresa rejects the role of hermit.

Teresa also treats Mary Magdalene as a martyr, not for physical but for spiritual suffering. She witnessed the Crucifixion, where she experienced a torment compounded, in Teresa's estimate, by abuse from an unruly crowd at the foot of the cross.

> How much the glorious Virgin and this blessed saint [Mary Magdalene] must have suffered! How many threats, how many wicked words, how much shoving about and rudeness! For the people around them were not exactly what we would call courteous! No, they were people from hell, ministers of the devil. (*Road* 26.8)[74]

Like the Mary Magdalene in some medieval legends, Teresa's figure experiences martyrdom in her grief for Christ after His death, a martyrdom she shares with Paul: "What must St. Paul and the Magdalene and others like them have undergone, in whom this fire of the love of God had grown so intense? It must have been a continual martyrdom" (*Life* 21.7).[75] Further, she suffers what Teresa calls the martyrdom of feeling inadequate for the divine favor she has received. Teresa's occasional touches of the hermit and martyr in her portrait of Mary Magdalene, however, fade beside the far more complete delineation in the role of apostle.

The tradition Jacobus follows in naming Mary Magdalene as the "apostle to the apostles" in the *Golden Legend* originates in the Gospel of John, which identifies her as the first person to speak with the risen Christ (20:1–18).[76] According to John, the risen Christ appears to Mary Magdalene as she weeps over the empty sepulchre. Mistaking Christ for a gardener, she demands to know if he has moved the body. Christ speaks her name, "Mary," and she responds with words of recognition, "Rabboni (which is to say, Master)" (John 20:16), and He gives her the first news of His Resurrection and dispatches her to spread the word: "'Go to my brothers, and tell them that I am now ascending to my Father and your Father, my God and your God'" (John 20:17). With her report to the disciples, "'I have seen the Lord!'" (John 20:18), Mary Magdalene became the first apostle. Yet, as both Mark and Luke assert, the male disciples discredited her: "She went out and carried the news to his mourning and sorrowful followers, but when they were told that he was alive and that she had seen him they did not believe it" (Mark 16:10, 11; also see Luke 24:11). Teresa does not address this rejection directly, but with her provision that the Samaritan woman "was believed," she corrects the Gospels' version.

With the integration of Martha into her Mary Magdalene, Teresa creates a figure that combines the contemplative life, in which her soul communes with God, and the active, in which she carries out works in the world. In the *Life*, Teresa designates these works as "charity" and "business affairs," but she also draws on the attribution of the "greatest eloquence" to both Mary and Martha in the *Golden Legend*.[77] In the *Interior Castle*, Teresa names the work as "bringing Him souls."

> Mary and Martha must join together in order to show hospitality to the Lord and have him always present and not host Him badly by failing to give Him something to eat. How would Mary, always seated at His feet, provide him with food if her sister did

not help her? His food is that in every way possible we draw souls
that they may be saved and praise Him always. (*Castle* 7.4.12)[78]

Addressing those nuns in her audience who might recoil from
this forbidden task by citing their incapacity, Teresa names the
role of apostle: "The other objection you will make is that you
are unable to bring souls to God, that you do not have the means;
that you would do it willingly but that not being teachers or
preachers, as were the apostles, you do not know how" (*Castle*
7.4.14).[79] She backs away from the (negatively stated) proposition that women might serve as apostles by calling her statement
metaphorical, as meaning that even if they cannot convert souls,
they can help their sister nuns achieve spiritual perfection. Yet
after all her pleas for heroic action, her consolation to them, that
"the Lord doesn't look so much at the greatness of our works as
at the love with which they are done" (*Castle* 7.4.15), expresses
more resentment than conviction. Unlike Mary Magdalene and
the other New Testament women, they must await permission
from the Church for the opportunity to fulfill the tropological
meaning of Scripture.

The order that Teresa gives to her disorderly life consists in
reading it figurally as a fulfillment of the lives of the New Testament women. Given her Inquisitional audience Teresa cannot
make her claim to similar authority overtly; instead she conceals it, rather thinly, with irony: "I then look at the life of
Christ and of the saints, and it seems to me I'm going in the opposite direction since they didn't advance except through contempt and insults" (*Life* 31.12). In chapters 3, 4, and 5, I argue
that her *Life* demonstrates that her life, in part because of the
contempt she has suffered, is indeed moving according to the
pattern of a saint's.

3

TERESA'S REPRESENTATION OF HER "OLD LIFE"
Life 1–10

Like Augustine, Teresa uses imagery of rebirth to describe her life after conversion. Augustine writes of having "slain my old self" and "purposed to renew my life" (*Conf.* 9.4). Teresa considers that conversion divides her life into two segments, a "new life" so separate and distinct from her "old life" that she introduces the narrative as a different text: "This is another, new book from here on—I mean another, new life" (*Life* 23.1).[1] In both function and perspective, then, the preconversion narrative of the *Life* corresponds to the retrospective narrative of the *Confessions*, in which Augustine narrates "the twisted tangle of knots" (*Conf.* 2.10) that comprise his life prior to conversion and confession of faith.

Against Augustine's adventures in the "cauldrons of lust" at Carthage and Rome, however, many critics find Teresa's narrative of her old life uninformative and uninteresting. Gari Laguardia expresses that dissatisfaction.

> The reader who turns to Teresa's text expecting the type of revelations found in other works of the same genre—those of Saint Augustine or Rousseau, for example—is bound to be disappointed. While Teresa is fond of berating herself for her sins, she gives the reader few specific examples to justify her bad conscience. . . . [I]t is surprising that she does not take the opportunity to utilize the first section as an exemplary catalogue of sinful activity. On the contrary, those chapters which concern her life before taking up her religious vocation are the vaguest of all.[2]

While this complaint misses the point that Augustine provides few specific details and that many of the sins he confesses, such as the theft of pears, refer generically to the sins of all humankind, it does correctly remark the cryptic nature of Teresa's confessions in the *Life*.

Critics have explained this vagueness about her sins in various ways. Many biographers have assumed that as a prospective saint, Teresa had few if any sins to confess. Laguardia argues that Teresa lacks the Augustinian conviction of sin because she transforms her unacceptable carnal emotions into justifiable spiritual desires.[3] Both explanations, however, mistakenly assume that the *Life* reflects Teresa's emotion and action straightforwardly. Instead, as we have seen, she wrote in a perilous rhetorical situation that precluded sincerity while demanding the appearance of it. For this reason, Weber's explanation based on rhetoric more nearly accounts for Teresa's evasiveness about her sinfulness. Defining her situation as a double bind, the necessity of presenting herself with the contradictory qualities of virtue and humility, Weber argues that Teresa "engages in contradictory speech acts, pleading innocent and guilty at the same time. . . . Teresa executes speech acts whose *force* is confessional . . . but the rhetorical *effect* is defensive."[4] An extension of rhetoric to include genre provides an even more complete answer. Having been commanded to write judicial confession, Teresa does not select the events of her past based on the remorse they caused her. Neither did she choose incidents that demonstrated her sinfulness or that illustrated her theology and anthropology, the principles of selection Augustine used.[5] Instead Teresa concentrated on narrating those circumstances and events from her early life that could raise suspicion of heresy, as well as those that might serve to counter the charge.

Ascertaining the significance Teresa herself attaches to any particular situation or event, particularly those of her childhood, presents insurmountable difficulties in many instances. Teresa's assessment of her father's affections for his children, for example, defies interpretation even while clamoring for it.

> We were in all three sisters and nine brothers. All resembled their parents in being virtuous, through the goodness of God, with the exception of myself—although I was the most loved of my father. And it seemed he was right—before I began to offend God. For I am ashamed when I recall the good inclinations the

Lord gave me and how poorly I knew how to profit by them. (*Life* 1.3)[6]

Until recently many critics and biographers have restated such assertions as historical fact. With no apparent source but this passage, Efrén and Steggink write that "all of the others [in the household] revolved around her."[7] Reading even more literally, it seems, Lincoln suggests that this love nearly resulted in incest.[8] Contemporary critical methods might provide an array of possible meanings, including the psychoanalytic suspicion that she might be expressing the fantasy of an unfavored child. Without a way to verify the emotions of Teresa's father, the modern reader can reliably conclude only that Teresa found it important to represent herself as the child he loved most.

Reading the discourse of the *Life* as a play of genres provides a means of understanding the principles of selection Teresa followed, if not always the significance of particular details. In Bakhtinian terminology, the retrospective narrative of the *Life*, in chapters 1 through 10, can be understood as a hidden polemic against the genre of judicial confession conducted with the inflections of hagiography and Christian spiritual autobiography. In the hidden polemic Teresa anticipates the questions an Inquisitor might raise about her heritage, and she addresses both general and particular accusations of sexual sin by giving her early years the structure of a saint's life.

A Response to the Inquisitional Questionnaire

The retrospective narrative of Teresa's *Life* may be read as a response to a hypothetical interrogation covering those subjects on the Inquisition's questionnaire as well as the events in her life that, possibly because they had prompted some gossip, were already known to some of her early readers.

Sixteenth-century Inquisitional practice of interrogation established the autobiographical narrative as the principal form of evidence. Starting in the early 1500s, the Inquisition systematically asked every accused person to tell the story of his or her life.[9] In the *Directorium*, Nicolau Eymerich stipulates the questions to be asked.

The Inquisitor will interrogate the accused about his or her place of birth and place of residence. About his parents (are they alive?

Deceased?). He will ask where the accused was brought up, by whom, and where he has lived. He will be especially wary of changes of domicile: has the accused left the places of his childhood? Has he traveled in regions infected with heresy, and if so, for what reason?[10]

The *Directorium* further instructs the Inquisitor to determine the extent and quality of the accused's education in Christian doctrine by asking, for example, "if he has ever heard talk of the poverty of Christ, or of the apostles, or of the beatific vision." If the Inquisitor continues to have doubts, the *Directorium* recommends, he "might ask the accused to recite ordinary prayers, one might interrogate him about Christian doctrine, and finally one might ask him where, when, and to what priests he has confessed his sins."[11] From these standard questions, Inquisitors turned to inquiry related to the specific charges.

For every accused person, the Inquisition filed written responses, which were either taken down by a notary or, on occasion, written out by the accused. Later, Inquisitors would ask the same questions and compare the answers with the record, often seizing on the omission of details or contradictory stories, whether related to the charge or not, as proof of the accused's guilt. The archives of the Inquisition burgeoned with autobiographical narratives that even persons once found innocent might be called on to duplicate at any moment.[12] While Teresa never stood formal trial, she, like all conversos and others who were automatically suspect, might well have considered herself continuously on trial. Much of the detail of the opening chapters of the *Life* suggests that she had assimilated the charges implied in the Inquisitional questionnaire and formulated her responses in anticipation of an accusation.

Teresa was not alone in attempting to adapt this Inquisitional autobiographical narrative to her own purposes. Adrienne Schizzano Mandel shows that María de San Jerónimo used her deposition to construct a life that would be recognizable rather than invisible to the authorities. María, who had been adopted by the prominent Lutheran Agustín Cazalla (burned at the stake in 1559) and then was converted to Islam by her Moorish fiancé, denounced herself to the Inquisition in 1581. Mandel observes that this uncoerced statement provided her the position of a speaking subject: "The judicial inquiry, which gives the architectural structure to her account, permits her the use of official writing to register her discourse, the pen of the notaries furnishing her with a power that the dominant ideology had explicitly denied her."[13] Perry adds that women also sought influence by taking the Inquisitional roles of accuser and witness.[14] Teresa's commands to write specified that she use the discourse of judicial confession, but rather than writing the script of self-condemnation demanded by the genre, Teresa deployed it to the end of self-defense.

Teresa opens the *Life* with an enigmatic statement about her relationship to her parents: "To have had virtuous and God-fearing parents along with the graces the Lord granted me should have been enough for me to have led a good life, if I had not been so wretched" (*Life* 1.1).[15] The sentence has most often been read as a formulaic admission of sinfulness (see the discussion of this sentence in the preface). A 1636 version of the *Flos Sanctorum*, like most subsequent biographies, recast the sentence into a statement of her family's nobility: "Both [her parents] were noble, and excelled in all kinds of piety and virtue."[16] The sentence is neither so simple nor so artless, however. Márquez Villanueva correctly notes that Teresa does not actually say that her parents belong to the nobility or that they have the "clean blood" required for such social status.[17] Teresa's use of the subjunctive for the main verb, *to suffice*, undermines the apparent certainty of the assertion of their virtue. In disavowing the influence of such ambiguous parental influence, Teresa might even be seen to distance herself from her family.

Many, if not most, of Teresa's contemporaries would have known that she was descended from Jewish lineage on her father's side. Teresa's grandfather, Juan Sánchez (1440–1507), a successful textile merchant, had converted to Christianity, but like many other conversos in the fifteenth century, he returned to Jewish observances and educated his sons in them, or so his brother-in-law complained to the Inquisition.[18] When a traveling tribunal visited Toledo to offer the edict of grace, a temporary provision that offered absolution to those who denounced themselves, Juan Sánchez declared himself and his family guilty of unspecified acts of heresy and apostasy against the Catholic faith.[19] In 1484, he complied with the ritual for absolution, the humiliation of walking, on seven consecutive Fridays, through the streets of Toledo wearing a *sambenito*, a bright yellow knee-length tunic embroidered with black crosses and flames to identify him as a Judaizer.[20] Teresa's father, six years old at the time, accompanied him on these walks. As a reminder of their disgrace, their tunics were put on permanent display in the cathedral.

Her grandfather's acceptance of the edict of grace permitted him to avoid the bankruptcy usually caused by the long period of presumed guilt and self-defense required under the more severe edict of faith enacted in 1500, but he did not escape the stigma that Spain attached to Jewish heritage.[21] Although some clergy had expressed the hope that baptized Jews would be regarded simply as Christians, in fact converso families were identified as such and persecuted, at first informally and then institutionally, by both Church and state. Ignoring the stipulation of canon law that baptism is irreversible, the Church denied the efficacy of the Jews' conversion on the basis of what Henry Kamen calls a "racialist doctrine of sin."[22] First formulated in the late fifteenth century, the statutes of racial purity (*limpieza de sangre*) prohibited converted Jews from entering universities, holding public office, joining religious orders, and conducting most types of financial transactions and eventually excluded them from nearly every outlet for participation in society. It is not too extreme to characterize these statutes as, in Juan Ignacio Gutiérrez Nieto's words, instruments for the sociopolitical death of the conversos.[23]

When her grandfather's Toledo business deteriorated as a result of his denunciation, he moved his business and family to the nearby Castilian town of Avila. Attaching his wife's Old Christian surname to his own, he assumed the name Juan Sánchez de Cepeda. Gossip did reach Avila about his condemnation in Toledo, but at this time Spanish society provided many ways of fabricating an Old Christian background. In 1500, he purchased a certificate of pure blood (*ejecutoria*), which permitted him to step into the social role of a nobleman. He followed the typical practice of attempting to assimilate the next generation by marrying his sons into Old Christian families, most of them, like the family of Teresa's mother, in a state of financial decline that induced them to accept the larger dowries conversos offered. With the certificate he and his sons also gained the right to conduct a variety of businesses, including tax collection, which royal decree prohibited to recently converted Jews. It was business competitors rather than religious zealots who brought a lawsuit charging his sons with false nobility in 1519, when Teresa was four. They prevailed by having friends testify that the family had lived as nobility in Toledo. The apparent ease of the settlement belies the danger such a suit presented to the family. Writing anonymously in 1515 a converso assesses the impact of the statutes: "Before the Inquisition the *conversos* were the most wealthy, powerful, and feared segment of society but now they are the most abject and least respected, particularly if one of their grandfathers had been punished by the Inquisition."[24] The words Teresa is reported to have spoken on her deathbed, "I die a daughter of the Church," might be taken in part as an expression of a wish to secure a posthumous identity apart from her biological parentage.

Teresa nowhere acknowledges her converso heritage directly, but she almost certainly knew about it. Castro argues that conversos recognized each other by their condition in life and the means by which they concealed their origins: "For the *conversos* themselves it would not have been as difficult as it is for us to know who was and who was not [a converso]."[25] Of Teresa's works, the *Foundations* provides the most concrete evidence: she describes a prospective nun, Teresa de Layz, as of "pure blood" (20.2), and she discusses the role of lineage in some of the business transactions (15.15). Many of her contemporaries also indicate that they knew. Diego de Yepes, who met Teresa in 1576, virtually acknowledges her heritage in his 1587 biography of her.

> Although knowing the origin of the parents that a servant of God had on this earth matters little, in order that this account not be lacking in truth or fact, I will have to relate those of this saint. She was, then, born in Avila, and of noble lineage on both sides.[26]

Another early biographer who also knew Teresa, Francisco de Ribera, mentions the lawsuit against her father and even as he denies its significance by attributing it to the move from Toledo, provides a detail that would have signaled the likelihood of converso heritage to Inquisitors instructed to be "especially wary of changes of domicile."[27] In the hearings for Teresa's canonization conducted throughout Spain from 1591 through 1610, many witnesses who had known her gave guarded responses to questions about her lineage: Báñez, who evaluated the manuscript of the *Life*, states that "no one denies her parents' nobility"; Yepes bases his confirmation of her nobility on the report that the Marqués de las Navas had said that "Teresa's lineage was older than his own."[28] In 1591, the current mayor of Avila testifies to her Old Christian heritage by referring to a genealogical investigation that had cleared one of her nephews.[29] About her canonization Teresa might have commented ironically, as she did about her success in overcoming financial obstacles to making her foundation in Caravaca, "It could not be because I am from the nobility [literally, illustrious blood] that He has given me such honor" (*Foundations* 27.12).[30]

Teresa's Jewish descent remained publicly unmentioned until 1946, when Narciso Alonso Cortés presented records of her grandfather's reconciliation with the Inquisition in the *Bulletin of the Spanish Royal Academy*.[31] Even having the documentary evidence, many biographers continued to describe her ancestry as Old Christian. Efrén and Steggink, authors of the most comprehensive modern biography, admit that they suppressed the information in the first (1968) edition "to mitigate the moral effect of the surprise to readers"; another recent biographer attempts to demonstrate that her grandfather was an Old Christian who made a superfluous conversion out of exaggerated piety.[32]

Teresa's Jewish heritage, then, gave her particular reason to stress her parents' contributions to her Christian education. Because those conversos who returned to Jewish traditions generally did so by observing household rituals rather than by gathering publicly, the Inquisition found descriptions of early religious instruction revealing. A child's mention of lighting candles or eating particular foods sometimes led to denunciation of the entire family. The succeeding sentences in the first paragraph of the *Life*, which accentuate her parents' virtue, might also be considered to anticipate questions about her family's religious practices.

> My father was fond of reading good books, and thus he also had books in Spanish for his children to read. These good books together with the care my mother took to have us pray and be devoted to Our Lady and to some of the saints began to awaken me when, I think, six or seven years old, to the practice of virtue. (*Life* 1.1)[33]

On this subject also, Teresa's praise of her parents is muted by ambivalence. An inventory of her father's books made after the death of his first wife reveals that he did own several devotional books, the "good books" to which Teresa refers, as well as a collection of Spanish literature and classical works in translation.[34] A later chapter, however, reveals that for instruction in reading "good books," she awaited a visit at age twenty-three to her uncle, who introduced her to Osuna's *Third Spiritual Alphabet*, the book she relied on for spiritual instruction (*Life* 3.4).

In the meantime, Teresa's mother taught her to read the bad books of the day, novels of chivalry.

> She loved books of chivalry. But this pastime didn't hurt her the way it did me, for she did not fail to do her duties; and we used to read them together in our free time. . . . Our reading such books was a matter that weighed so much upon my father that we had to be cautioned lest he see us. I began to get the habit of reading these books. And by that little fault, which I saw in my mother, I started to grow cold in my desires and to fail in everything else. (*Life* 2.1)[35]

Teresa's father was not alone in disapproving of the novels of chivalry. Even though the knights in the Spanish novels of chivalry, such as *Amadís de Gaula* and *Las sergas del Esplandián*, often defended Catholicism against infidels, their sexual license defied contemporary standards of morality. Intellectuals and clergy alike attacked the novels as instruments of vice. Revealing a similar attitude, Teresa links her budding adolescent sexual desires to her insatiable pursuit of the chivalric chain of signifiers: "I was so completely taken up with this reading that I didn't think I could be happy if I didn't have a new book. I began to dress in finery and to desire to please and look pretty" (*Life* 2.1, 2).[36] Teresa excuses her mother's indulgence in the forbidden novels as an escape from "the great trials she had to bear" (*Life* 2.1), which she does not specify but which might refer to the circumstances of her mother's life that led her prematurely to adopt the dress of an old woman. Already pregnant when she married Teresa's father at age fourteen, Beatriz de Ahumada (1495?–1528) bore ten children in fewer than twenty years; she died soon after giving birth to Teresa's sister Juana.[37] Anxiety aroused by Teresa's identification with her mother's reading might explain the exchange she attempts to make between her sexually bound mother and the inviolable Virgin Mary: "I remember that when my mother died I was twelve years old or a little less. When I began to understand what I had lost, I went, afflicted, before an image of our Lady and besought her with many tears to be my mother" (*Life* 1.7).[38] After the litany of complaints against her parents, her exoneration of them rings rather hollow: "If I start to complain about my parents, I am not able to do so, for I saw nothing but good in them and solicitude for my own good" (*Life* 1.8).[39] Her later ecstatic vision of Joseph and Mary as benevolent parents outfitting her with jewels (*Life* 33.14), which conversos were forbidden to wear, might be interpreted in psychological terms as an attempt to replace her own parents with others who could suitably reward her.

With the remainder of the retrospective narrative, which recounts events after she left her family home, it is equally difficult to ascertain Teresa's motives for selecting particular incidents: the tone of paranoia belies the vagueness of the details. The Inquisition's policy of withholding information about the exact nature of the charges against the accused, quoted below from the *Directorium*, could have caused her to review every event in her life with anxiety.

> In the matter of heresy, one proceeds the same way [as in civil law]: it is necessary that the accused not know the specific thing with which he is charged. It is necessary to arrive there by a constant digression, posing questions about the bill of indictment itself to bring the accused to confess or perhaps to remember the crime that he had forgotten. Mentioning the bill of indictment to the accused so that he might escape the snares of the interrogatory constitutes, in Inquisitorial terms, a very grave offence.[40]

While the burden of prospective accusation provoked some persons to denounce themselves, it spurred Teresa to defend herself.

Unlike Augustine in the *Confessions*, Teresa does not narrate her actions as a confession to God: the principal audience for the *Life* is man, not God, even though she sometimes addresses Him directly. Unlike God, who judges her by her intentions rather than her actions, the human beings for whom she writes have already judged her by appearances. She sometimes complains that they have been too lenient with her because God has allowed her to masquerade as a virtuous person: "I was doing deeds that uncovered what I was, and the Lord was covering my evils and uncovering some little virtue, if I had it, and making it great in the eyes of others so that they always esteemed me highly" (*Life* 7.18).[41] At the same time she protests that they have wrongly accused her: "Often times [in the novitiate year] I was accused about things without my being at fault" (*Life* 5.1). As Weber shows, Teresa retracts or qualifies every concession she makes in the *Life*. When she does confess to a misdeed, she shifts the responsibility to others: "In falling I had many friends to help me; but in rising I found myself so alone that I am now amazed I did not remain ever fallen" (*Life* 7.22).[42] Because these friends were either known to or included among her readers, she necessarily proceeds with circumspection, concealing while seeming to reveal.

Teresa summarizes the nearly twenty years between her monastic vows and her conversion experience as a "battle and conflict between friendship with God and friendship with the world" (*Life* 8.3). In a losing battle much of that time, she broke her monastic vows.

> I don't know how I am going to continue here when I remember the kind of profession I made and the great resolve and happiness with which I made it and the espousal that I entered into with You. I cannot speak of this without tears; and were they tears of blood and were they to break my heart, the sentiment would not make up for the way I offended You afterward. (*Life* 4.3)[43]

Ribera found these admissions of sin sufficiently alarming to cause readers to believe that "she must have sinned against her chastity and virginity." After making written inquiries into her conduct, he identifies her sin as "open dealing and friendly conversations with men," not as innocuous as it now seems for its implication of flirtation, but not mortal sin. Drawing mainly from exculpatory evidence in Teresa's *Life*, Ribera certifies that her sins were venial rather than mortal.[44] Teresa blames her confessors for this betrayal of Christ. While she obscures the specific nature of their complicity in her sin, she does express three general complaints against them: they did not correctly distinguish venial and mortal sin; they failed to instruct her in mental prayer; and they did not discourage those friendships and activities that distracted her from spiritual development. Lincoln explains this criticism by positing Teresa's romantic involvement with one or more confessors, but she provides no substantiating evidence. Whatever the reason, Teresa expresses considerable bitterness toward them. In addition to explaining or justifying events that apparently had provoked gossip or criticism, every episode Teresa narrates demonstrates her confessors' failings.

In one of the most detailed episodes, Teresa relates that she stole an amulet from her confessor at Becedas, who is identified by editors as Pedro Hernández. In spending several months in the spring of 1539 at a nearby spa to attempt to recover from the first stages of an illness that would develop into nearly total paralysis, she learned that a local woman held the parish priest under a magical spell of love with a copper figurine he wore around his neck. Convincing the priest to give her the amulet, Teresa threw it in the river. Teresa admits doing wrong here, though she mitigates her offense by stating her desire to do good: "My intention was good; the deed bad. For in order to do good, no matter how great, one should not commit the slightest wrong" (*Life* 5.6). Yet it is difficult to know exactly what wrongdoing she admits. Teresa implies that deception and theft may be her sins, yet the Inquisition would almost certainly have approved the destruction of such a tool of witchcraft, a practice treated as heresy.[45] Teresa also implies that she might have sinned by showing Hernández the affection necessary to make him surrender the figurine, but she continues by speculating that his desire rather than hers actually accomplished the benefit, reinforcing her earlier insinuation that he was the one who demonstrated the inappropriate affection.[46] Finally, while confessing to venial sins, if not to mortal ones, Teresa accuses the priest, whom she describes as "learned, although not greatly so," for misleading her about the nature of her sins.

> I have come to see by experience that it is better, if they are virtuous and observant of holy customs, that they have little learning. For then they do not trust themselves without asking someone who knows, nor do I trust them; and a truly learned man has never misguided me. Those others certainly could not have wanted to mislead me, but they didn't know any better. I thought that they really know and that I was obliged to no more than to believe them, especially since what they told me was liberal and permissive. If it had been rigid, I am so wretched that I would have sought out others. What was venial sin they said was no sin at all, and what was serious mortal sin they said was venial. (*Life* 5.3; also see 4.7, 8.11)[47]

Teresa takes the blame for relying on this misinformation: "It was on account of my sins, I believe, that God permitted these confessors to be mistaken themselves and to misguide me" (*Life* 5.3). Nevertheless, the episode as a whole functions to condemn the system that gave even priests with little education and doubtful intelligence total authority over women.

In another intriguing though even more enigmatic episode, Teresa confesses to what she calls pastimes, vanities, and "occasions" (translated by Peers as "situations"). On one of these "occasions," which she describes as a prolonged intimate conversation with a person she does not identify, she saw a huge toad approaching them (*Life* 7.8). While the twentieth-century mind might explain this apparition as an actual toad (as Lincoln suggests), an optical illusion, or a hallucination, for Teresa it signified a warning from God. Lincoln identifies the other person as García de Toledo, then vice rector at St. Thomas in Avila and one of Teresa's longtime confessors; Efrén and Steggink do not identify the person.[48] Whatever the nature of the toad or the conversation, it is unlikely that these startling events would have gone unreported in the convent. An Inquisitional audience would have considered the rumor of such an unnatural occurrence as possible evidence of heresy, and the hint of any romantic or sexual relationship would similarly have led to investigation. Teresa's narrative of this incident can plausibly be seen as a defense against real or imagined accusations by the Inquisition. For her indulgence in "occasions" like these Teresa blames the system of open convents that allowed nuns and their visitors of either sex to come and go without restriction or supervision. Although she begins with the assertion, "The convent where I resided was not at fault" (*Life* 7.1), two paragraphs later she charges, "It did me great harm not to be in an enclosed monastery" (*Life* 7.3).[49] Efficient with her rhetoric here as elsewhere, Teresa makes an argument for stricter discipline while also explaining, even if not entirely justifying, her well-known "occasions."

The only episode in which Teresa truly accuses herself involves deceiving her father about her own spiritual condition just prior to his death. Teresa herself notes the anomalous character of this anecdote: "I don't know why I have told this" (*Life* 7.16).[50] Indeed, for its confession of wrongdoing as well as its entirely private nature, it is atypical. For more than a year, Teresa relates, she allowed her father to believe that her chronic illnesses, daily vomiting and severe chest pains, prevented her from engaging in the discipline of prayer when she knew her lapses attributable to her "occasions." Nearly identical phrasing suggests that with this episode Teresa rehearses her earliest relationship with her father. In introducing her father, she offers that "he was very honest" (*Life* 1.1), a trait she emphasizes again here: "He did not lie, and by this time, in accord with the things I spoke of to him, I shouldn't have lied either" (*Life* 7.12).[51] By this time, Teresa implies, she should not again have deceived her father, as she had in reading novels of chivalry and conducting the adolescent sexual experimentation that led him to send her at age sixteen to the Augustinian convent of Santa María de Gracia as a kind of reform school. Yet she implicates him in the blame, for here, as in her childhood, his "esteem and love" for her incapacitate him for carrying out his parental responsibilities, or in the terminology Laguardia uses, he is a "bad 'reader' of her discourse," unable to "decipher her code."[52] In addition to reiterating her complaint against him and expressing remorse for this now irreparable evasion, Teresa uses the episode to deflect any speculation that he might have reverted to Judaism. In his principal symptom, severe shoulder pain, Teresa remarks the physical effects of carrying burdens equivalent to the Cross.[53]

Even in the most apologetic and personal of her narratives, then, Teresa keeps the Inquisitional questionnaire in her peripheral vision. While she does not mention her identification with Mary Magdalene in this section of the *Life*, those readers knowing Teresa's interpretation of her as a "woman of nobility" who was criticized not for prostitution but for her high social station might have transferred the attributes of chastity and nobility to Teresa.

Hagiography in the First Person

With the *Confessions* Augustine made the figural reading of one's own life an essential generic feature of Christian autobiography. While Augustine interprets himself with numerous biblical figures, including St. Paul and Christ, he makes the prodigal son of Luke 15:11–32 the most important figure for self-interpretation.[54] From the perspective gained in conversion, then, Augustine sees that the young man pursuing sensual pleasure in Carthage and professional advancement in Rome was replicating the itinerary of the prodigal son into forgetfulness of God. Because Augustine considers that the prodigal son's journey away from God does not take place in spatial terms, neither does the return. Like the prodigal son, who eventually "return[s] to himself" (Luke 15:17), Augustine begins his own return when he accepts the Neoplatonic concept that God can be found within himself (*Conf.* 7.1). With his conversion, he reenacts the homecoming of the prodigal son, receiving a forgiving welcome and the assurance that God places particular value on his love for its having been lost. The parable of the prodigal son also provides Augustine with his epistemology, formulated as "I believe in order to know" (*"credo ut intelligam"*).[55] Now casting himself as one searching for something lost, he reasons that he could not even conceive the search for knowledge of God unless he had some memory of it. The answer to his question, "How, then, do I look for thee?" (*Conf.* 10.20), is that he must search his memory, which contains not only what he has learned about God but also, as part of its nature, the Truth or Word.

Teresa's figural reading of her life, then, locates the work in the tradition of Christian autobiography Augustine inaugurated in the *Confessions.* For reasons considered in chapter 1, her references to her paradigm, Mary Magdalene and other New Testament women, are not nearly as systematic as Augustine's. In the retrospective narrative of the *Life* preceding the conversion scene, where she makes explicit her identification with Mary Magdalene, she casts herself as a more generic saint.

Teresa represents her early life as a quest to imitate the lives of the saints she read in the *Golden Legend.* In childhood play she tries out the paths of both the martyr and the hermit, which in his structural analysis of the *Golden Legend*, Alain Boureau considers as strands of the category of the "witness saints." Witness saints, Boureau explains, make their lives an imitation of the life of Christ, the martyrs with physical suffering and the hermits with spiritual suffering.[56] When Teresa finds obstacles to these roles, she experiments in play with being a nun, but with, as she puts it, considerably less desire. Through spiritual marriage with Christ, she eventually finds a route to Him that combines two categories of saints in the *Golden Legend* that Boureau considers to encompass the suffering of the witness saints while augmenting it with additional functions: the defenders, who protect the Church by attacking heresy and extending the physical territory of the Church, and the preachers, who in addition to the activities of both the witness and defender, convert souls.[57]

In an episode of the *Life* made famous by George Eliot in *Middlemarch*, Teresa tells of running away from home to make herself a martyr. She identifies martyrs as those saints who achieve an immediate enjoyment of God: "When I considered the martyrdoms the saints suffered for God, it seemed to me that the price they paid for going to enjoy God was very cheap" (*Life* 1.4).[58] In the case of St. Catherine, a fourth-century virgin martyr from Alexandria to whom Teresa later dedicates a poem, the price Teresa considered "cheap" included beatings with scorpions, starvation, and torture on the wheel; and when these methods failed to kill her, beheading.[59] Teresa convinced an older brother, usually identified as Rodrigo, to help her achieve her goal of martyrdom: "We agreed to go off to the land of the Moors and beg them, out of love of God, to cut off our heads there" (*Life* 1.4). Several witnesses in the canonization hearings testified that Teresa told them that the two had reached the Adaja Bridge at the edge of Avila before an uncle, dispatched on horseback by their mother, recovered them.

Rather than martyrdom, Teresa's principal desire seems to have been rejection of society. Martyrdom, Alison Goddard Elliott explains in *Roads to Paradise*, takes place *within* society: "Literal martyrdom is unimaginable divorced from its political and social context."[60] The most significant portion of a martyrdom is a courtroom scene, in which the prospective martyr engages in a verbal confrontation with the social authorities. The *Golden Legend* portrays St. Catherine successfully disputing the emperor with "diverse modes of the syllogisms, by allegory and metaphor, by logic and mystic." Her persuasive rhetoric converts the fifty orators lined up against her, the emperor's wife, the captain of the army, and two hundred soldiers. Rather than emphasizing her own relationship to society, however, Teresa defines the journey as a thwarted attempt to escape from society, specifically, her family: "Having parents seemed to us the greatest obstacle" (*Life* 1.4).[61] Just as she crossed into liminal space, however, her family reintegrated her.

Teresa and her brother then tried out the mode of spiritual suffering represented by the hermit saints, whose experience does occur in liminal space. In contrast with the public drama of martyrdom, the suffering of the hermit takes place in solitude, sometimes becoming known to the world only when another hermit seeking a cave finds the corpse along with evidence of self-imposed deprivation and suffering. The first move toward this sainthood is a flight from society, often on the eve of an occasion that signals irreversible incorporation into society, such as marriage. The prospective saint then shows the capacity to endure suffering by taking little, if any, food and water on the journey to the site of hermitage, usually a natural cave rather than a human construction of any kind. Their experiment confined to their own backyard, Teresa and her brother saw their gestures toward such sainthood collapse immediately: "In a garden that we had in our house, we tried as we could to make hermitages piling up some little stones which afterward would quickly fall down again" (*Life* 1.5). Teresa abandoned this project also, but late in life when confronted with the example of Catalina de Cordona, a hermit who founded a monastery on the site of her cave, Teresa suffered severe regret that she had not persisted in taking this path.

Teresa also uses play to try out the role of nun, which has been considered a less extreme point on the continuum of spiritual suffering that culminates with the hermit. Charles F. Altman argues that the lives of the hermit saints display an ethos of gradation between good and evil that differs from the binary opposition in the plots of the martyr saints, where martyrdom represents the only good. While the extreme measures taken by the hermit may represent the best religious life, intermediate stages such as an ascetic or a monastic life are judged merely not quite as good rather than as unacceptable.[62] Rather than external obstacles, as with martyr and hermit, Teresa faces internal resistance to the role of nun: "When I played with other girls I enjoyed it when we pretended we were nuns in a monastery, and it seemed to me that I desired to be one, although not as much as I desired the other things I mentioned [martyr and hermit]" (*Life* 1.6).[63] Teresa eventually takes this route, and when she does, she makes an escape characteristic of the hermit saints. Unlike those saints, however, her motive consists in fear rather than love. Without her father's permission and in part because she "feared marriage" (*Life* 3.2), she persuaded another of her brothers, Antonio, to accompany her in an early morning escape from home. Her ambivalence caused her tremendous suffering: "When I left my father's house I felt that separation so keenly that the feeling will not be greater, I think, when I die. For it seemed that every bone in my body was being sundered." (*Life* 4.1).[64] Laguardia and Weber argue that her conflict did not cease until she transferred her emotions from her father to God.

Even having entered the Carmelite convent of the Incarnation in Avila, Teresa continued to test herself in various saintly roles. Among her colleagues she observed a nun who suffered patiently through a particularly painful, repellent illness: "There were some holes in her abdomen which caused obstructions in such a way that she had to eject through them what she ate" (*Life* 5.2). After her death, Teresa undertakes to imitate this model of sainthood, essentially a martyrdom in which the prospective saint flaunts physical suffering as a means of devaluing this world: "I asked God that, dealing with me in like manner, He would give me the illnesses by which He would be served" (*Life* 5.2). She relates that God answered this prayer with an illness no "less painful or laborious" than the other nun's. In 1538, she developed dizzy spells and chest pains which were diagnosed as consumption, and then a seizure that left her unconscious for four days, probably 15 through 19 August 1538. The ensuing paralysis, which at its most extreme permitted her movement of only one finger of her right hand, lasted for three years. In part because her muscles did not deteriorate during these years as they would have if she had had an illness, many doctors have judged the paralysis to be neurotically produced.[65] Josef Breuer and Sigmund Freud pronounce Teresa "the patron saint of hysterics," and indeed her descriptions of her illness coincide with their definition of hysteria as the discharge of an affect in a somatic reaction.[66] Teresa herself links her physical symptoms to spiritual malaise, describing the suffering in mental and emotional as well as physical terms: "Everything seemed to be disjointed; the greatest confusion in my head; all shriveled and drawn together in a ball" (*Life* 6.1). This illness nearly permitted Teresa the opportunity for a martyr's death. After she had lain unconscious for a couple of days, doctors and priests, convinced that she was already dead, sealed her eyes with wax and dug her grave. On her revival, she decided, "I would be able to serve God much better if I were in good health" (*Life* 6.5). By the time she had finished the *Life* and made her first foundation, she had exchanged the model of the martyr for the role Boureau defines as the preacher, a decision she reaffirms here: "When we read in the lives of the saints that they converted souls, I feel much greater devotion, tenderness, and envy than over all the martyrdoms they suffered" (*Foundations* 1.7).[67] Over time she extended that role to include the functions of defender of the faith.

In chapter 4, I describe Teresa's path to mystical union with God, where she receives the equivalent of Christ's words to Mary Magdalene, "Go in peace." These words, Teresa argues, make her an apostle. St. Paul similarly uses visionary experience to substantiate his claim to apostleship: "Am I not an apostle? Did I not see Jesus our Lord?" (1 Cor. 9.1).

4

TERESA'S ANALOGIES FOR
HER MYSTICAL EXPERIENCE
Life 11–22, *Interior Castle*

Teresa describes the terminus of her mystical experience as a "complete transformation of the soul in God" (*Life* 20.18) analogous to the alteration Christ made in Mary Magdalene with His words, "Go in peace." Although instantaneously awarded to Mary Magdalene, this transformation requires an extended exercise of the soul from those who succeed her: "What He did in a short time for the Magdalene His Majesty does for other persons in conformity with what they themselves do in order to allow Him to work" (*Life* 22.15). Teresa describes her own progression toward the required discipline throughout her works, most systematically in the section of the *Life* known as Four Ways of Watering the Garden (chaps. 10–22) and the *Interior Castle*. This chapter examines the verbal and theological resources Teresa marshaled to communicate her own experience of spiritual transformation to her multiple audiences, which here, as for other works, ranged from skeptical priests to sisters eager to follow her path to perfection.

Although like every mystic Teresa considers her experience ineffable, or inexpressible in linguistic or conceptual terms, she frequently attempts to explain it by using what she calls "comparisons" between material and spiritual phenomena.[1] Critics usually define those works in which she extends these comparisons—the Four Ways of Watering the Garden and the *Interior Castle*—as allegories, while also pointing out their problematic standing within the genre: of the *Interior Castle* Weber writes, "Although an allegory, its coherence is elusive, for there is no one-to-one correspondence between literal signifier and allegorical signified"; and Concha demonstrates that Teresa's allegories dissolve rather than develop.[2] As these observations themselves suggest, Teresa's comparisons are more accurately identified as analogies than as allegories.

Teresa puts her comparisons not principally to the didactic, logical, or aesthetic ends associated with allegory but rather to theological purposes: she makes analogies between material and spiritual worlds as a means of understanding the spiritual. And while she does press the analogies into expository and pedagogical service, to convince confessors of the orthodoxy of her experience and to encourage her nuns, she often appears to be attempting to extend her own understanding of her spiritual experience by trying out various analogical avenues. Even within a single chapter she sometimes uses the same object to explain distinct experiences that she may have no interest in relating one to another, and when one analogy does not serve fully to explain a spiritual phenomenon, she continues to introduce more analogies until she has either given a sufficient explanation or exhausted her stores of comparison. With respect to genre, these sections of Teresa's works are not allegories but treatises on mystical theology in the form of an anatomy of her own soul. In defining Four Ways of Watering the Garden and the *Interior Castle* as treatises or commentaries on mystical theology, I decline to consider them as mystical texts, which Michel de Certeau defines as those texts that speak with the voice of the Other, texts effectively written not by the mystic but by God.[3] While Teresa sometimes invokes the mystical topos, as when she implores God to use her as a vehicle for His speech as in *Interior Castle* 1.1.1 or when she tells of writing in an inspired frenzy, she most often speaks with her own voice. Her lack of education and empowerment prevent her from writing texts recognizable as theological, which Certeau considers the antithesis of the mystical text, but her treatises on mystical theology may be said to conduct a female mystic's dialogue with the abstract systems of theological texts.

The vocabulary that persists through even the most protean of Teresa's analogical constructs is Augustine's terminology for the faculties, or functions, of the soul: memory, understanding, and will. Beginning with the observation that love is constituted of a triad—lover, loved, and love—Augustine developed the theory that spiritual self-knowledge entails the interaction of three faculties: the memory brings forgotten knowledge of the soul to the faculty of understanding, and when the soul is thus known to itself, the faculty of will binds all three together in love. Because the human soul is constructed in the image of God, Augustine reasoned, the exercise of the faculties in knowing the self leads toward, though not actually to, knowledge of the interrelations among the triad of Father, Son, and Holy Ghost. Teresa applies the theory of the soul's faculties, developed by Augustine for the purpose of explaining the operations of the Trinity, to spiritual self-interpretation. Discarding Augustine's idea of equality and interrelation of the faculties, Teresa describes battles and defections among them that reflect her own spiritual conflicts and capacities.

The significance Teresa gives to the Augustinian functions of the soul are idiosyncratic, devised from her experience, not from any system. While Augustine's notion of the will emphasizes its function as the instigator of action, Teresa privileges capacity for emotion in her descriptions of will (*voluntad*), thereby representing her struggle against insensitivity. Teresa's descriptions of the process of knowing, which she assigns to both understanding and memory, diagnose her difficulties with mental activity. With Augustine, she defines the understanding (*entendimiento*) as mental apprehension, an intuitive function of knowing both the self and God, but she distinguishes it more definitively from reason (*razón*). While Augustine designates reason the highest of human attributes, Teresa considers it an inferior mode of knowing. In addition to treating memory (*memoria*) as the Augustinian recollection of mental images,[4] Teresa considers it the faculty for acquiring such images from God. And she often equates memory with thought (*pensamiento*), an unreliable mental operation for her, and with the imagination (*imaginación*), which conjures fancies and hallucinations. By adding these erratic aspects to memory, Teresa represents her own difficulties with unwanted reminiscence ("the deaths and worries of the world are nonsense, at least when grief or love of relatives and friends endures a long time" [*Testimony* 1.24]),[5] and she portrays her struggle to discern diabolical deceptions from divine truth.

Augustine treats the will as the most intractable of the faculties, the one that causes his agonizing delay before conversion: "The mind orders itself to make an act of will, and it would not give this order unless it willed to do so; yet it does not carry out its own command. . . . The reason, then, why the command is not obeyed is that it is not given with the full will" (*Conf.* 8.9). Augustine comes to understand that original sin causes his will to be divided and that only God's grace, won by Christ on the Cross, can repair it. Teresa's misquotation of a line from the *Confessions* illustrates her lack of concern with will in this Augustinian sense. In book 10, after confessing to persisting desires for carnal pleasure, Augustine pleads that God keep his will steadily directed toward spiritual objects: "Give me the grace to do as you command, and command me to do what you will!" (*Conf.* 10.29). Teresa refers to these lines several times, and although indicating direct quotation, she alters them to delete the request for the healing of the will: "Understanding this [that I couldn't do anything by myself] helped me very much; and also what St. Augustine says; 'give me, Lord, what you command, and command what You desire'" (*Life* 13.3; also see *Meditations* 4.9, *Exclamations* 5.2).[6] This plea to be given what He commands, rather than the grace to do as He commands, suggests that Teresa's inability to act requires not God's reparation of her will but His intervention with external, societal forces. For Teresa the most problematic of the faculties, the one whose progress defies human effort, is the memory.

Augustine conducts the introspective operation of the faculties as a means of knowing God: "Who is this Being who is so far above my soul? If I am to reach him, it must be through my soul" (*Conf.* 10.7). Teresa, by contrast, considers the exercise of the faculties as a means of preparing the soul for His appearance in the soul. She recommends contemplating the disparity between God's grandeur and human lowliness, for example, not as an end in itself but as a means of strengthening the faculties: "Our intellects and wills, dealing in turn now with self now with God, become nobler and better prepared for every good" (1.2.10). For this reason, the condition and activity of the faculties serve Teresa for taking the measure of the soul's development in Four Ways of Watering the Garden and the *Interior Castle*. Teresa's definitions of the faculties, because so personal, alter somewhat with her own development, yet within a given work, this vocabulary of the faculties remains relatively steady while her comparisons multiply and succeed one another.

Rather than on the sequence of correlations or analogies, then, my discussion of the mystical treatises centers on the particular faculties whose development Teresa chronicles in each of her mystical treatises. While Teresa's mystical works have been considered as a progression in the sense that the later ones include additional heights of experience, other differences in emphasis have not yet been identified. In bringing Augustine's construction of the soul to Teresa's analyses, I find that she isolates, with some consistency though not with absolute rigor, different faculties for scrutiny in each of the works: the will in Four Ways of Watering the Garden, the understanding in the first three dwelling places of the *Interior Castle*, and the memory in the next three. In the seventh dwelling place, soul and spirit divide, with the repaired faculties assigned to conducting the soul's work in the world while the spirit is instructed by God.

The Extension of the Will: The Soul as Garden (*Life* 11–22)

Teresa defines her subject in Four Ways of Watering the Garden as the process of becoming a "servant of love," a state the soul achieves by following "the ascent to possession of perfect love" (*Life* 11.1). Teresa's choice of a comparison to describe this development, the analogy between the soul and a garden, conveys the nature of her own principal obstacle to loving God, the incapacity to feel.[7] Observing the nuns' displays of emotion in the first convent she entered, she discovers that she feels nothing: "So hard was my heart that I could read the entire Passion without shedding a tear" (*Life* 3.1).[8] Water, as she implies here, alleviates the principal symptom of the disabled emotions, aridity of the soul, or "that great dryness" (*Life* 4.9).[9] Defining the soul as a garden, then, makes it a repository for water from every possible source: tears, underground springs, irrigation, mists, clouds, drenching rains. Teresa specifies that water in whatever form is a manifestation of love: "By 'water' I am referring to tears and when there are no tears to interior tenderness and feelings of devotion" (*Life* 11.9).[10] As early as the second stage, however, Teresa begins to identify God's gifts to the soul in terms of fire as well as water. She develops the flame along with water as a sign of the developing love until the two

analogies meet in a confrontation that, logically and aestheti-
cally speaking, should extinguish the flame but does not: "The
driving force of that fire is quenched by a water that makes the
fire increase. This sounds like gibberish, but that's what happens" (*Life* 19.1).[11] As Teresa's parallel analysis of this spiritual
development in the terminology of the faculties demonstrates,
water serves Teresa for describing a reversible process, such as
the development of the will's capacity to feel, but it does not
describe the transformation of the will that occurs at the heart
of the mystical experience she chronicles here. Water, as Teresa
herself acknowledges in the *Interior Castle*, does not describe
all spiritual experience: "I don't find anything more appropriate
to explain *some* spiritual experiences than water" (4.2.2; my emphasis). When she comes to experience not explicable with water, the analogy of the soul as garden also loses its explanatory
power.

Teresa's ways of watering the garden, like all her explanations of spiritual development, divide into two stages, the natural and the supernatural: those that require human exertion
alone (the first way of watering), and those in which God assists
the soul in increasingly greater proportion (the second, third,
and fourth ways).[12] In the first grade of prayer, the soul culti-
vates the garden, which is at this point a wasteland of "very
barren soil, full of abominable weeds" (*Life* 11.6), entirely by its
own effort: "You may draw water from a well (which is for us a
lot of work)" (*Life* 11.7).[13] Before collecting even one drop, the
soul may spend long periods "letting the pail down into the well
and pulling it back up without any water" (*Life* 11.10). While
Teresa acknowledges that the understanding, even discursive reasoning, may be useful for some persons at this stage, she designates the will as the faculty that develops; even when the understanding does not work, the "will is being strengthened and
fortified" (*Life* 11.15). Thus she recommends mental prayer, a
practice independent of understanding and reason, as the best
means for the soul to rehearse its prospective emotional relationship with God. All of the soul's "manual labor" here yields
only a drop or two of water, not enough to irrigate the garden but
sufficient to demonstrate the incipient will to love.

In the Second Way of Watering the Garden, which Teresa labels both prayer of quiet (*oración de quietud*) and first recollection (in later works she separates these two states), the soul begins to receive some divine assistance with its watering. She

gives this supernatural intervention the form of mechanical devices: "Or you may get it by means of a water wheel and aqueducts in such a way that it is obtained by turning the crank of the water wheel" (*Life* 11.7). The watering accomplished through human and divine collaboration begins to transform a wasteland into a verdant, fragrant garden that eventually will provide fruits with which the soul can display His grace to the world: "These trees are beginning to bud so as to blossom and afterward give fruit—and also the flowers and carnations so as to give forth their fragrance" (*Life* 14.9). To keep these fragile plants thriving, the soul must vigilantly root out the weeds, or sins, that compete for territory in the garden. Even as she develops the analogy of the garden, she begins to replace water with fire as the sign of divine love: "This [second] prayer, then, is a little spark of the Lord's true love which He begins to enkindle in the soul" (*Life* 15.4).[14] In the conflict of the elements at this stage, water prevails: "However much [the soul] may desire to light the fire and obtain this delight, it doesn't seem to be doing anything else than throwing water on it and killing it" (*Life* 15.4). Yet she forecasts the priority she will give fire: "And if we don't extinguish it through our own fault, it is what will begin to enkindle the large fire that (as I shall mention in its place) throws forth flames of the greatest love of God" (*Life* 15.4). In the fourth stage, fire succeeds water as the principal analogy for God's gift to the soul and its reciprocal expression of love.

Teresa's treatment of this stage with the terminology of the faculties reinforces the importance of the shift of analogy from water to fire. While the will had been impervious to feeling, it now can receive God's love: "Only the will is occupied in such a way that, without knowing how, it becomes captive" (*Life* 14.2).[15] The extraneous activities of the understanding and memory here, however, have the potential to "make the will tepid" (*Life* 15.7), that is, to choke off the fire: the understanding, which she likens to a millstone, casts about for reasons that the soul might not merit such favors, composes speeches using "rhetorical artifices" rather than the emotions of humility and reverence, and searches for ideas and explanations; the memory races around, bringing back her past sins and other disruptive thoughts, while the imagination represents images of the distractions in which the other faculties indulge.[16] These extraneous activities of the understanding and memory cause so much interference, which Teresa describes as noise, that she recommends the will ignore them to enjoy "the beginning of a love of God that has much less self-interest" (*Life* 15.14).

Teresa returns to the analogy of watering the garden for the third stage of prayer. Here the soul expends little of its own effort to obtain water: "It may flow from a river or a stream. (The garden is watered much better by this means because the ground is more fully soaked, and there is no need to water so frequently—and much less work for the gardener)" (*Life* 11.7.) Now the soul has only to direct the flow of the water because Christ virtually takes over as gardener. Teresa's explanation with the analogy of the garden makes this way of watering seem instantaneously achieved, but with the terminology of the faculties, she reveals the intricate process of its achievement. This third stage actually comprehends three different configurations of the faculties. In the first of these, "the will is held fast and rejoicing" (*Life* 17.4) as if in the posture of Mary Magdalene sitting in contemplation at Christ's feet, while the understanding and the memory remain free for work in the world as Martha: "In this prayer [the soul] can also be Martha in such a way that it is as though engaged in both the active and contemplative life together" (*Life* 17.4).[17] The soul can conduct business negotiations and do acts of charity, yet because its will resides with God, it avoids excessive attachment to worldly things and the consequent misplacement of its energy. In the second phase, the understanding joins the will in union with God. The memory, often in alliance with the imagination, attacks and torments the faculties held by God, bringing her to a desperate plea for the unification of the faculties: "'When, my God, will my soul be completely joined together in Your praise and not broken in pieces, unable to make use of itself?'" (*Life* 17.5).[18] Governing the memory, like saturating the garden, requires divine assistance, however, which it receives in the culmination of the third stage, a "sleep of the faculties" (*sueño de las potencias*) from which not even the memory can stray: "The faculties are almost totally united with God but not so absorbed as not to function" (*Life* 16.2).

Teresa's fourth way of watering comprehends two spiritual states, union and elevation: "The union, as I understand it, is different from the elevation. . . . Though they are one, the Lord works differently in each case" (*Life* 18.7).[19] While Teresa manages briefly to use the analogy of the garden for explaining union, she abandons it for elevation. Even before she begins to write, Teresa perceives a compositional impasse: "When I began to write about this last water it seemed impossible to know how to speak of it without making it sound like Greek [literally, Arabic]" (*Life* 18.8). After attending Communion to request divine guidance, she makes a self-conscious attempt to begin developing the analogy: "Well now, let us speak of this heavenly water that in its abundance soaks and saturates this entire garden" (*Life* 18.9). By the end of the sentence she changes the subject to the absence of water and suggests that the soul compensate for such a loss by drawing on alternative sources. The next time she takes up the original analogy at any length, she proceeds from showing how the fruits of the garden benefit others to the ways in which the garden, even after having flourished, can be lost (*Life* 19.3). Teresa's description of union in the vocabulary of the faculties explains the deterioration of the analogy. In the union Teresa describes in the *Life*, even though all the faculties are absorbed in God, only the will actually performs its function, which is to love.

> This bothersome little moth, which is the memory, gets its wings burnt here; it can no longer move. The will is fully occupied in loving, but it doesn't understand how it loves. The intellect, if it understands, doesn't understand how it understands; at least it can't comprehend anything of what it understands. (*Life* 18.14)[20]

Further, this configuration of the faculties holds only a moment, for memory and understanding, withdrawing from the union, begin their interference again: "It is the will that holds high the banner; the other two faculties quickly go back to being a bother" (*Life* 18.12).[21] Spiritual development through the stage of union, as Teresa's analogies and confessions of her lapses illustrate, can be reversed.

The experience of elevation, which Teresa also defines as rapture, transport, and flight of the spirit, makes an enduring alteration in the soul, however: "Rapture produces much stronger effects and causes many other phenomena" (*Life* 20.1). Teresa's garbled, digressive explanations of this phenomenon in the *Life*, by comparison with more lucid passages in the *Meditations* and the *Interior Castle*, suggest that she does not comprehend it as fully as she will after further experience. Reading this section of the Four Ways of Watering thus requires searching out submerged associations between images and ideas. Admittedly making some connections not quite visible in the *Life*, I argue that Teresa requires the analogy of fire to complete her explanation of the transformation of the will.

With the vocabulary of the faculties, Teresa describes the requirements for an analogy appropriate to explaining elevation, as she presents it here. The mystical experience related in the *Interior Castle* produces a division in the soul: "There is some kind of difference, a difference clearly recognized, between the soul and the spirit, even though they are both one. . . . [T]he one functions differently from the other" (7.1.11).[22] In the *Life*, however, she asserts the unity of the soul: "Neither do I understand what the mind is; nor do I know how it differs from the soul or the spirit. It all seems to be the same thing to me" (18.2).[23] In her descriptions of the parallel experience of corporeal elevation, Teresa reveals the anxiety that the prospect of this division causes: "Although this experience is delightful, our natural weakness causes fear in the beginning" (*Life* 20.4). To the end of maintaining the integrity of the soul throughout mystical experience, Teresa deploys the analogy between the soul and fire.

> The way this happens is comparable to what happens when a fire is burning and flaming, and it sometimes becomes a forceful blaze. The flame then shoots very high above the fire, but the flame is not by that reason something different from the fire but the same flame that is in the fire. (*Life* 18.2)[24]

In a later chapter she attempts to use the analogy of water, which all along has the dual function of describing the soul itself as well as gifts from God, proposing that God raises the soul as "clouds gather up the earthly vapours." Teresa herself acknowledges its failure: "I don't know if this comparison is holding together, but the truth of the matter is that this is what happens" (*Life* 20.2).[25] This analogy, as she conceives it here, does not convey the soul's expansion in ascent, but with the analogy of fire, she succeeds in explaining how although soul and spirit remain one, "the soul sometimes goes forth from itself" (*Life* 18.2).

Teresa's description of elevation in terms of the faculties reveals that she also requires an analogy to describe the transformation of the soul. In elevation, God suspends all the faculties for extended periods, and even though the understanding and the memory detach themselves occasionally, they defer to the will's continuous experience of loving. As a kind of graphic illustration of spiritual elevation, God sometimes carries the body away with the soul. This rapture, manifested to other persons as something like a state of unconsciousness or sometimes, Teresa claims, as an elevation of the body, results in the healing of physical ailment. Teresa describes the concomitant transformation of the soul with the analogy of fire. Now, however, the soul becomes the implement made malleable in the divine fire.

> A small fire is just as much a fire as is a large one. Through this example one can see the difference there is between union and elevation of the spirit. In a small fire it takes a lot of time for a piece of iron to become red-hot. But if the fire is great, the piece of iron, even though large, will in a short time lose its entire being—or it will appear to do so. (*Life* 18.7)[26]

In an oblique way, then, Teresa uses fire to introduce the notion of the divisibility of the soul, because once having entered the fire, the spirit wishes to remain, while the soul pulls to rejoin the body: "The soul seeks a remedy so as to live—much against the will of the spirit, or of its superior part, which would not want to break away from this pain" (*Life* 20.14).[27] In this fire, the soul, now become a piece of gold, is purified, fashioned, and enameled by God (*Life* 20.16). When the soul reemerges, God possesses the keys to its will: accordingly, the soul, a "servant of love," functions as custodian of the garden, keeper of a fortress flying the banner of God, mayor of a city. The soul experiences this state as a burning love equal to that of the apostles: "What must St. Paul and the Magdalene and others like them have undergone, in whom this fire of the love of God had grown so intense?" (*Life* 21.7). For relief from this painful fervor Teresa prescribes works.

As if traveling beneath the surface for several chapters of the *Life*, the image of fire returns with the scene known as the transverberation, in which she describes the piercing of her heart by one of the cherubim.

> I saw in his hands a large golden dart and at the end of the iron tip there appeared to be a little fire. It seemed to me this angel plunged the dart several times into my heart and that it reached

deep within me. When he drew it out, I thought he was carrying off with him the deepest part of me; and he left me all on fire with great love of God. (*Life* 29.13)[28]

Teresa articulates this experience in overtly sexual imagery, as Bernini's sculpture in Santa Maria della Vittoria in Rome suggests. Bernini ignores her strenuous cultivation of feeling that prepared her to receive God's love, however. Unlike the merely phallic arrow of Bernini's cherub, which is aimed at her genitals, God's dart pierces Teresa first through the heart.

The Elaboration of the Understanding: The Soul as Castle (*Interior Castle* 1–3)

Teresa takes the process of becoming a servant of God as her subject in the *Interior Castle* also, but here she makes the determination to serve God a function of knowledge rather than emotion, the obstacles to it ignorance rather than insensitivity. The soul Teresa represents in the *Interior Castle* rather naturally enters into the enjoyment of loving God that the soul of the *Life* begins to experience only at the end of the third way. In fact, the most natural course for the will circumvents the understanding: "Once God is found the soul becomes used to seeking Him again through the work of the will, the soul doesn't want to tire itself by working with the intellect." The will depends on the understanding for its function of loving, however: "To avoid [using the understanding] will be impossible, especially before the soul reaches these last two dwelling places; and the soul will lose time, for the will often needs the help of the intellect so as to be enkindled" (6.7.7).[29] In the stages of natural experience (the first three dwelling places), Teresa considers the understanding as the principal working faculty, while in the supernatural stages (the final four stages), as she suggests, she leaves behind the understanding to explore the role of the memory.

Many recent critical analyses of the *Interior Castle* seek to understand why Teresa does not develop the comparison between the soul and a castle into a consistent allegory.[30] Teresa does not drop the analogy of the castle, but she relies on numerous other analogies: the soul as crystal and diamond; as palmetto and tree of life; as silkworm, turtle, and hedgehog; as butterfly, fledgling, and dove. Traditional explanations focus on her lack of formal education and the obvious haste with which she wrote. More recently critics have speculated that she deliberately chose the cascade of competing analogies. Helmut A. Hatzfeld judges that her pedagogical aims took precedence: "An overall image chosen at the start undergoes a considerable extension and produces a galaxy of accompanying images taken from quite different domains to make the experimentally gained insights clearer and clearer."[31] Catherine Swietlicki emphasizes her aesthetic aims, speculating that she was influenced by "Zohar stylistics, in which mixing metaphors and interrelating simultaneous symbol systems is considered an art."[32] Weber considers that the "proliferation of conflicting comparisons" in the *Interior Castle* serve as a "rhetoric of obfuscation": "disorder, digression, and imprecision—these are the tactics that disguise a charismatic text as women's chatter."[33] Rather than the pedagogical, aesthetic, or rhetorical aims of comparison, I think the heuristic function paramount for Teresa. Teresa's choice and orchestration of the multiple analogies of the *Interior Castle* can best be understood in relation to problems she confronts, the process by which the soul comes to know God and in consequence of this knowing, to serve God.

Even the initial presentation of the analogy of the castle indicates that Teresa considers it a heuristic device rather than a definitive comparison to be extended for either literary or pedagogical effect. In constructing an otherwise realistic castle of diamond or crystal, Teresa suggests at the outset that the castle will not suffice for her project of diagramming the soul.

> Today while beseeching our Lord to speak for me because I wasn't able to think of anything to say nor did I know how to begin to carry out this obedience, there came to my mind what I shall now speak about, that which will provide us with a basis to begin with [sic]. It is that we consider our soul to be like a castle made entirely out of a diamond or of very clear crystal, in which there are many rooms, just as in heaven there are many dwelling places. For in reflecting upon it carefully, Sisters, we realize that the soul of the just person is nothing else but a paradise where the Lord says He finds His delight. (1.1.1)[34]

Teresa makes the rooms of the castle, which correspond to the dwelling places promised in heaven, the most vital aspect in her extension of the comparison. Thus God's dwelling place coincides with the innermost room of the soul. The wall surrounding the castle offers an apt analogy for the body, not simply because it is exterior but also because it suggests that some physical barrier obstructs the entrance, and the image of the soul contaminating the outer rooms by the things it brings along, vanities and honors represented by wild beasts and snakes, conjures an effective image of a person walking on a carpet with muddy feet. A few of the allusions to the castle seem more like nearly moribund metaphors, however, such as the designation of prayer as a door to the castle (1.1.7) and then as a foundation for the castle and the admonition that the castle must not be built on the sand of expecting rewards for one's efforts (2.1.10). Occasionally she acknowledges the artificial nature of her development of the comparison, simply determining to stick with "the image I have taken for my explanation" (4.3.2). The intermittent and occasionally strained development of the metaphor suggests that Teresa's castle functions only to a minimal extent as what Certeau calls the "borrowed space in which it [the soul] can mark its movements, [which] is itself the inarticulable echo of an unknown Subject."[35] God does appear to Teresa in the center of her soul, but rhetorically speaking, the castle, rather than a location from which God speaks, is principally a means of sketching some of the configurations of her soul.

The crystal or diamond Teresa also introduces here functions not simply as a building material for the castle but also as an analogy that contributes essential features to Teresa's description of the soul. The crystal provides a spherical image, which, while conflicting with most architectural design for castles, emerges as an aspect of the space Teresa seeks to describe: "This castle has, as I said, many dwelling places: some up above, others down below, others to the sides; and in the center and middle is the main dwelling place where the very secret exchanges between God and the soul take place" (1.1.3). The emphasis on this concentricity avoids the tradition of ascent to God, which locates God at the top of the castle's highest tower. Also with the crystal, which she considers an entity that emits light (rather than reflecting it as the material object does), Teresa emphasizes God's communication with the faculties and senses, which guard the exterior of the soul, from the center: "There is a Sun in the interior of the soul from which a brilliant light proceeds and is sent to the faculties" (7.2.6). From this image Teresa moves to explain the darkening of the outermost compartments of the soul, which she does not do as vividly with the castle. In the sinful soul, a layer of pitch or a black cloth covers the rays at the center of the soul (1.2.3; 1.2.4) in the same way that, as she puts it in the *Life*, the mirror of the sinful soul is covered with a grime that prevents it from reflecting the image of God. Here as elsewhere Teresa invests her energy not in the consistency of the analogy but in the qualities of the soul it allows her to delineate.

Teresa identifies the understanding (*entendimiento*, often translated as "intellect" by Kavanaugh) as the faculty responsible for exploring the crystalline castle of the soul: "I don't find anything comparable to the magnificent beauty of a soul and its marvelous capacity. Indeed, our intellects, however keen, can hardly comprehend it, just as they cannot comprehend God" (1.1.1).[36] In the first three dwelling places, Teresa defines the object of the understanding as spiritual self-knowledge (*propio conocimiento*). Failure to use the faculty of understanding to acquire this knowledge results in ignorance as ludicrous as not knowing one's own name.

> It is a shame and unfortunate that through our own fault we don't understand ourselves or know who we are. Wouldn't it show great ignorance, my daughters, if someone when asked who he was didn't know, and didn't know his father or mother or from what country he came? Well now, if this would be so extremely stupid, we are incomparably more so when we do not strive to know who we are, but limit ourselves to considering only roughly these bodies. (1.1.2)[37]

Teresa recommends the exercise of comparison and contrast between God and the soul as the means to this self-knowledge: "We shall never completely know ourselves if we don't strive to know God. By gazing at His grandeur, we get in touch with our own lowliness" (1.2.9).[38] The very activity of making this comparison benefits the faculty of understanding: "[In Christ and the saints] we shall learn true humility, and the intellect will be enhanced" (1.2.11).[39]

In the second dwelling place, the understanding plays the decisive role in urging the soul to continue pressing forward to its center. At the outset, faith counters reason (*razón*), which attempts to deceive the soul, by reminding the soul that its fulfillment lies in spiritual rather than worldly things. In the concurrent dispute among the faculties, the understanding prevails. While the other faculties function to some extent, the memory presenting images of transient worldly things and the will inclining to love, the understanding provides a profusion of reasons for abandoning the outside world: "The intellect helps it realize that it couldn't find a better friend. . . . [T]he intellect tells the soul of its certainty that outside this castle neither security nor peace will be found. . . . [T]he intellect will ask who it is that finds everything he needs in his own house" (2.1.4).[40] The principal preparation for meeting God, she explains in the third dwelling place, which otherwise merely extends the exhortation to persistence with little reference to analogy, consists in understanding oneself (3.2.3).

The Imprinting of the Memory: The Soul as Silkworm (*Interior Castle* 4–6)

The fourth dwelling place marks the transition to the supernatural phases of prayer, which, as in the second water of the *Life*, she labels the prayer of quiet (4.2.2).[41] Teresa continues to identify knowing as the route to perfection in these stages.

> O Lord, take into account the many things we suffer on this path for lack of knowledge! The trouble is that since we do not think there is anything to know [*saber*] other than that we must think of You, we do not even know how to ask those who know nor do we understand what there is to ask. (4.1.9)[42]

The repeated use of the verb *saber*, meaning to know information, rather than *conocer*, to be acquainted with, indicates a transition to a different kind of knowledge. In the supernatural phases, Teresa more often refers to this knowledge as certainty or assurance (*certeza* or *certidumbre*) than as understanding. Rather than being achieved by the exercise of a human faculty, this knowledge derives from supernatural forces.

> The certitude is so strong that even in things that in one's own opinion sometimes seem impossible and in which there is doubt as to whether they will or will not happen, and the intellect wavers, there is an assurance in the soul itself that cannot be overcome. (6.3.7)[43]

The faculty Teresa shows receiving this kind of knowledge is the memory (and occasionally the understanding). In keeping with Teresa's continual complaint that she has no control over her own memory, attaining this knowledge does not depend on the exercise of the human faculty but instead is received as the impression from a divine stimulus. "The wax," she explains, "doesn't impress the seal upon itself; it is only disposed" (5.2.12).[44]

With a different kind of knowing at stake, Teresa again takes up the problem of mind. While previously linking mental activity and the understanding, now she associates the mind with the imagination, which, as we have seen, she frequently attaches also to the memory: "I came to understand through experience that the mind (or imagination, to put it more clearly) is not the intellect" (4.1.8).[45] Teresa expresses preoccupation with the faculties she associates with mind by making the head an anatomical referent for the soul. After reflecting that the constant movement of "the interior world" resembles the motion of the heavens, she links both to the commotion in her head.

> While writing this, I'm thinking about what's going on in my head with the great noise there that I mentioned in the beginning. It makes it almost impossible for me to write what I was ordered to. It seems as if there are in my head many rushing rivers and that these waters are hurtling downward, and many little birds and whistling sounds, not in the ears but in the upper part of the head where, they say, the higher part of the soul is. (4.1.10)[46]

Continuing in a more optimistic vein, she speculates that she might be able to put the action in her head to some use: "I wouldn't be surprised if the Lord gave me this headache so that I could understand these things better" (4.1.10). Yet although the mind makes a "great noise" as distracting as the beat of a catch against a grindstone, she can learn only to ignore it, not to control it: "We must let the millclapper go clacking on, and must continue grinding our flour and not fail to work with the will and the intellect" (4.1.13). In this fourth dwelling place God begins to divulge His secrets, first in the form of rising water and then as warmth from burning embers. While the will and understanding have the capacity to evaluate these phenomena correctly, the memory and imagination, particularly in those persons with "weak heads and imaginations," mislead the soul.

In the fifth dwelling place Teresa introduces the comparison between the silkworm and the soul, which conveys, better than any she has previously used, the miraculous transformation of the soul. Ignoring the concept of sexual reproduction, Teresa explains that the apparently dead seed comes to life as a worm "by the heat of the Holy Spirit."

> You must have already heard about His marvels manifested in the way silk originates, for only He could have invented something like that. The silkworms come from seeds about the size of little grains of pepper. . . . When the warm weather comes and the leaves begin to appear on the mulberry tree, the seeds start to live, for they are dead until then. (5.2.2)[47]

Teresa acknowledges that she relies in part for this seemingly fantastic claim on the technique of the nascent scientific movement, observation, though at second hand: "I have never seen this but heard of it, and so if something in the explanation gets distorted it won't be my fault" (5.2.2). Then, she relates with complete amazement, the developed worm disappears into a cocoon, and a butterfly emerges: "Now if this were not seen but recounted to us as having happened in other times, who would believe it?" she asks rhetorically (5.2.2). The difference between a soul before and after experiencing union, then, corresponds to the disparity between the "ugly worm" and "a little white butterfly," and the transformation is equally marvelous: "Truly, I tell you that the soul doesn't recognize itself" (5.2.7).[48] Unable to "go back where it came from" but also unable to serve God, the butterfly suffers from its desire, as will the transformed soul.

Now betrothed to God, the soul endures a seemingly indefinite wait for God's call in the sixth dwelling place. As reassurance God gives the soul a variety of interior sensations, including powerful feelings in the soul, locutions, raptures, and visions. Everyone around her questions the provenance of the gifts, however. A confessor with little experience "fears everything and finds in everything something to doubt because he sees these unusual experiences. . . . Everything is immediately condemned as from the devil or melancholy" (6.1.8). Understanding even less, the public subjects her to scorn and ridicule, and God, wishing to test her love, subjects her to serious illnesses and torments: "Many are the things that war against it with an interior oppression so keen and unbearable that I don't know what to compare this experience to if not to the oppression of those that suffer in hell" (6.1.9). Under this assault the soul begins to doubt its own knowledge and certainty, to wonder whether all its spiritual experiences "have been dreamed up or fancied" (6.1.11). To identify the gifts as divine or demoniacal, the soul attempts to read their signs (*señales*), most significant among them the imprint they leave on the memory.

As one demonstration of His love, God gives the soul locutions, which Teresa defines as words coming from within the soul. Knowing that the devil can still intervene in the stage of spiritual betrothal to prevent the marriage, the soul must evaluate every locution. A locution, when divine rather than demoniacal or imaginary, leaves these effects in the soul: words with the power to fulfill what they signify; a "great quiet" bestowed on the soul; and the persistence of the words in the memory: "These words remain in the memory for a very long time, and some are never forgotten, as are those we listen to here on earth" (6.3.7). Even without the assent of the understanding, the soul can confidently base worldly action on these locutions.

With the two most precious gifts she describes, the intellectual vision and the imaginative vision, the devil tries even harder to shake the soul's certainty: "The devil can stir up doubts, as he does with temptations against matters of faith, that do not allow the soul to be firm in its certitude" (6.9.10). The principal difference between the two visions inheres in the way they are remembered. The secrets God reveals in imaginative vision, she proposes, "remain so impressed on the memory that they are never forgotten" (6.4.5).[49] Teresa likens the ultimate imaginative vision to opening a chest or reliquary finally to view the amulet that even before being seen has provided protection. The sight is a brilliant "inner vision" of God revealed in His human aspect: "He shows it clearly His most sacred humanity in the way He desires; either as He was when He went about in the world or as He is after His resurrection" (6.9.3). By comparison with a painting of Christ or with the images that the imagination or an "overly active intellect" might conjure, both of which she describes as dead, the imaginative vision is "something alive" (6.9.4).

While the soul can relate all the details of the imaginative vision, "when the visions are intellectual, the soul doesn't know how to speak of them" (6.4.5). To explain the soul's certainty that it has had such experience while not being able to remem-

ber many, if any, details, Teresa relates an autobiographical anecdote that at the same time reveals her essentially ascetic temperament more effectively than her exhortations for austerity
in the convents. She recalls that when she entered the Duchess
of Alba's treasure room, she was so overwhelmed by "the con-
glomeration of things" that while retaining a clear memory of
having visited the room, she remembered nothing in particular;
similarly, "after it returns to itself, the soul is left with that representation of the grandeurs it saw; but it cannot describe any
of them" (6.4.8). An intellectual vision brings the soul not images but the sensation of the continual presence of God, Christ,
or the Virgin, who are sometimes accompanied by saints.[50] The
intellectual vision thus cures the soul's loneliness, and more
important, the "continual companionship" brings an intimate
knowledge of God. These representations, although not images
imprinted on the memory, are "inscribed in the very interior
part of the soul and are never forgotten" (6.4.6).[51] Having received
such visions, the soul need not echo Pilate in asking, "'What
is Truth?'": the soul knows with certainty that "God alone is
Truth" (6.10.5).

With spiritual marriage, which takes place in the seventh
dwelling place, God makes a "division in the soul," actually a
division between soul and spirit.

> One understands with certitude that there is some kind of differ-
> ence, a difference clearly recognized, between the soul and the
> spirit, even though they are both one. So delicate a division is
> perceived that sometimes it seems the one functions differently
> from the other, and so does the savor the Lord desires to give them
> seem different. (7.1.11)[52]

While Teresa occasionally slips into using the word *soul* for both
the soul and the spirit in this section, in general she distinguishes their functions and experiences. While the spirit, represented by Mary, experiences the pleasures of marriage in the
center of the interior castle, the soul continues its worldly work
in the person of Martha.

In spiritual marriage, God and the soul, which might have
been separated in any previous stage, become irrevocably united
through the spirit: "The soul, I mean the spirit, is made one
with God" (7.2.3).[53] Water, Teresa explains, serves her better than

fire to explain the resulting indivisibility: while two matches joined to make a larger flame can always be separated, "in the spiritual marriage the union is like what we have when rain falls from the sky into a river or fount; all is water, for the rain that fell from heaven cannot be divided or separated from the water of the river" (7.2.4).[54] God strips the spirit of the faculties and the senses, blinding it as He did Paul on the road to Damascus so that he can teach it by spiritual means alone: "God now desires to remove the scales from the soul's eyes and let it see and understand, although in a strange way" (7.1.6). With intellectual visions, which do not proceed through either the bodily eyes or the eyes of the soul, God gives the spirit understanding of the truths of the Christian faith. In particular, the soul perceives the truth about the Trinity, that while completely distinct, "all three Persons are one substance and one power and one knowledge and one God alone." The three Persons converse with the spirit, making their interrelationship vivid in a way that Scripture does not, and they provide perpetual companionship to the spirit. While God occasionally permits the understanding to watch the instruction of the spirit, which like Solomon's work on the temple at Jerusalem (1 Kings 6:7) proceeds silently, this education proceeds independent of human faculty.

The faculties remain with the soul during and after spiritual marriage. Now repaired by the previous spiritual experience, they cause only the occasional disturbance or distraction. The soul no longer desires spiritual delights, and the interior union of the spirit provides the peace necessary for devoting full energies to the service of Christ. As the spirit communicates its understanding outward to the faculties and senses, the soul perfects its desire and capacity to imitate Christ, acquiring qualities such as forgetfulness of self, desire to suffer, love for persecutors, and disdain of death: "All these things must come to the soul from its roots, from where it is planted. . . . What is there, then, to marvel at in the desires this soul has since its true spirit has become one with the heavenly water we mentioned?" (7.2.9). In the terminology of the Christian life, the contemplative spirit provides water that sustains the growth of the active soul.

Teresa expresses certainty that her spirit has been transformed with allusions to the Pauline baptismal formula. In passages such as Galatians 2:20, "I live not now but Christ lives with me," Paul assures the prospective convert to Christianity that he or she will acquire an entirely new nature, one shared with Christ. While Teresa refers to this formula several times— to mark God's rescuing her from death (*Life* 6.9) and to describe the final stage of the Four Ways (*Life* 22.10)—here she takes the passage as a reference to spiritual marriage, which marks the culmination of the transformation that began with her conversion.

> Perhaps this is what St. Paul means in saying that "He that is joined or united to the Lord becomes one spirit with him" [1 Cor. 6:17] and is referring to this sovereign marriage, presupposing that His Majesty has brought the soul to it through union. And he also says: "For me to live is Christ, and to die is gain" [Phil. 1:21]. (7.2.5)[55]

While Teresa considers the spirit definitively transformed, the soul can always revert to its "natural state" of sin and confusion if it is attacked by the poisonous creatures of the outer rooms of the castle. Still, she proposes, the soul also can pronounce its conversion in Pauline terms: "The soul as well [as the spirit], I think, can say these words now because this state is the place where the little butterfly we mentioned dies, and with the greatest joy because its life is now Christ" (7.2.5).[56] This use of Pauline language underlines the difference between Teresa's concept of transformation and Augustine's: while for Augustine conversion consists in the perfection of the will through grace, for Teresa, both in the narrative of the *Life* and in this recapitulation, conversion requires certainty of the interior presence of God.

In summarizing the experience of both spirit and soul, Teresa leaves analogy for scriptural allusion: "Who would know the many things there must be in Scripture to explain this peace of the soul!"

> He brings the soul to Himself with this kiss sought by the bride, for I think this petition is here granted [Song 1.1]. Here an abundance of water is given to this deer that was wounded [Ps. 42.2]. Here one delights in God's tabernacle [Rev. 21:3]. Here the dove Noah sent out to see if the storm was over finds the olive branch as a sign of firm ground discovered amid the floods and tempests of this world [Gen. 8:8–12]. (7.3.13)[57]

These scriptural passages can be translated into the same array of analogies she deployed in describing all the previous stages of spiritual passage. God consummates spiritual marriage with the kiss the Bride has requested—"Let Him kiss me with the kiss of His mouth"—a kiss that, as we have seen in her *Meditations on the Song of Songs*, ignites the flame of love in the soul. Like the deer of Psalm 42, to which Teresa gives a wound that recalls the piercing of her heart, the Bride receives water for the garden of the soul. The soul arrives at the center of its interior castle, where it finds both itself and God. Finally, as Noah's dove, which Teresa frequently substitutes for the little butterfly, the soul finds solid ground (*tierra firme*) on which to build His Church.

5

TERESA'S REPRESENTATION OF HER "NEW LIFE"
Life 32–36, *Foundations*

Teresa's representation of her new life in the role of apostle begins in the *Life*, principally in the chapters narrating the founding of the St. Joseph convent in Avila, and it emerges fully realized in the *Foundations*. The latter work, begun in late 1573, comprehends a retrospective narrative of the foundations made since Avila and a memoir of Teresa's activities to mid-April 1582, a few months before her death on 4 October. Teresa's least-known text, the *Foundations* portrays her in the role she had demanded for so long: as early as 1590, Ribera describes her as an apostle, another St. Paul; Bilinkoff, in detailing the circumstances of the Avila foundation, defines Teresa's project as "apostolic [and] missionary."[1] While in her account of the founding of St. Joseph in the *Life* she emphasizes the contemplative aspect of the composite figure of Mary Magdalene, in the *Foundations* she acts more as Martha, though without naming her. One should cease contemplating God, she advises, when He needs her works in the world: "It would be a distressing thing if God were clearly telling us to go after something that matters to Him and we would not want to do so but want to remain looking at Him because that is more pleasing to us" (5.5).[2] The occasional locution and vision from God guide her, but she no longer talks with God frequently or experiences raptures. Always ceding the ultimate responsibility for her achievements to God, she nevertheless accentuates the importance of her own work: "The

Lord desired that no foundation be made without great trial on my part" (24.15; my translation).[3]

Although more unified with respect to genre than her previous writing, the *Foundations* is not simply a historical narrative. Teresa justifies her apostolic mission with a motive that Spain used for its imperialist enterprise, evangelism. As a result, the *Foundations* shares some features with the genre of New World chronicle; Teresa's figure of the apostle includes an aspect of the conquistador. And as Teresa realizes that death will force her to cede her position, she turns the *Foundations* to biographical purpose, making her chronicle a frame for the lives of several of the first Barefoot Carmelite nuns. Together these stories constitute a work that, like Christine de Pizan's *The Book of the City of Ladies*, may be considered, as Maureen Quilligan designates Pizan's work, "an allegory of female authority," albeit a very simple one.[4] Insofar as the New World chronicle bolsters the rhetoric of nationalism, which some theorists consider anchored in the inequality of gender roles, it clashes with the allegory of female authority.[5] While Teresa conceives her foundations as the expression of a female system of kinship, New World chronicle rests on the patriarchal model, in which, as Claude Lévi-Strauss formulates it, women are objects of exchange. Teresa's apparent blindness to this contradiction probably permitted her to proceed with her project, but it also restricted the scope of her success and drained her of satisfaction in it, as some of the miniature biographies reveal.

In her account of the founding of the first Barefoot Carmelite monastery, the convent of St. Joseph at Avila in 1562 (*Life* 32–36), Teresa portrays herself as an uncertain, sometimes even unwilling accessory to the action, probably in part to placate her opponents. Also, her engagement with the project did develop slowly. The idea was conceived in an informal gathering of nuns in Teresa's cell at the Carmelite convent of the Incarnation in 1560. María de Ocampo suggested, apparently rather idly, that if they could not observe a stricter rule within their convent, which followed the mitigated Carmelite rule approved by Pope Eugene IV in 1432, they might follow the example of a group of Franciscan nuns in Madrid, the Royal Barefoot Nuns who followed a strict rule of discipline in a convent founded by King Philip II's sister, Juana. Teresa liked the idea because after a terrifying vision of hell, she had promised God that she would compensate for the souls lost to Protestantism by conducting her spiritual life more rigorously. The idea also took root in the other young women, who were frustrated by the secular, social atmosphere of the Incarnation, which allowed the nuns extended journeys and unlimited visitors. Their plan, in Teófanes Egido Martínez's words, was "as enthusiastic as it was naive," however.[6]

On reflection, Teresa had some ambivalence about founding a new convent, because as she puts it, "I was very happy in my own monastery." The dowry she brought allowed her private quarters, and much of the time she enjoyed her lengthy stays outside the convent. Although she had already mentioned the plan to her friend Guiomar de Ulloa, who had agreed to finance it, she admits that her discussions were not very serious: "I hadn't done so with as much determination or certitude as was necessary to bring it about" (*Life* 32.12). Then God gave her a locution that forced her to action: "One day after Communion, His Majesty earnestly commanded me to strive for this new monastery with all my powers. . . . He said it should be called St. Joseph" (*Life* 32.11).[7] As she was instructed, she spoke with her confessor, Baltasar Alvarez, while Guiomar talked to the provincial administrator, Angel de Salazar. After some initial interest, both Alvarez and Salazar expressed reservations. In the meantime, nearly everyone in Avila had heard of the plan, and nearly everyone opposed it. They articulated their opposition as concern about the convent's scanty endowment, a real consideration in this impoverished city, but Bilinkoff speculates that they actually had more important objections, such as resistance to the disruption of the social arrangement that allowed wealthy families to locate a daughter in a convent while having her essentially in their control, as well as fear that Teresa's devotional practices, especially mental prayer, represented a defiance of Church orthodoxy and establishment.[8] It was at this time she wrote the spiritual testimony for Pedro Ibáñez (discussed in chap. 1).

Teresa gives the active roles to others in her narrative of this first foundation. Even after negotiations had been made to have her sister and brother-in-law buy a house without revealing their intention for it, Teresa did not fully understand the details of primitive Carmelite rule, which as formulated in the 1229 bull of Gregory IX mandated collective poverty and mendicancy. Teresa relates that she learned the details of this primitive rule from María de Jesús, a nun from Granada who passed through Toledo while Teresa was staying there. Showing greater determination than Teresa, María had walked to Rome to secure permission to found a Carmelite convent under reformed rule. Teresa, who still awaited the return of a letter to Rome, now decided to found her convent in accord with these principles. When she returned to Avila she found others already planning the clandestine consecration of the house. Teresa does not say who did what, but with several priests she renovated the house and celebrated the reservation of the Sacrament in a secret ceremony on 24 August 1562. Even though Teresa had allowed for thirteen nuns including a prioress, only four women took vows that day. Afterward, Teresa experienced a paralyzing attack of emotional conflict, which was resolved by a vision of Pedro de Alcántara (a spiritual advisor who had recently died) supporting her decision to found in poverty, and she faced a lawsuit that required two years of litigation in the city council. While her advocates negotiated a settlement, Teresa remained in the Incarnation under orders from the prioress not to intervene in any affairs of St. Joseph. Teresa was permitted to join the new convent in February 1563, six months after its dedication.

By the time she began writing the *Foundations*, in late 1573, her convent at Avila had already filled its ranks and spawned a chain of Barefoot Carmelite foundations throughout Castile: for women, convents at Medina del Campo (1568), Malagón (1568), Valladolid (1568), Toledo (1569), Pastrana (1569), Salamanca (1570), and Alba (1571); for men, monasteries at Duruelo (1568, moved to Mancera) and Pastrana (1569). Soon afterward, she founded another at Segovia (1574) and then moved outside this Castilian orbit to make the Andalusian foundations at Beas (1575) and Seville (1575). While she still had a skeptical faction in her audience, now principally the Carmelite establishment that had begun to worry about the extent of her reach, she also wrote for present and future members of her new order. With less reason to minimize her role, Teresa portrays herself as founder, the one who conceives what Edward Said calls the "beginning intention," the "created *inclusiveness* within which the work develops."[9] She relates that when Giovanni Battista Rossi (known in Spain as Rubeo), father general of the Carmelites in Rome, visited St. Joseph in Avila, he deemed it such a beginning intention: "He rejoiced to see our manner of life, a portrait, although an imperfect one, of the beginnings of our order" (2.3).[10] "With the desire that this beginning go forward," Rubeo gave her documents authorizing the foundation of more monasteries and censuring any local official who might hinder her efforts. Teresa now visualized the "inclusiveness" of the project: "And thus in seeing the strong desire of our Most Reverend General that more monasteries be founded, it seemed to me I saw them founded" (2.4).[11] While this intuition of the shape of the whole provides the impetus to begin, it also shows her the end, as she says here. As much as by a recognition of beginning, the *Foundations* is dominated by the "sense of an ending," or as Teresa puts it, a growing awareness of "how soon everything comes to an end" (29.33).

A Domestic New World Chronicle

Teresa defines the impetus for the additional foundations in relation to Spain's evangelical enterprise in the New World. After a Franciscan friar told her about the millions of non-Christians in the Indies, she pleaded with God for a part in the project of conversion.

> I was so grief-stricken over the loss of so many souls [in the Indies, actually Mexico] that I couldn't contain myself. I went to a hermitage with many tears. I cried out to the Lord, begging Him that He give me the means to be able to do something to win some souls to His service, since the devil was carrying away so many, and that my prayer would do some good since I wasn't able to do anything else. (1.7)[12]

God answered her prayers with a prophecy: "'Wait a little, daughter, and you will see great things.'" Rubeo's permission for additional foundations fulfilled this promise: "Remembering the words our Lord had spoken to me, I now perceived some beginning to what before I could not understand" (2.4).[13] In narrating the events motivated by her desire to contribute to Spain's evangelical and imperial project, she writes a domestic version of the New World chronicle.

Others have remarked heroic aspects of Teresa's self-representations. James V. Mirollo treats Teresa and Benvenuto Cellini as contributors to innovation in Renaissance heroism.[14] Gaston Etchegoyen compares Teresa to the knight of chivalry: "Amadís of Gaul and Saint Teresa could both have taken for their motto: 'To love in order to act.'"[15] While traces of the novel of chivalry might be seen in the episodic succession of triumphs in the *Foundations*, Teresa confines most of her allusion to the genre she loved as a child to narratives of her spiritual life, where she defines her desires in erotic and romantic terms and portrays herself as military defender of God's castle. The chivalric plot plays out in the realm of the marvelous, while Teresa's path in the *Foundations* leads through this world.

The New World chronicles are quite various, of course, some concentrating on description, others on defense of native populations or economic considerations.[16] The writings of Hernán Cortés serve particularly well to illustrate the aspects of Teresa's persona that resemble the New World conqueror for several reasons: the element of self-dramatization, the close identification between self-interest and national interest, the interest in governance, and the comprehensiveness of his vision of a future society. In seeking to promote himself as the true governor of Mexico, Cortés wrote a history of his activities in the form of letters to the king of Spain. Cortés's letters, like those of many other explorers, reached Spain soon after they were written, and beginning in 1515, his father had them published. While Teresa probably never read any printed chronicles, she certainly would have heard oral accounts of the same kinds of exploits and she received frequent letters from her brothers who fought with Spanish armies in Peru and Chile. Cortés wrote his letters in an attempt to displace the Spanish aristocracy in Mexico, and probably as a result, the publication of further letters was banned in 1527.[17] In addition to the adventure, the challenge made to the nobility would have interested Teresa.

The interplay of political with evangelical motives in Cortés's writings provides a way of understanding Teresa's self-representation in the *Foundations*. Mario Hernández Sánchez-Barba argues that Cortés considered his conquest to have a double purpose, "religious (evangelization) and political (foundation),"[18] his principal political interest being to make Mexico a province of Spain rather than merely a colony or a territory. Teresa's motives similarly weave together the political and evangelical. As well as spiritual perfection for individuals, she intends an alteration in the sociopolitical order.

Like Dante in his *Divine Comedy*, Teresa measures the human reality of the world she knows against the divine order she has perceived in mystical vision. Like Dante also, although with deeds rather than words, Teresa undertakes to reform that human reality. Her foundations, she argues here with respect to the value of women, will make the eternal order visible in this world.

> How differently will we understand these ignorances on the day when the truth about all things shall be understood. And how many fathers and mothers will be seen going to hell because they had sons and also how many will be seen in heaven because of their daughters. (20.3)[19]

In addition to the devaluation of girls and women, Teresa diagnoses other defects in the worldly order, such as attribution of honor based on lineage and the definition of wealth in strictly material terms. The order she seeks to impose alters these values in accordance with the eternal order. Because God measures piety rather than lineage, Teresa does not take family background into account in admission to the convents. Further, as in Toledo, she does not hesitate to accept patronage from the converso population: "He told me that lineage and social status mattered not at all in the judgment of God" (15.16). Because the "estates, inheritances, and riches" that parents confer on their children mean nothing in eternity, Teresa does not require a dowry. And because God values women equally with men, she devotes most of her energies to the spiritual education of women. Teresa's project in the *Foundations*, then, consists in making her convents and monasteries "a heaven, if there can be one on earth" (*Road* 13.7).

For Cortés, the evangelical aspect of his mission justifies any means of achieving it. His letters reveal no awareness of the Indians' perspective or remorse for the dispossession, injury, and death he inflicted. His explanations of retribution, as here to the observers of the execution of an Indian, intertwine political with religious grounds.

> I had come by Your Majesty's command to protect and defend both their persons and their property and to teach them how they were to believe in and worship the One God. . . . Likewise I said I had come to tell them of Your Majesty whom Divine Providence has decreed that the whole world shall serve and obey.[20]

Teresa's textual persona operates on a similar assumption of divine right. To a greater extent than the biographies of Yepes and

Ribera, her account of the foundations shows her relying not simply on shrewdness but on deceit. Weber describes Teresa's deceptions as the technique of a *pícaro*, the character of the rogue introduced with *Lazarillo de Tormes*, anonymously published in 1554. Like the boy from Tormes whose poverty drives him to a life of service for cruel and unscrupulous masters, Teresa exposes society's faults from the margins: "Teresa, at odds against a collection of inept bureaucrats, waffling ecclesiastics and petty landlords, outwits hierarchical authority with ingenuity and determination."[21] As Weber also shows, this stance provides some of the ironic humor of the work. While agreeing that Teresa's stance toward society has something of the picaresque, I would characterize it as more than "mischievous."[22] Teresa portrays herself as quite a ruthless operator.

In making the foundation at Burgos in 1581, she displays a range of deceptive techniques, which while not exactly crimes, were not victimless either. On arriving in Burgos, Teresa had permission for the foundation from nearly everyone except the archbishop presiding there, Cristóbal Vega. Before sending word of her arrival to him, however, Teresa had already cleared the hurdle she knew would be the most difficult, permission from the city council, which all but preempted a negative decision from the archbishop.

> There was little use telling him that once we had the permission of the city, as he had asked of us, nothing else was left to be done than simply make the foundation and that the bishop of Palencia had told me (for I had asked him if it would be good that I come without letting the archbishop know) that there was no reason for asking the permission because the archbishop had already said how much he desired the foundation. (31.21)

Besides, she adds, "if we had openly informed him, he would have told us not to come" (31.21). Apparently cornered, the archbishop imposed several conditions on the license: that the foundations have an income, that funds to buy the house not be taken out of monies the nuns had brought with them, and that the purchase be concluded before issue of the license.

Teresa arranged to buy a house in Burgos from an owner who had given power of attorney to a priest. When the contract was signed, other potential buyers accused the priest of taking too little for the property, indeed of virtually making it a gift, and argued that the sale should be canceled "because of the great fraud [*engaño*]" (31.37). Teresa reports that the owners were pleased with the purchasers' plans for the house, but, as she admits, they had no choice because they had already made a binding contract: "They were so happy that their house was being made into a monastery that they approved, although there was nothing else they could now do" (31.37). Before notifying the archbishop of the purchase, Teresa moved the nuns into the house and began alterations. When he forbade the saying of mass in the house, Teresa flamboyantly walked her nuns to another church every Sunday. After the archbishop had given the license, she canceled her agreement for the money she had borrowed to provide the specified income: "With the permission of the Father Provincial, we nullified in the presence of a notary the contracts concerning the money she had given us and returned all the documents." She justifies the secrecy of this default on her agreement with mock concern for the archbishop's feelings: "This was done in great secrecy so that the archbishop wouldn't know of it, for he would have been hurt" (31.48). Even if deception of the archbishop might be considered fair in this war, the negotiations apparently left some persons shortchanged and, more important, nuns trying to survive in a convent thought to have an endowment but actually dependent on charity.

No less than Cortés, Teresa wrote with a view to establishing her reputation for posterity. To this end Cortés narrates not only his battles but the difficulties he faced in devising strategies for them. Cortés uses an account of an attack on Indians who had been fortifying themselves against the Spaniards not simply to record the event but to demonstrate his command of the situation: "And I, knowing this and knowing how cunning and astute they are in war, had often considered how we might invade and attack them relatively unprepared."[23] Teresa also portrays herself as a talented founder, with political acuity, resourcefulness, good judgment, organization, and a canny eye for assessing value in real estate.

Even with her patent from Rubeo, the Barefoot monasteries usually faced strenuous opposition from residents in the town, many of whom feared the financial demands of a monastery without an income or endowment, and from other orders, which resented competition for public benevolence. As Teresa states with regard to the foundation at Medina, "Since the monastery is to be founded in poverty, permission is everywhere difficult to obtain" (3.1). Weber and Bilinkoff detail numerous other causes of this antagonism: her insistence on poverty constituted a critique of the Church's wealth, a charge made also by Protestants; the attraction of her convents to conversos, which raised alarm about religious and political subversion; her defiance of a papal order against contemplatives' making foundations.[24]

Obtaining the license from local and Church authorities to found the monasteries required skillful political maneuvering, which she usually accomplished with her talent for, in Weber's words, "dismantling monolithic authority into lesser competing authorities [and] seeking out an authority whose will coincided with her own."[25] In Medina, Teresa first approached a former Jesuit confessor she knew to be friendly to her idea, Baltasar Alvarez, sending him and Julián de Avila, the chaplain of her first convent, to negotiate on her behalf. According to Efrén and Steggink, the bishop, Alvaro de Mendoza, marshaled numerous prominent lay and religious men against the foundation. After he was somehow persuaded to give the license, the council leaders who had responsibility for actually issuing it began a campaign against Teresa. The public charges that she resembled the still infamous Magdalena de la Cruz suggest the depth of hostility against her. When the plans appeared to be at a stalemate in Medina, Julián asked the bishop of Salamanca to set up a review panel. Julián and Teresa collected favorable witnesses, and after two months of rancorous public and private debate the license was issued.[26]

In Segovia, she found no pliable authority short of King Philip II, who had been convinced, by Teresa and others, that her project coincided with the national interest. She had made the foundation and celebrated mass with only oral permission given to a second party, an arrangement she disingenuously professes to have thought acceptable: "This gentleman didn't bother about getting the permission in writing, nor did this seem to me to matter" (21.5). When the vicar general learned of the foundation, he arrested the priest who had said mass there, ordered destruction of the altar, and posted a guard at the door of the house. Although he was eventually persuaded that the license had been given, he withheld the Sacrament from the convent. Teresa proceeded to press her case through her friends, in this case, a nephew of the bishop. She relates that when the license for the foundation at Caravaca appeared with the unexpected proviso that the house would be subject to the council of the Order of Knights, she appealed to the king: "The king is so fond of favoring religious who he knows are faithful to their profession that once he had learned of the manner of life in these monasteries and that we follow the primitive rule, he favored us in everything" (27.6). He resolved this dispute in Teresa's favor, as he did also the rivalry between the Barefoot Carmelites and the Carmelites several years later.

Teresa also portrays herself as financier and fund-raiser, even as she denies her capacity for this most essential function: "How could a poor wanderer like myself get credit for a loan unless the Lord would give it?" (3.2). Ribera cites her apparently miraculous accumulation of capital as a reassurance to nuns about the future: "She entered Seville to found the monastery there with only half a maravedí, and before she left, she bought a house that cost 6,000 ducats and a year or two later she bought another one that cost 13,000."[27] Egido Martínez judges that she "possessed a clear mind for economics" and that she understood investment, credit, and contracts.[28] José Antonio Alvarez Vázquez considers that Teresa developed a "capacity for negotiation [more literally, haggling]" that she used to obtain the best possible prices.[29] When a house was not given to Teresa, she solicited money from many sources, including the parent Carmelite order, benefactors (usually conversos), and, after continuing economic decline forced her to allow endowments, from dowries. In Medina, Teresa first secured money to rent a house from a woman who wished to be included in the convent, but when the nearby Augustinian friars prevented the nuns from moving in, she was forced to try to buy a house. This time she appealed for help to a priest, Fray Antonio de Heredia, who found someone willing to sell him a house in Medina "without her asking for any surety or binding force other than his word" (3.3). In Toledo, her expulsion from a house she had rented aroused sympathy among the converso population, who raised 12,000 ducats for one of the nicest houses in town. For the foundation in Seville, which otherwise seemed impossible, Teresa's brother Lorenzo de Cepeda returned after thirty-four years in the New World with the money to guarantee a loan for the entire purchase price.[30] One way or another, Teresa herself raised most of the capital for her foundations.

Teresa's narrative of her travels around Spain can be read as an imitation of the explorers' transatlantic voyages. As she tells it, she braved the equivalent of the torments of hell, the roads of Spain, and she makes those trials vivid for future generations. While late in her life the order insisted that she travel with a priest, initially she made her trips, sometimes weeks long, with one or more nuns as companions. Riding at first in two-wheel carts, then in horse-drawn wagons, with a cloth cover the only protection, they endured extremes of heat and cold: "I tell you, Sisters, that since the sun was beating on the wagons, getting into them was like stepping into purgatory" (24.6). On other trips, extreme cold impeded their travel: "Once it didn't stop snowing the whole day" (13.3). A hostel room without windows and a mattress "like sharp stones" became bearable only when she considered that while she could exchange one discomfort for another (the heat of the wagons seemed preferable), the damned in hell suffered the same pains for eternity: "Never will there be any change at all, for even a change from one trial to another brings with it some relief" (24.9). Teresa gives few details about the course of the journeys, but the occasional glance at the frustrations she faced suggests the forbearance they must have exacted. Often she had to cede control of physical aspects of the journey to careless and incompetent drivers. Having put the wagons on a barge to cross the Guadalquivir River, she then watched them float downstream because "those who were holding the rope let it go, or I don't know what happened" (24.10). And after waiting hours for a permit to pass over a bridge into Seville, they found that the wagons' wheels were too wide, a problem that required sawing off part of the axles. Teresa's travels, more than occasionally comic, take on a heroic aspect for the stamina and patience they required.

Teresa's deeds form a homely counterpoint to the battlefield victories of the *conquistadores*. The houses she bought were usually in ramshackle condition, at best. The house at Medina "had completely collapsed except for one room." Although Teresa and her retinue of nuns managed to make a chapel from the unplastered walls by hanging tapestries and bed curtains, the decayed condition of the courtyard walls prevented them from living there. Eventually a local merchant offered to let them occupy one floor of his house, which to her delight even included a "gilded room" for a chapel, while the reconstruction proceeded at the other house. In Salamanca, university students still occupied the house when she arrived, and to follow her practice of moving in before her presence and purpose became known, she had to prevail on a friend to have it vacated in one afternoon. This house was not decrepit, but to describe it as dirty would have been to understate its condition: "[The students] must not have had a gift for cleanliness" (19.3). When the several disadvantages of the house, including the location, forced Teresa to find another for them, she drew the designs for partitioning the larger rooms into cells. She supervised a hurried renovation and whitewashing and moved the nuns in before the contested sale of the house had been completed.

In addition to construction and design, Teresa's Mary Magdalene, a composite of the contemplative Mary and the active Martha, does the housework she also recommends to her nuns: "The Lord walks among the pots and pans helping you both interiorly and exteriorly" (5.8). The occasional descriptive detail Teresa includes about furnishings in a narrative that otherwise ignores the physical world suggests that she takes pleasure in making the house she buys into homes for the nuns she calls her daughters.

> And as though I were to live in that house [in Salamanca] for the rest of my life, I sought to obtain everything, even the smallest thing that would contribute to the tranquility suitable for the life, and so it gave me great happiness to see that everything was in good shape. (19.6)

Teresa tells of shopping excursions for household items, including wool blankets, straw mattresses, utensils, even nails. She particularly attends to the texture and color of fabric, specifying that the material of a borrowed bedspread she uses to cover broken wall plaster is blue damask and that for the pennants hanging from the rafters in the chapel at Toledo she chose taffeta in bright red and yellow, a fortuitous choice since these colors seemed to prove fire-resistant. She describes the habits she designed for the nuns—"the veils, the white, coarse woolen mantles we wore, and our sandals of hemp" (24.13)—with the pride of a mother who has taken particular care in dressing her children.

Wishing like Cortés to portray herself as a governor as well as a founder, Teresa includes several chapters of advice to prioresses that can be considered analogous to the regulations, laws, and instructions that appear in his letters, as well as in separate documents. She devotes chapters 5 through 9 to advising prioresses about handling their charges. Throughout she stresses the importance of requiring absolute obedience. She relates with satisfaction the story of a nun who knew better following her instructions to plant a cucumber sideways. Teresa thus urges prioresses to enforce strict discipline, denying fixations such as taking Communion every day, implementing rigorous work regulations to curb flights of imagination, and exercising caution about the source of visions. Weber argues that this authoritarian stance betrays Teresa's revolt against authority, denying autonomy and liberty to others.[31] Certainly Teresa's regulations for the convents, which she articulated in the *Constitutions*, seem extraordinarily harsh, prohibiting, for example, singing in harmony, touching each other on the face or hands, laughter, and games. Given what we can glean about Teresa's own playfulness and sense of humor, they seem inordinately repressive. Yet they should not be judged anachronistically by contemporary or secular standards of freedom. Teresa interpreted Scripture to mean that salvation requires obedience to God, and some of her disciplinary measures can be seen as training in the subordination of personal desire to divine will: "He is pleased more by obedience than by sacrifice" (6.22). Also, far from being coerced, women came voluntarily to Teresa's foundations, presumably because they preferred the life to any alternative. Teresa's statement on governance, which in 1576 she made a separate work, *On Making the Visitations*, extends Teresa's portrait of herself in the *Foundations* as a severe but supportive, even affectionate, leader. And, as the *Foundations* comes to closure, she permits others to succeed her by, in Said's terms for authorization, incorporating continuity into her beginning intention.[32]

An Allegory of Female Authority

In late 1575, Rubeo brought Teresa's wagons to a halt. Angered at the autonomy claimed by some groups of Barefoot Carmelite friars and by Teresa's defiance of his order against making foundations in Andalucía, he ordered Teresa and several others confined in Castilian monasteries. Teresa stayed in the convent at Toledo more than four years. Certain that she had made her last foundation, she wrote a conclusion to the *Foundations* in November 1576 (27.8). Teresa eventually did take to the road again, making four more foundations—Villanueva de la

Jara (1580), Palencia (1580), Soria (1581), Burgos (1582)—but during the hiatus, a feeling of old age had overtaken her. Even while telling of obstacles to these last foundations more serious than she had faced before, she expresses awareness that whatever her own accomplishments, others will take her place as founders: "Each one who enters in the future bear in mind that with her the observance of the primitive rule . . . begins again" (27.11).[33] Further releasing her hold on future members of the order, she warns them against allowing pride in their beginnings to distract attention from its current condition.

Teresa prepares for this moment throughout the *Foundations* by splicing biographical narratives of several young women into the chronicle. These women, the "stones" and "cement" of her work, are themselves the foundations: "Some of the new ones entering the monastery it seemed the Lord had chosen as the kind of cement that is suited to an edifice like this" (9.1).[34] Thus Teresa writes an allegory of female construction reminiscent of Pizan's *The Book of the City of Ladies*, in which Lady Reason appears to Christine and commands her to "establish and build the City of Ladies": "For the foundation and completion of this City you will draw fresh waters from us as from clear fountains, and we will bring you sufficient building stone, stronger and more durable than any marble with cement could be."[35] The stones with which Christine builds are the lives of famous women from all of Western history: Antigone, Sappho, Dido, Xanthippe, Penelope, Mary Magdalene, and so on. With God as her director, Teresa constructs her city of ladies with women she had met in Spain: Casilda de Padilla, Beatriz de la Encarnación, Teresa de Layz, Catalina Godínez, Catalina de Cardona, and Beatriz de Chávez. Expressing literary intentionality for the first time in all her writings, she gives as her reason for telling one of the stories, "It will give you pleasure" (26.1). As Weber points out, Teresa here includes some detail that seems purely novelistic.[36]

Critics have disagreed about whether Teresa's project of foundations reproduced the patriarchal order or whether they can be considered in any way protofeminist. Claire Guilhem judges Teresa's exclusion of *beatas*, those women who wished to live independently in female communities but not to enter an order, an indication of her collusion with the official misogyny.[37] In contrast, Lerner, writing of the medieval women mystics in general, considers that while their spiritual experience itself did not produce social change, "it was different with the utopian visions of the religious sectarians, in whose lives personal experiences and communal expressions merged. . . . They went from the private to the public realm and acted in it, that is, they made their lives political." As the transcripts of the hearings for Teresa's canonization (discussed in chap. 6) demonstrate, Teresa shared with these other mystics "the capacity to make their private ecstatic experiences part of the collective experience."[38] The biographies that constitute Teresa's allegory of female authority suggest that her foundations did challenge the social and economic order of patriarchy, even if her ambitions did not extend to radical change.

The women to whom Teresa's foundations appealed had learned early that they had no value in themselves. Teresa de Layz had disappointed her parents at birth by becoming their fifth daughter. On her third day of life they neglected her for an entire day, "as though she mattered little to them" (20.4). Suspecting that the baby might have died, a woman arriving that evening hurried to Teresa's room, where she found a baby miraculously empowered with precocious speech that saved her life.

> Weeping, the woman took the baby into her arms and complaining of the cruelty said: "How is it, my daughter, are you not a Christian?" The baby girl lifted her head and answered, "Yes, I am," and spoke no more until reaching that age at which all children begin to speak. (20.4)

With this act Teresa finally won a place in the family: "Her mother began to love and cherish her from then on" (20.4). Beatriz de Chávez, who entered the convent at Seville, took last place in her parents' affections while her brothers were alive: "Although she had had older brothers, they had all died, and she, the less loved by her parents, was left" (26.7).

Having reluctantly raised these girls, parents wished to exploit their exchange value in marriage. They arranged early marriages with the men they thought best able to preserve or enhance the family fortune, severely punishing any refusal or attempt to escape. When the family inheritance passed from an older sister to Casilda, she was engaged to an uncle as a means of keeping the wealth in the family, and when she took refuge in a convent, her parents obtained a court order to remove her.

Beatriz's parents made a marriage contract for her at the earliest possible moment: "When she reached the marriageable age, though she was still but a girl, her parents came to an agreement on whom she should marry" (26.7). Beatriz nearly died for her resistance.

> Since they had already given their word and their not following through on it would have been taken as an affront by the other party, they gave her so many whippings, inflicted on her so many punishments, even to the point of wanting to hang her, for they were choking her, that it was fortunate they didn't kill her. (26.8)

Catalina Godínez tried to disfigure herself by getting severe facial sunburns to thwart her parents' attempts to marry her. When that failed, she developed an astonishing array of illnesses—breast cancer, consumption, tuberculosis, dropsy, inflammation of the liver, gout, and sciatica. After eight years in bed, she proposed that if God were to give her complete health within a month she should be allowed to petition for a license to found a convent rather than marry. When she was cured at the appointed time, her family released her from her nuptial obligation. Her successful appeal to Philip II resulted in the foundation at Beas.

The divine intervention that effects rescue in many of these narratives emphasizes the exigency of women's situations. Casilda received the miraculous gift of skillful argumentation that stunned her elders, who seem to have had quite low standards for women's speech. When relatives attempt to convince her that she is too young to decide to enter a convent, she asks why they considered her old enough to be married; when her fiancé argues that she could serve God more by giving alms than by becoming a nun, she retorts that he should give the alms. So clever were her responses considered that they "made it appear that it wasn't she who was speaking" (11.4). When Casilda's first escape plan failed, she devised another, which was typically elaborate. While her mother was at confession, Casilda sent the governess to ask for a mass. Left alone for a moment, she ran toward the convent. She might easily have been stopped by the bystander her governess signaled for help, but he was stricken with immobility: "He said afterward that he wasn't able to move, and so he let her get away" (11.10). When the governess reached the convent, Casilda had already taken the habit.

These stories end happily from Teresa's point of view, with a transfer of wealth to the convents. Teresa de Layz, who received a sign that she should marry a man who would help support the order rather than join it herself, rejected having children in order to leave their estate to the convent at Alba de Tormes. Catalina de Godínez (and her sister) left their inheritance to the order "without any conditions, so that even if they were not admitted to profession the money would still belong to the order" (22.24). Previously vehicles for their fathers' accumulation of wealth, these women now diverted it to other women.

Teresa uses the vocabulary of kinship to describe this new social organization. Catalina Godínez's conversion gave her a new definition of lineage.

> The Lord worked a complete change in her: She had been thinking of a marriage that was being sought for her, which was better than she could have hoped for, and saying to herself: "With what little my father is content, that I become connected with an entailed estate; I am thinking of becoming the origin of a new line of descendants." (22.5)[39]

The Spanish original is even more emphatic, closer to "I mean my lineage to begin with me." Teresa's system of female kinship provides for inheritance—but not principally of worldly goods. Teresa characterizes Casilda de Padilla's entering the convent at Valladolid as a rejection of her family's mistakenly material definition of inheritance. Christ, who possessed nothing in this world, passed on the only inheritance of value, the emblems of His suffering: "What could we, your descendants, inherit from You? What did You possess, my Lord, but trials, sufferings, and dishonors?" (10.11). Similarly, Teresa plans that her nuns will endow their descendants with the wealth of their suffering, and ultimately those with sufficient courage will "inherit His kingdom."

Two of the women on whom Teresa builds her foundations took roads to sainthood that she had tried out in youth: Beatriz de la Encarnación, the martyr, and Catalina de Cardona, the hermit. Because the details of the lives of many of these women resonate with Teresa's life, their biographies function as specular autobiographies, self-representations written in the act of gazing at others, from a stance of some regret. In them she finds reason to regret the course of her own life. When Beatriz entered the convent at Valladolid, she already showed extraordinary virtue: "Both the nuns and the prioress affirmed that they had never noticed in any aspect of her life anything they would consider an imperfection" (12.1). Always willing to suffer to save souls, Beatriz found an opportunity when she learned that the Inquisition was to burn several men at the stake for heresy. She begged God to give her sufferings enough to save their souls, and that night a fever signaled that her prayer had been answered. From that moment she lived with hideous pain of several diseases, including an intestinal abscess "so internally located that the medicines they gave were of no help" (12.4) and an abscess on the throat that prevented her from swallowing. Throughout she cheerfully carried out all her duties as if she were well. The nuns in her convent gathered around her deathbed to witness her ascension, and at her funeral a sweet fragrance emanating from her body and a candle that burned but did not diminish confirmed her sainthood.

Teresa admires Beatriz, but she does not cause her to reassess her own vocation, as does Catalina de Cordona. A noblewoman who had been governess to the sons of both Charles V and Philip II, this Catalina embraced the hermit's life at age forty-four.[40] With the assistance of a male hermit, she found "a tiny cave hardly large enough for her" (28.24). He left her with three loaves of bread, the same number that St. Mary of Egypt took with her, and when these were gone she lived on herbs and roots for the next eight years. Although she disciplined herself two hours a day with a heavy chain, her greatest torment came from the devils who appeared to her in the form of huge dogs and snakes. Using her connections at court to obtain a license, she founded a monastery for Barefoot Carmelite friars on the site of her cave, which thus became a cornerstone of the foundation. Her life challenges Teresa's belief that the path she has chosen, that of the apostle, leads to sainthood.

> I saw that the one who had done such harsh penance there was a woman like me, but more delicate because of her background, and not so great a sinner as I. . . . The desire alone to imitate her, if I could, consoled me; but not much, for all my life has passed in desires, but the deeds I do not perform. (28.35)[41]

Given Teresa's string of foundations, her discouragement here would not seem objectively explicable. By placing it within the context of these other lives, however, Teresa associates it with the contradictions inherent in her attempts to valorize women within a patriarchal institution and society. Beatriz's heroism has a certainty and Catalina's a purity that Teresa's activity lacks. Her energy falters until a vision reassures her that she has Catalina's approval.

As fatigue and illness slow her pace, Teresa requires more and more divine encouragement and reassurance and, possibly, Alvarez Vázquez speculates, more external resistance.[42] In declaring her satisfaction at having provided enclosed spaces for others, she expresses nostalgia for the contemplative aspect of her own life: "So it is with souls accustomed to living in the running streams of their Spouse. When taken out of them and caught up in the net of worldly things, they do not truly live until they find themselves back in those waters" (31.46). Although very weary and even despondent, she continues her active life in the world until God announces the end she had conceived at the beginning: "'Everything is now finished; you are free to go'" (31.49).

6

THE ROLE OF TERESA'S BOOKS
IN THE CANONIZATION
PROCEEDINGS

Efficacious as Teresa's writing was for her protection and advancement, the text that finally convinced her contemporaries of her special relationship with God was not verbal but carnal. According to Ribera's account of the postmortem events in Teresa's life, nuns at the Alba de Tormes convent, where she had died on 4 October 1582, began to detect a sweet aroma, a scent like honeysuckle or jasmine, emanating from the chapel wall into which her coffin had been sealed. These odors were said to intensify on days commemorating Teresa's favorite saints, and it was reported that nuns who happened to fall asleep during their vigils beside her shrine were awakened by noises recalling them to prayer. These occurrences having aroused curiosity, the nuns requested Jerónimo Gracián to excavate the already crumbling wall, and on 4 July 1583 they opened the coffin. In his biography of Teresa, Ribera relates that although the wood had decayed and the shroud had rotted, they found her body incorrupt, "sound and whole as if they had just buried her."[1] Ribera, who saw the body himself some years later, gives graphic and gruesome detail that now seems more appropriate to the discourse of the autopsy report than the biography. In brief, he attests that even though her body had not been eviscerated or embalmed, it remained impervious to worms and mold and that in consistency it resembled a live body.

Rivalry for possession of the body, now considered one of the signs Christ had promised would come to the Church, ensued. Almost immediately Gracián took the left hand to the recently founded Barefoot Carmelite convent in Lisbon, keeping a finger for himself. When some Barefoot Carmelite priests secretly moved the body to Avila in 1585, they left behind the left arm to console the nuns at Alba. The convent at St. Joseph displayed the body to pilgrims who journeyed from all over Spain to read the signs of a miracle. While most religious sought ocular verification of the physical evidence, Alonso de la Fuente, who led the offensive in the posthumous Inquisitional trial of Teresa's books, relied on Teresa's words. Asserting in 1589 that "the book is corrupt," he concludes that "this being the case, the miracle that is said of the nun Teresa de Jesús, that she is today complete and incorrupt, is a fabulous business conjured by Satan, or an invention of heretics."[2] Those who went to St. Joseph, however, confirmed that Teresa's body did indeed signify her sanctity.

When the bishop of Salamanca observed the condition of the body for himself in 1591, he initiated preliminary interrogatories for her canonization, which were made in Alba and Salamanca. The questions in this first fact-finding procedure exhibit a somewhat skeptical approach, as if they were designed in part to put an end to outlandish claims; for example, witnesses were asked "how they know that she received certain gifts from Christ in prayer, whether because she told the witness; or if they heard from other persons, how and from whom, where and for what purpose, and whether the information was publicly known."[3] These interviews apparently yielded a preponderance of affirmative information, or at least that is what Silverio de Santa Teresa collects in his edition of the transcripts. The movement for sanctification gained real momentum, however, only after King Philip II saw a cloth stained with her blood, which was said to retain its color and to emit a fragrance. He ordered the second round of depositions to be taken in numerous Spanish cities. In 1597, Bernabé del Mármol took these transcripts to Rome, where he presented them to Pope Clement VII with letters of support from the king and his sister, the empress María. The Congregation of Rites, the papal body charged with preparing briefs for the canonization trials, determined the additional information required and delegated to Spanish authorities the administration of two additional inquiries, a brief "remittal on general issues," conducted in 1604, and an extensive "remittal on particulars," a set of 117 propositions that witnesses in 1609–1610 were asked to confirm or deny as "true, public, notorious, and obvious."[4] One of these articles asserted that as well as her body and the relics devised from her belongings, her books smelled sweet.[5]

While Fuente had asserted in 1589 that no woman could have written the books ascribed to Teresa, concluding that she had help from the devil, the initial investigation attempted to verify that she was in fact the author of the books published under her name. Witnesses presented a number of proofs: Isabel de Cristo, a Barefoot Carmelite in Segovia, asserted that the style resembled Teresa's speech; María de San José, a Barefoot Carmelite from Lisbon, related that she had seen Teresa writing them; Garciálvarez, confessor for a brief time to the convent at Seville, observed that in style and syntax they resembled the letters she had written to him; Alonso de Andrada, who as a student had assisted with the foundation at Toledo, testified that he recognized her script in the manuscripts he had copied for binding.[6]

As reformulated in Rome, however, the documents on canonization asserted, in agreement with Fuente but specifying divine rather than demonic dictation, that Teresa did not write her books herself. Article 54 proposes that the lack of revision indicates that she wrote in a state of ecstasy, and possibly to rationalize earlier testimony based on her handwriting, it explains that "after returning to herself she found things written in her script but not by her hand." Article 56 asserts that the doctrine in these books was "not acquired or taught by human industry, but infused by God through the medium of prayer." In affirming the latter proposition, many witnesses cited the prevailing belief that no woman was capable of writing such books. The Carmelite bishop of Avila, Lorenzo Otaduy, judged the doctrine "elevated beyond the resources of any woman, particularly one without study of theology."[7] Even a familial relationship apparently did not serve to mitigate this gender-based judgment. Diego de Vera, a nephew by her half-brother from her father's first marriage, asserted that "it is taken for impossible that she could have written her books, especially the *Castle*, even if she had had much more learning than any woman can claim."[8] In giving Teresa sainthood, the Church deprived her of authorship, or tried to.

While Teresa's books had long been said to produce beneficial effects in readers, now they were perceived to have supernatural effects. Witnesses in the final hearings told of miraculous conversions, cures of diseases such as melancholy and toothache, dedications to the monastic life, and reforms in conventual life attributable to readings of Teresa's books, which now were read principally in the several printed editions.

Even a soiled copy produced a miraculous effect. Pablo Bravo de Córdoba y Soto Mayor relates that Dr. Alonso de Anaya, president of the chancellery of Valladolid, was skeptical about Teresa's vision of Bernardino de Mendoza ascending from purgatory to heaven. Mendoza had deeded a house and garden to the Barefoot Carmelites for a convent at Valladolid, but Teresa considered the property too far from the city and wished to settle elsewhere. The conditions of his will prohibited her moving, however. In the *Foundations* Teresa asserts that after Mendoza died, Teresa received a message that he would enter heaven after a mass had been said in his house. When Teresa held the mass, he appeared to her in a vision, thanking her for her intervention on behalf of his ascent to heaven and in effect releasing her from the contract. Anaya sent a friend to the convent at Valladolid for a copy of Teresa's book to verify reports of the vision. When informed by the prioress that a nun had spilled cooking oil on their only copy, the friend returned empty-handed, thinking better of giving this man, who was known for fastidiousness, an oily book. Anaya insisted on having it anyway, and he found it a page-turner: he read 257 pages "without stopping to eat lunch or dinner, to sleep, or to perform any other obligation."[9] After reading of Teresa's miracles and considering her recent death, he received a sign that he should prepare for his own death. He contracted a minor illness, informed unconcerned doctors that he would die of it, and did so on the ninth day, amid signs of his certain salvation.

While this death rewarded piety, in another case a premature death punished a negative opinion about Teresa's books. Count Pedro Lasso de la Vega testified that the Dominican Juan de Lorenzana, who had joined Fuente in condemning Teresa's books before the Inquisition, suffered divine retribution. Several priests tried to change his mind, and having failed, they wrote to Diego de Yepes, confessor to the king, for evidence that might convince him before he disillusioned anyone else. During the exchange of post, Lorenzana developed a fever, and "when the letters arrived from San Lorenzo [the royal summer palace], the priest had already been buried two or three days."[10] In part because of such events, many witnesses considered Teresa's books holy relics.

The papal document treats the *Life* as a case apart from the other books. Specifying that she wrote it "without any thought that it would circulate publicly" and naming all the confessors who commanded her to write the book or had been closely associated with her, article 55 implies that the *Life* does not have the divine provenance of the other works. The article adduces purely human evidence for its truthfulness, including her reputation for sincerity and examinations made by numerous priests and the Inquisition. While apparently attempting to relegate the *Life* to a secondary position, the papacy actually elevated it to principal authority for the portion of the canonization brief that presents a biography of the prospective saint. This biographical section of the brief also draws from the *Foundations*, particularly for her locutions from God, but possibly because information about these events also came from eyewitnesses and participants, Teresa's interpretations figure less prominently.

Most of the witnesses in the earliest investigations had actually known Teresa, and as a result, they relied on personal interaction with her and observation. Because they narrated their own interaction with Teresa, few details of her early life emerged. On points where witnesses had no firsthand knowledge, they more or less restated the questions or cited the remarks of those Church authorities who had known Teresa, especially Domingo Báñez, Pedro Ibáñez, Francisco de Ribera, and Julián de Avila. Teresa's books were adduced mainly as secondary evidence, as in Julián de Avila's blanket referral to her books for everything he was not able to mention.[11]

The bill of particulars that returned from Rome, however, relied heavily on Teresa's books for its propositional material. Article 1 states that Teresa "was born of the nobles Alfonso [*sic*] de Cepeda and Beatriz de Ahumada," and article 2 relates that "from early childhood her parents raised her with Christian piety."[12] In assenting to these propositions about her heritage, some witnesses, like the Carmelite Blas de San Alberto, cited the *Life* as evidence: "Thus this witness had read in the book of the *Life* of the said Teresa de Jesús."[13] Many witnesses stated the assumption that necessarily remained unstated, that, in the words of Dr. Pedro de Tablares, "she is of noble lineage, without any Jewish or Moorish blood by her parents, paternal grandparents or maternal grandparents."[14]

The document continues by narrating the principal episodes of the *Life*, sometimes nearly verbatim. Witnesses were thus asked to affirm that she "had the custom of repeating the words 'forever, forever, forever'"; that her reading of the saints' lives "ignited a fervent desire for martyrdom"; that "after finding execution of this desire impossible," she and her brother "made hermits' caves in their father's orchard"; that after her mother's death Teresa begged the Virgin Mary "to take the role of mother to her"; that on reading Augustine's *Confessions*, "it seemed to her as if she had heard the voice in the garden"; and that she seized an enchanted amulet to release a priest from its spell.[15] The bill not only rehearses incidents from the *Life* but interprets them in her favor, stating, for example, that the Virgin accepted Teresa's request that she act as her mother, that Teresa's building a hermit's cave prefigured her founding of convents, and that the devil instigated the opposition she faced in founding St. Joseph and other convents. Teresa could not have hoped for a more credulous reading of her self-interpretations.

Pope Paul V beatified Teresa on 24 April 1614, giving Spain permission to venerate her as a saint, and on 12 March 1622, Gregory XV inscribed Teresa in the book of saints of the universal Church.

7

EPILOGUE
Psychoanalytic Interpretations of Teresa's Mystical Experience

Readers of Teresa's life and works have understood her experience in many vocabularies. On finding her body uncorrupted after a year of burial, her contemporaries initiated the process of designating her a saint. She has remained important in the Catholic faith and other religious traditions, but increasingly she receives secular attention as well. In the nineteenth century, many women writers considered Teresa an ideal of female heroic action, a view Eliot's narrator expresses in the prelude to *Middlemarch*: "Theresa's passionate, ideal nature demanded an epic life. She found her epos in the reform of a religious order."[1] Teresa's life also has significance for this century. Several of France's most important thinkers, including Jacques Lacan, Julia Kristeva, and Luce Irigaray, have given psychoanalytic meanings to her mystical experience. All these theorists equate mystical with pre-Oedipal experience, an anthropocentric concept that when fitted onto the mystics creates numerous distortions, most important in Teresa's case, a failure to account for her action in the world.[2] Yet these translations of religious into psychoanalytic experience also raise significant questions about the experience Teresa reports, in particular, the relationship between mystical union and the formation of her subjectivity.

Irigaray and Kristeva, both trained in Lacanian psychoanalytic theory, have turned to the medieval women mystics, Teresa among them, for their formulation of a feminist politics and a feminine psychology, respectively. Lacan introduced Teresa into the French psychoanalytic discussion of female sexuality by using her in "God and the *Jouissance* of Ŧħє Woman" as evidence that women reside outside language. In that lecture he cites Hadewijch of Brabant and Teresa to support his theory that women experience a "supplementary *jouissance*," which he defines as an encompassing enjoyment exceeding that of phallic, orgasmic sexuality. Lacan points to Bernini's sculptural representation of St. Teresa reclining in ecstasy as a display of this supplementary jouissance: "You have only to go and look at Bernini's statue in Rome to understand immediately that she's coming [*qu'elle jouit*], there is no doubt about it." Yet according to Lacan, she cannot explain or express her experience: "And what is her *jouissance*, her *coming* from? It is clear that the essential testimony of the mystics is that they are experiencing it but know nothing about it."[3] Having effectively silenced women with his gendering of language as the Law of the Father, Lacan proceeds to ridicule them for not telling him about female sexuality: "What gives some likelihood to what I am arguing, that is, that the woman knows nothing of this *jouissance*, is that ever since we've been begging them—last time I mentioned women analysts—begging them on our knees to try to tell us about it, well, not a word!"[4] Irigaray counters caustically that Lacan has been looking when he should have been listening: "In Rome? So far away? To look? At a statue? Of a saint? Sculpted by a man? What pleasure are we talking about? Whose pleasure? For where the pleasure of the Theresa in question is concerned, her own writings are perhaps more telling."[5] In a chapter of *Speculum of the Other Woman* entitled "La mystérique," Irigaray attempts to force Lacan to hear what the mystics tell in language by using their writings, including Teresa's, to create an intertextual tapestry of mystical discourse.[6] In that essay, she makes the most often-quoted statement about the power that accrued to women mystics, "this [the stance of the mystic] is the only place in the history of the West in which woman speaks and acts so publicly." Ironically, Irigaray leaves her "mystérique" in the same realm to which Lacan confines woman: the imaginary, a place anterior to consciousness and subjectivity.

Irigaray's "La mystérique" functions more effectively to further *Speculum*'s project of exposing the patriarchal bias of Western philosophy than to understand the mystics' representations of their experience. In the persona of the "mystérique," Irigaray leads the *Speculum's* male philosopher—a composite figure of Plato, Descartes, Freud, and Lacan—into the unconscious, which she defines as the repository of the repressed feminine in Western culture. There below consciousness "he can no longer find himself as 'subject,'" and his logic and geometry do not provide the mastery to which he is accustomed. While Irigaray designates herself and the male philosopher together as one feminine "soul" ("*elle*"), the "mystérique" separates herself at every turn to mock his discomfort in her territory. She leaves his questions unanswered and eventually abandons him flailing as helplessly as the silent film heroine tied to the track before an oncoming train: "But alone and without help, alas! the soul cannot prevent herself from being buried and sealed off in her crypt."[7] After the soul submits to such incapacitation, she enters a mystical relationship, for which, following the nuptial tradition in medieval mysticism, Irigaray borrows the imagery of human marriage. Irigaray defines this "courtship" as "reciprocal identification" ("*co-identification réciproque*"), a relationship that in Irigaray's schema would preclude productive activity. This scenario does serve to humiliate the male philosopher but not to portray the mystic. Yet because Irigaray situates this treatment of female mysticism within the context of her evolving theory of gender difference and relationship, she does provide, more fully in her subsequent works than in *Speculum*, a conceptual framework for explaining the experience of the women mystics.

For Irigaray, gender difference varies according to its construction in any given society. She defines the relationship between man and woman in patriarchy as one of complementarity, a binary opposition in which one of the terms is defined as the absence of the other. Woman, defined solely by opposition to the male, has neither independent subjecthood nor attributes of her own; in Elizabeth Grosz's notation for relationship in the works of Irigaray, the male is *A*, the subject, and the female is *not-A*, the object.[8] This patriarchal couple, *A and not-A*, makes a unit of one, Irigaray explains in *Ethique de la différence sexuelle*: "Until the present, generally, love took place within the One. The two did not make more than one."[9] As an alternative to this cancellation of feminine identity in patriarchy, Irigaray initially proposed, in "When Our Lips Speak Together," that women seek their subjectivity in relationships between and among women. There Irigaray enacts a union between her feminine persona and another woman who is "neither mother (pardon me, mother, for

I prefer a woman) nor sister. Neither daughter nor son." That is, a woman not related to her by patriarchal lineage or law. Neither the same nor different, but un-different, these lovers make "neither one nor two," a configuration Irigaray also uses to describe the female genitals.[10] Binary opposition does not govern this relationship, which can be designated as A_1 and A_2, but the complete reciprocity prohibits creative interchange between the lovers: "Everything is exchanged, yet there are no transactions."[11] Without transactions, however, each of the lovers remains unaltered, thus unproductive. More recently, Irigaray has envisioned a relationship between man and woman that supersedes the patriarchal, a relationship of alterity, which Grosz designates as A and B.[12] Even in union, each subject affirms its essential difference from the other. "Never will I be in the place of the man, never will a man be in my place. Whatever identifications may be possible, one will never occupy precisely the place of the other—they are irreducible one to the other."[13] This dynamic of irreducible difference, which she considers indispensable for providing women the subjectivity they have been denied, remains to be realized, however.

The mystical union Irigaray presents in "La mystérique" more nearly resembles a relationship of un-difference, which I will call connaturality, than of alterity. In the Irigarayan "cauldron of identification" that is mystical union, the soul, having shed names and properties (status as property), encounters not God but "God" ("*Dieu*"), who likewise has "renounced modes and attributes." The secret of their union, she confides, is that "she is transformed into Him."

> Each becomes the other in consumption, the nothing of the other in consummation. Each will not in fact have known the identity of the other, has thus lost self-identity except for a hint of an imprint that each keeps in order the better to intertwine in a union already, finally, at hand. Thus I am to you as you are to me, mine is yours and yours mine, I know you as you know me, you take pleasure with me as with you, I take pleasure in the rejoicing of this reciprocal living—and identifying—together.

Some of the imagery of Irigarayan mystical union recalls her descriptions of women's relationships with women.

> We are both singular and plural, one and ones, provided that nothing tarnishes the mirrors that fuse in the purity of their exchange.

Provided that one, furthermore, does not exceed the other in size
and quality. For then the other would be absorbed in the One [as]
to infinity.[14]

A union as connatural as this one sounds would deprive the
soul of the "self-identity" required for independent subjectivity.

As evidence for the connatural nature of mystical experience,
Irigaray takes an epigraph from Angela of Foligno's *Book of the
Experience of the Truly Faithful*: "The Word was made flesh in
order to make me God."[15] Teresa also makes many statements
that might similarly be taken as claims to complete identification with God, such as, "In the spiritual marriage the union is
like what we have when rain falls from the sky into a river or
fount; all is water, for the rain that fell from heaven cannot be
divided or separated from the water of the river" (*Castle* 7.2.4).
Did Teresa, then, consider herself deified through mystical experience, as Irigaray suggests by including her in the figure of
the "mystérique"? For the most part, she did not. Irigaray may
mean to intimate that a woman's mystical experience discovers
a female God, thus sacralizing the feminine, but even so, Teresa
would not fit in her scheme. Although Teresa occasionally uses
the imagery of Jesus as nurturing mother, the God she most
often portrays is unequivocally male. And rather than finding
the divine within herself, a consequence more common to East-
ern than to Western mysticism, Teresa attains relationship and
dialogue. She insists on difference between herself and God:
"This castle is a creature and the *difference*, therefore between
it and God is the same as that between the Creator and His
creature" (*Castle* 1.1.1; my emphasis).[16] And in accord with Irigaray's contention in *Ethique* that "in order to love there must
be two," she specifies the alterity and reciprocality of her relationship with God: "I have always seen in my God much greater
and more extraordinary signs of love than I have known how to
ask for or desire!" (*Exclamation* 5.2). Still, she does sometimes
yearn for thorough identification with God, presumably also for
the divinization it would require. As we have seen, Teresa resolves conflicting desires for union with and separation from God
by splitting spirit away from soul: "The soul, I mean the spirit, is
made one with God" (*Castle* 7.2.3). This compromise allows her
spirit to remain with God while her soul operates in the world.

The difference Teresa describes between God and herself might
be considered merely the distinction of complementarity in the

patriarchal couple, in which she would have the place of *not-A*. For Irigaray, complementarity both creates and perpetuates a structure of specularization that denies woman an image of herself. In patriarchy, the male projects his own ego onto the world, which then functions as a mirror that reflects his image wherever he looks. The flat mirror that reflects him does not serve for woman, in part because she is a component of which the mirror is made and in part because her nature requires the concave mirror of the speculum, an instrument used for gynecological examination. Some of Teresa's mirror imagery does suggest that mystical union gives her an image not of herself but of Christ, the culminating vision of the *Life*, for example: "It seemed to me I saw Him clearly in every part of my soul, as though in a mirror. And this mirror also—I don't know how to explain it—was completely engraved upon the Lord Himself by means of a very loving communication I wouldn't know how to describe" (*Life* 40.5).[17] Elsewhere, however, Teresa separates her self-image from Christ's. This 1577 poem, Christ's part of a dialogue with her, suggests that her image, while available only within Him, is not identical to His: "By love you were created / beautiful, lovely, and / painted thus in my interior. / If you should lose yourself, beloved / Soul, you must seek yourself within Me. / I know that you will find / Portrayed in my breast / and so very lifelike / that it will please you when you see it / regarding yourself so well depicted" (*Poetry* 8, lines 8–17; my translation).[18] In later years especially she speaks more often of acquiring than of losing "self-identity" through mystical experience.

While Irigaray marshals philosophy and feminist politics to critique Lacanian theory, Kristeva attempts to elaborate it to include the feminine. Her continuing reliance on Lacan signals not simply her commitment to psychoanalytic practice but also, Juliana Schiesari shows in *The Gendering of Melancholy*, the misogynistic cast of some of the ideas she applies to mysticism.[19] Kristeva's theory, however, goes farther than Irigaray's toward explaining Teresa's transformation through mystical experience: Kristeva's unconscious, like Teresa's soul, is individual rather than collective, and more important, Kristeva's use of religious vocabulary allows her texts to resonate sympathetically with Teresa's. And like Kristeva, Teresa did not entirely shed the misogyny of her society.

Kristeva defines mystical union in psychoanalytic terms as a regression to absolute and completely enveloping maternal love of infancy. In *Tales of Love*, she takes Jeanne Guyon (1648–1717) as her example of the mystic because she displays the symptoms of withdrawal into archaic narcissism, which Kristeva defines in *Black Sun* as melancholia: "Those in despair [melancholics] are mystics."[20] Kristeva considers the same symptoms to be more disguised in Guyon's predecessors, Teresa and John of the Cross, because of their "greater talent" and closer affiliation with the temperament of their times. Born at the moment that Descartes sealed the subordination of passion to thought, Guyon illustrates for Kristeva the loving subject of Christianity in conflict with the new Cartesian knowing subject. Guyon's object is "the amorous presence of the Loved One," which she pursues by annihilating every attribute of self. The means Guyon advocated for seeking mystical experience, which Kristeva describes as "outside method and thought but also outside language," led to her conviction for the heresy of Quietism, a movement that developed from Illuminism. The divergence of Teresa's mystical theory from Illuminism provides one indication of the inadequacy of this comparison with Guyon.

While Freud and Lacan left the pre-Oedipal or imaginary landscape unarticulated, Kristeva attempts to describe its features. In doing so, she develops a vocabulary for talking about the mother's contribution to the acquisition of language and consciousness. To describe the most primitive phase of the maternal realm, Kristeva adopts the Platonic term *chora*, which she defines as "a nonexpressive totality formed by the drives and their states in a motility that is as full of movement as it is regulated."[21] Here the maternal body presses the energy of drives through the infant, engraving both physical and psychical marks. The infant keeps the archaic striations made in the *chora* as affects, which appear in what Kristeva calls the semiotic aspect of language. Kristeva reconceives the transition that Lacan's mirror stage represents from specular to linguistic terms, and, following Freud, who specifies that narcissism develops not in the symbiotic connection between mother and child but as a supplementation of it, she substitutes a dual process that entails the simultaneous imprinting of what she calls an Imaginary Father and the "abjection [a Kristevan neologism for rejection of something that is not an object] of the mother." Kristeva defines the Imaginary Father as the mother's expression of her desire for the father, or because the infant in this period knows no distinction between the sexes, for any object the mother loves beyond the infant and herself. Primarily vocal rather than visual, linguistic rather than specular, this Imaginary Father is not an object but a model to be copied in the inscriptions made by sympathetic physical and psychical vibration. As the infant assimilates the markers of the Imaginary Father from the mother's emotion, it simultaneously attempts to "abject" the potentially engulfing chaos of the maternal identification. This process leaves the traces of both similarity and difference, a difference within unity that is a precondition for entering the Oedipal stage, or the symbolic order.

The infant with a melancholy future, the future mystic, fails to read an inscription of mother's desire for the Imaginary Father, for an object beyond the narcissistic union. Although the cause of such an archaic dyslexia may be biological, most frequently it resides in faintness of the markings, even their absence. Cynthia Chase points out that "the marks of maternal care must be *read* to signify the mother's desire . . . [but] they may *not* signify."[22] That is, they might not signify anything beyond the mother. Also, the person functioning as Imaginary Father must be capable of attracting the mother's desire out of exclusive focus on her infant. When unannounced by the Imaginary Father, the Law of the Father, or language, does not operate to allow for mourning, which Kristeva defines linguistically as replacement of the preobject in verbal representation. Because signifiers operate as symbols only in the absence of the object, a failure of the Imaginary Father to intimate the future separation portends devitalization of meaning. Language, as Kristeva understands it, comprehends heterogeneous elements: the semiotic, an affective modality deriving from the inscriptions of drives in the imaginary realm, and the thetic, a syntactic modality introduced by the Law of the Father. Melancholy divorces the symbolic signifier from its necessary underlying affect as well as from the thing signified. Rather than with meaning, signs fill with paralyzing affects that prevent the attachments of the metonymic chain: "The possibility of concatenating signifiers (words or actions) appears to depend upon going through mourning for an archaic and indispensable object."[23]

The melancholic erects a "defensive shell" to attempt to hold the primitive union with the unmourned preobject. Not a comforting cradle or Edenic garden, the imaginary place of melancholy withdrawal is rather a "psychic tomb" that the melancholic, prey to an "inspective obsession," scrutinizes ceaselessly.[24] Within the walls the melancholic finds only semiotic marks of imprisoning attachment rather than liberating signifiers. Confined to this place, the melancholic suffers the loss of any object whatsoever with the force of the original trauma of separation from the mother. Women fall prey to melancholy more frequently than men, perhaps even inevitably, Kristeva believes. Separation from the mother through matricide requires of a daughter putting to death part of herself: "For a woman, whose specular identification with the mother as well as the introjection of the maternal body and self are more immediate, such an inversion of matricidal drive into a death-bearing maternal image is more difficult, if not impossible."[25] According to Kristeva, men more easily recover the maternal object with an erotic object than do women, who must expend tremendous psychic energy to change gender of the desired object.

Was Teresa melancholic, as Kristeva suggests? She would not have described herself as such even though the word *melancholy* was in her vocabulary. Developing the premise of the humoral theory of the origin of melancholy, she considers it a physical ailment, which she thought often attributable to excesses of asceticism. At the same time she diagnoses intellectual symptoms deriving from demonic influence, including manifestations often mistaken for legitimate spiritual experience, especially interior voices and hallucinations, as well as a range of emotional symptoms, such as willfulness and selfishness. Like Kristeva, Teresa found women more often ravaged by it than men. While this analysis coincided with the misogynistic doctrine of the Church, she more often used it to cure than to condemn. She advises prioresses at some length about the diagnosis and treatment of melancholy in the *Foundations*, urging them to alleviate the symptoms whenever possible, to prescribe remedies of red meat and reduced periods of mandatory prayer, but above all, to require obedience. At the same time, perhaps by intuitive recognition that the illness exceeds the physical, she seems to despair of curing most melancholics, particularly those with what she calls a weak imagination, which would retard or preclude disciplined spiritual experience.

For her own suffering, Teresa uses words with connotations of spiritual sensitivity rather than physical disability: affliction or anxiety, grief, sorrow, oppression, anguish, and interior trials.

The *Tesoro* shows that some of these words had theological connotations, *tristeza*, for example: "[Tristeza] derives from the memory of sin and of having offended God. This sadness has a rationale; Christ Our Lord had it for the sins of the sinner, and St. Paul for his own sins and those of others."[26] Teresa similarly identifies these feelings with the Passion of Christ: "If you are experiencing trials or are sad, behold Him on the way to the garden: what great affliction He bore in his soul; for having become suffering itself, He tells us about it and complains of it" (*Road* 26.5). For Teresa, then, many of the symptoms of the Kristevan melancholic would have distinguished her as a member of the spiritual aristocracy that shares Christ's dejection about the sinfulness of humanity.

Teresa's images of the sinful soul do resemble Kristeva's "psychic tomb" of melancholy, however. Teresa describes the soul without God as a wasteland, deserted but for the signs of sin, which might be considered in psychological terms as the marks of self-hatred: insects and vermin inhabit the courtyard of the undeveloped soul in the *Interior Castle*; in the *Life*, weeds choke out all other growth in the arid "dungheap" that is the soul before it has begun spiritual progress. The emotional deceleration Kristeva diagnoses in the melancholic recalls Teresa's description of sin as spiritual paralysis: "These unfortunate souls [those not in a state of grace] are as though in a dark prison, bound hands and feet, in regard to doing anything good that would enable them to merit, and blind and deaf" (*Castle* 7.1.3). In that "dark prison," the only light that can penetrate is reminiscent of Nerval's paradoxical black sun, "dazzling with black invisibility," which Kristeva finds evocative of melancholy: "There was no light, but all was enveloped in the blackest darkness. I don't understand how this could be, that everything painful to see was visible" (*Life* 32.3). Kristeva's melancholic experiences time as stagnant, "the psychic object . . . belong[ing] to lost time, in the manner of Proust," and Teresa herself sounds Proustian in her description of her mystical experience as a recovery of lost time: "Now it can be known whether my soul understands itself in being aware of the time it has lost and how in a moment You, Lord, can win this time back again" (*Soliloquy* 4.1). Also, Teresa's complaints about linguistic activity resemble the symptoms of verbal deceleration and devalorization of signification that Kristeva attributes to the divorce of the semiotic and thetic functions of language in melancholy: "At the level of the sign, splitting separates the *signifier* [the symbolic] from the *referent* [the signified] as well as from the drive-related (semiotic) *inscriptions* and devalorizes all three."[27] In narrating the years before her conversion Teresa often complains of various kinds of linguistic incapacity, such as "my intellect disturbs me because I cannot think anything about God. If I read, I don't understand" (*Testimony* 1.22). After conversion, and particularly after mystical union, she remarks a release from anxiety about language and other symbolic activity: "If souls now see a devout image or hear a sermon (before they would not even have heard it) or music, they are not agitated as was the poor little butterfly" (*Castle* 7.3.11). If Teresa is considered a melancholic in the Kristevan sense, then it must also be said that, unlike Jeanne Guyon, she finds a way to transform the melancholy crypt into an interior castle.

Kristeva's analysis of Christianity provides one explanation of what Teresa calls her transformation. Kristeva finds the symbols of Christianity perfectly suited to the relief of melancholy. The Virgin Mary represents an ideal mother in that she willingly gives up her Son for something she loves beyond him. Also, the fantasy of feminine immortality associated with the Virgin Mary, Kristeva believes, helps to allay anxiety about the "abjection" of the mother, the matricide required for formation of the subject. God functions as the ideal Imaginary Father because He can play the symbolic as well as the Oedipal father, blending "the two facets of fatherhood" in a way that links "the abstract and arbitrary signs of communication" to "the affective meaning of prehistorical identifications." As Imaginary Father, God breaks into the psychical tomb where the melancholic is held captive, bringing jouissance, which Kristeva defines as "the direct re-experiencing of the physical pleasures of infancy and of later sexuality." This jouissance is not Lacan's phallic identification with the male's symbolic power but an "*other jouissance* that fantasy imagines," the Imaginary Father "requir[ing] that the melancholy object blocking the psychic and bodily interior literally be liquefied."[28] And what Kristeva calls the hiatus between the Passion of Christ and His resurrection, which she finds represented in Hans Holbein's painting *The Body of the Dead Christ in the Tomb*, allows the subject to rehearse and consolidate the separation from the maternal. While such a theory about the operation of religious symbols does not admit confirmation or contradiction, it is interesting to recall that Teresa took the Virgin Mary as her surrogate mother. And while Teresa once envisioned Joseph as her father and often invoked him as her legal advocate, she also finds parental authority in God. The exchange of her human father for a divine father that many critics, including La Guardia, Weber, and Jane Tylus, have proposed as a way of understanding her life, might be seen in Kristevan terms as the acquisition of an alternative Imaginary Father, one with the power to release her from the melancholic tomb.

While the French psychoanalytic theorists have emphasized the contemplative aspect of Teresa's experience, the nineteenth-century women novelists concentrated on the active. Anna Burr Jameson had anticipated Eliot in formulating the question raised in the prelude to *Middlemarch*, whether or not a similarly talented woman living in another historical period might also lead a heroic life of action. In *Legends of the Monastic Orders*, Jameson answered the question affirmatively: "[St. Teresa] would have been a remarkable woman in any age and country. Under no circumstances could her path through life have been the highway of commonplace mediocrity. . . . [W]hat was strong, and beautiful, and true, and earnest, and holy, was in herself; and what was morbid, miserable, and mistaken, was the result of the influences around her."[29] Eliot's epilogue to *Middlemarch* answers in the negative on behalf of its nineteenth-century version of Teresa, Dorothea Brooke, who finds a vehicle for action only in her husband: "A new Theresa will hardly have the opportunity of reforming a conventual life. . . . [T]he medium in which their ardent deeds took shape is gone forever."[30] Awareness of historical context would preclude raising the question, yet the problem is intriguing because it forces a statement about the essential motive of Teresa's life. I find an answer from Abbot John Chapman, an English Benedictine, who quotes a spiritual mentor to support his own view: "St. John of the Cross is like a sponge full of Christianity. You can squeeze it all out, and the full mystical theory remains. . . . [Teresa] is first a Christian; only secondarily a mystic."[31] Roman Catholic Christianity gave Teresa an identity, releasing her from the marginalized positions of woman and converso, and her written accounts of mystical experience served the end of enabling her to live this identity in action.

APPENDIX A

CENSURE BY
BROTHER DOMINGO BÁÑEZ
[on the manuscript of the *Life*]

1) I have looked, with great attention, at this book in which Teresa de Jesús, a Carmelite nun and founder of the Barefoot Carmelites, gives a sincere account [*relación llana*] of all her spiritual experiences, for the purpose of being taught and guided by her confessors. And in it I have found nothing that in my judgment is bad doctrine, but only things that have value as education and advice for those who practice prayer. This religious woman's great experience, as well as her humility and discretion in always choosing confessors with illumination and learning, allows her to ascertain things about prayer that learned persons often cannot because of their lack of experience.

2) Only one thing in this book must be observed, and there is good reason to examine this closely, which is that it contains many revelations and visions, always to be greatly feared, especially in women, who too easily believe these come from God and attribute holiness to them even where it does not belong, before they have put themselves through the dangerous work of achieving perfection. Satan frequently transforms himself into an angel of light and deceives curious and arrogant souls, as we have seen in our times. But for this reason we should not deem that all revelations and visions come from the devil. Paul would not have said that Satan transforms himself into an angel of light if that angel did not sometimes illuminate us.

3) In ancient and in modern times, male saints have had

revelations, and female saints as well, such as St. Dominic, St. Francis, St. Vincent Ferrer, St. Catherine of Siena, St. Gertrude, and many others that could be counted. And as the Church of God is and must be holy until the end, not only because it professes holiness but also because it includes those with the most perfect piety and holiness, there is no reason to condemn and trample such visions without due consideration. They can be accompanied by great virtue and Christian faith. Rather we should follow the saying of the Apostle in chapter 5 of 1 Thessalonians: "Do not stifle inspiration, and do not despise prophetic utterances, but bring them all to the test and then keep what is good in them and avoid the bad of whatever kind." On this point, whoever reads St. Thomas will understand how diligently those in the Church who discover some gift that can be either useful or harmful to neighbors must be examined and how much caution examiners must have in order not to extinguish spiritual fervor for God in the righteous or cause others to lose courage in their exercise toward the perfect Christian life.

4) Although she is deceived in some things, this woman, as far as can be seen in this account, is not a deceiver, because she speaks plainly [*llanamente*], both the good and the bad, and with such a desire to express them accurately that she leaves no doubt about her good intentions. And however many reasons there may be to examine similar souls, because in our times there have been mockers who paint themselves virtuous, there is just as much reason to protect those who appear to have the hue of true virtue. It is strange that weak and worldly people may amuse themselves by seeing people with this kind of virtue deprived of authority [*desautorizados*].

5) A long time ago God complained through the prophet Ezekiel, chapter 13, about false prophets who harassed the holy and flattered the sinners: "You discouraged the righteous man with lies, when I meant him no harm; you strengthened the wicked." In some sense this can be said against those who frighten souls on the road of prayer and perfection, telling them that these are dangerous roads or other strange things such as that many have fallen into error on this road and that the safest road is smooth [*llano*], common, and heavily used.

6) It is clear that those who wish to follow the instructions and perfection of continual prayers along with great fasting, vigils, and spiritual disciplines are saddened by such words. On the

other hand, the weak and sinful become stronger and lose fear of God, because they find their path more secure.

7) This is the deception: calling the road smooth and secure. We lack knowledge and consideration of the danger and precipices where we all walk in this world, there being no other security than, with full awareness of our daily enemies, humbly invoking God's mercy if we would wish not to be made captive of them. And there are souls whom God constrains in such a way that they enter the road to perfection, but when the fervor ceases they cannot help going to the other extreme in sin. And it is necessary to watch and pray for these persons continually, since no one without passion ever rejected evil. Let each one place a hand on his heart, and he will know that this is true. I believe that if God ever tolerates tepid souls, it is because the fervent pray as follows: "And lead us not into temptation."

8) I have said this, not so that we can canonize those that seem to go by the road of contemplation, for this is another worldly extreme that covertly persecutes virtue, making saints of those with any version of virtue. For it gives them reason for vanity, and rather than making virtue honorable puts it in danger. When those who were so highly praised fall, the reputation of virtue suffers more than if they had never been so esteemed. And so I take this overestimation of the holiness of those that live in this world as the devil's temptation. It is right that we should have a good opinion of the servants of God, but however good they are, we should see them as human beings in danger and consider that the good are not manifest to us here. Only of this can we be certain at present.

9) On the basis of my consideration that what I have said is true, I have always proceeded cautiously in the examination of this account of prayer and the life of this religious woman. No one has been more skeptical than I in regard to her visions and revelations, though not in regard to her virtues and good desires. I have great experience of her truth, obedience, penitence, patience and charity with those who persecute her, and other virtues that anyone who deals with her will readily see. And I value these things as a sign of true love of God more than visions and revelations.

10) But neither do I underestimate her visions, revelations, and raptures, and I would attribute hers to God before those of some other holy persons. But in this case it is more certain to

keep fear and caution, because even once having assurance, the devil may take his aim, and what previously was from God may change and come from the devil.

11) And so I resolve that this book is not such that it can be communicated to anyone and everyone, but only to educated men who also have spiritual experience and Christian discretion. The book is very appropriate considering the purpose for which she wrote it, to give information about her soul for those who must guide her so that she might not be deceived.

12) Of one thing I am as certain as I can humanly be: that she is not a deceiver, and so her clear truths [*claridad*] merit everyone's help with her good intentions and good works. Because in thirteen years she has made at least a dozen, I believe, convents of barefoot Carmelite nuns, with superior rigor and perfection, as those who have seen them will testify, such as the provincial (a Dominican with a master's degree in theology), Brother Pedro Fernández, and Brother Hernando de Castilla, and many others.

13) This I submit as my critique of this book, subjecting my opinion to that of the Church and its agents.

Written in San Gregorio of Valladolid, on 7 July 1575.

Br. Domingo Báñez

APPENDIX B

JUDGMENT, ATTRIBUTED TO PEDRO IBÁÑEZ

1. God's goal is to bring a soul to Himself, and the devil's is to separate the soul from God. Our Lord never uses means that separate one from Himself, nor does the devil use those that bring a soul to God. All the visions and the other things that she experiences bring her closer to God, and make her more humble, more obedient, etc.

2. It is the doctrine of St. Thomas and all the saints that the angel of light is known by the peace and tranquility it leaves. She never has these experiences but that they leave peace and contentment and that all the combined pleasures of this world seem inferior.

3. She has no fault nor imperfection for which she is not reprimanded by an interior voice.

4. She never asked for or desired these things, but rather desired only to fully accomplish the will of God Our Lord.

5. Everything she says conforms with the Divine Scripture and to what the Church teaches, and it is also true in the rigorous scholastic sense.

6. She has great purity of soul, great integrity [*limpieza*], fervent desires to please God, and, by contrast, she tramples the things of this world.

7. She has been told that whatever she asks of God, provided it is right, will be done. She has asked many things and the Lord has granted her things too numerous to put in a letter.

8. When these things are from God, they always redound to individual or communal benefit. She and others have great experience of these benefits.

9. She deals with no one who has a wicked disposition or whose conversation does not lead to devotion, although she would not say such a thing about anyone.

10. Each day she increases in the perfection of virtue and always she teaches virtue with greater perfection. And thus, her daily speech and the visions themselves have grown continually, in accordance with the teachings of St. Thomas.

11. She never repeats gossip nor says impertinent things. She has said of some that they are filled with devils, always for the purpose of demonstrating what is a soul that has mortally offended God.

12. It is the devil's fashion [estilo], when he wishes to deceive, to advise that they keep quiet about what is said to them; but she has been advised to relate her experiences to learned men of God, and if she should ever keep quiet, she will be deceived.

13. So great is the benefit of these things to her soul and the good edification she gives by example that more than forty nuns live with great recollection in her convent.

14. These things ordinarily come to her after praying for a long time, being very close to God and burning with His love, or in taking communion.

15. These things give her a great desire to ascertain that she is not deceived by the devil.

16. These things produce the profoundest humility in her; she knows that what she receives comes from the hand of God and how little she has on her own.

17. When she is without these spiritual things, other things she may receive usually cause her pain and trial; when these experiences come to her, she has no memory of anything else, except a great desire to suffer, and from this desire such pleasure that it frightens her.

18. Trials, vicious gossip against her, illnesses—the terrible heart disease she has, her nausea, and other pains, which are all taken from her when she has visions—satisfy and comfort her.

19. She does great penance in the matters of fasting, self-discipline, and mortification.

20. She suffers the things of the world that can give content-

ment along with its trials, of which she has suffered many, with equal courage, without losing the peace and tranquility of her soul.

21. She has made a firm determination not to offend the Lord, and she has made a vow to understand that no thing is more perfect than that; she will not do it no matter who says it, even though she considers members of the Company of Jesus to be saints and believes that God gave her His mercies through them; she has told me that if she were to know that perfection does not include conversing with the Jesuits, she never would see or speak to them again, even though they are the ones who calmed her and led her to these visions.

22. The pleasures she normally has, the feelings for God, and the fusing with God are certainly frightening, and with these feelings she is usually occupied for an entire day.

23. In hearing someone talk about God with force and devotion she often swoons, and she cannot even try to resist; she then appears to those who see her to have the greatest devotion.

24. She cannot bear to deal with anyone who does not give her a reprimand for her faults, which she receives with great humility.

25. She cannot suffer those who having a state of perfection do not square it with their Institute or order.

26. She is fully separated from her relatives, family, friends; and she is a great friend of solitude; she has great devotion for the saints, and their feast days, and the mysteries that the Church represents, as well as great feeling for Christ Our Lord.

27. If all the Company of Jesus and all the servants of God on earth were to tell her that her experiences are from the devil and were to tell her that she should fear and tremble before the visions; if they were to cut her in a thousand pieces, they would not persuade her she converses and talks with anyone but God.

28. God has given her such a strong and courageous heart that it's frightening. She used to be timid; now she stomps on devils. She is above the frivolity and childishness of women, who are very much without scruples; she is extraordinarily virtuous.

29. With this the Lord has given her the gift of sweet tears, great compassion for her neighbors, knowledge of her faults, respect for her betters, disdain for herself. And I say with certainty that she has benefited many people, and I am one of them.

30. She always carries the memory of God and the feeling of His presence with her.

31. Nothing she has been told has either not been so or not been accomplished; and this is a great argument on her behalf.

32. These things produced in her an admirable clarity of understanding and insight into matters of God.

33. She has been told that an examination of Scripture will show that no soul who wished to please God was ever deceived for so long [as she has had visions].

NOTES

Introduction

1. Cited in *TVST*, 690.

2. Teresa de Lauretis, *Technologies of Gender: Essays on Theory, Film, and Fiction* (Bloomington: Indiana University Press, 1987), 9.

3. Silverio de Santa Teresa, *Procesos de beatificación y canonización de Santa Teresa de Jesús* (Burgos: Monte Carmelo, 1934–1935), 3: xxxviii.

4. Karl Joachim Weintraub, *The Value of the Individual: Self and Circumstance in Autobiography* (Chicago: University of Chicago Press, 1978), 220. For other early treatments of Teresa's *Life* as autobiography, see Roy Pascal, *Design and Truth in Autobiography* (Cambridge: Harvard University Press, 1960); Jean Starobinski, "The Style of Autobiography," trans. Seymour Chatman, in James Olney, ed., *Autobiography: Essays Theoretical and Critical* (Princeton: Princeton University Press, 1980), 73–83; Louis A. Renza, "A Veto of the Imagination: A Theory of Autobiography," in Olney, *Autobiography*, 268–295; Barrett J. Mandel, "Full of Life Now," in Olney, *Autobiography*, 49–72. On the Spanish context of autobiographical writing, see Randolph D. Pope, *La autobiografía española hasta Torres Villarroel* (Bern: Herbert Lang, 1974), 46–88.

5. Michel Foucault, *Discipline and Punish: The Birth of the Prison*, trans. Alan Sheridan (1975; New York: Random House, Vintage, 1979).

6. Antonio Márquez, *Literatura e Inquisición en España (1478–1834)* (Madrid: Taurus, 1980), 223.

7. Alison Weber introduces the very apt concept of the double bind as a description of Teresa's rhetorical situation in *Teresa of Avila and the Rhetoric of Femininity* (Princeton: Princeton University Press, 1990).

8. Gerda Lerner, *The Creation of Feminist Consciousness: From the Middle Ages to 1870* (New York: Oxford University Press, 1993), 159.

9. Elizabeth W. Bruss, *Autobiographical Acts: The Changing Situation of a Literary Genre* (Baltimore: Johns Hopkins University Press, 1976), 13.

10. Angela Selke, "Il iluminismo de los conversos y la Inquisición: Cristianismo interior de los alumbrados, resentimiento y sublimación," in Joaquín Pérez Villanueva and Bartolomé Escandell Bonet, eds., *La Inquisición española: Nueva visión, nuevos horizontes*. Papers presented at International Symposium on the Spanish Inquisition, Cuenca, 1978 (Madrid: Siglo XXI, 1980), 573.

11. Cited in I[da] B[eatrice] O'Malley, *Florence Nightingale, 1820–1856: A Study of Her Life Down to the End of the Crimean War* (London: Thornton Butterworth, 1931), 98–99. I am grateful to Susan Katz for this reference.

12. Lerner, *The Creation of Feminist Consciousness*, vii–viii.

Chapter 1

1. Enrique Llamas Martínez, *Santa Teresa de Jesús y la Inquisición española* (Madrid: CSIC, 1972), 228.

2. Nicolau Eymerich and Francisco Peña, *Le manuel des inquisiteurs [Directorium Inquisitorum]*, trans. and introd. Louis Sala-Molins (Paris: Mouton, 1973), 47. The *Directorium*, a widely copied manuscript by the fourteenth-century Aragonese Inquisitor Eymerich, was first printed in 1503, then revised by Peña and republished in Rome in 1578 (Edward Peters, *Inquisition* [1988; Berkeley, Los Angeles, and London: University of California Press, 1989], 60, 68).

3. Claire Guilhem, "L'Inquisition et la dévaluation des discours féminins," in Bartolomé Bennassar, ed., *L'Inquisition espagnole: XV–XIX siècle* (Paris: Hachette, 1979), 229; Caroline Walker Bynum, *Jesus as Mother: Studies in the Spirituality of the High Middle Ages* (Berkeley, Los Angeles, and London: University of California Press, 1982), 135–136.

4. Eymerich and Peña, *Directorium*, 48; Virgilio Pinto Crespo, "Institucionalización inquisitorial y censura de libros," in Pérez Villanueva and Bartolomé Escandell Bonet, eds., *La Inquisición española*, 533–535.

5. Stephen Haliczer, "The First Holocaust: The Inquisition and the Converted Jews of Spain and Portugal," in Stephen Haliczer, ed. and trans., *Inquisition and Society in Early Modern Europe* (Totowa: Barnes and Noble, 1987), 7–18; José Martínez Millán, "Aportaciones a la formación del estado moderno y a la política española a través de la censura inquisitorial durante el período 1480–1559," in Pérez Villanueva, *La Inquisición española*, 537; Henry Kamen, *Inquisition and Society in Spain in the Sixteenth and Seventeenth Centuries* (London: Weidenfeld and Nicolson, 1985), 30.

6. Jaime Contreras, "The Impact of Protestantism in Spain, 1520–1600," in Haliczer, *Inquisition and Society*, 56.

7. Alonso de la Fuente, "Primer Memorial," in Llamas Martínez, *Santa Teresa de Jesús*, 400. Fuente reviewed the first edition of Teresa's works, which were edited by Luis de Léon under the title *Los libros de la Madre Teresa de Jesús, Fundadora de los monesterios de monjas y frayles Carmelitas Descalzos de la primitiva Regla . . . En Salamanca, por Guillermo*

Fóquel, 1588. León included the *Life,* the *Road to Perfection,* the *Interior Castle,* the *Exclamations,* and the *Avisos.* He declined to publish the *Foundations,* giving as his reason the fact that many of the people it names were still living, and he omitted *Meditations on the Song of Songs* without comment (294–295).

8. In a related context, Alison Weber remarks that Fuente was "a very good reader of Teresa, alert to her ambiguities and rhetorical strategies" (*Teresa of Avila and the Rhetoric of Femininity,* 161).

9. E. Allison Peers, trans. and ed., *The Complete Works of Teresa of Avila* (London: Sheed and Ward, 1944), 1: 55.

10. Américo Castro, *Teresa la santa y otros ensayos* (Madrid: Alianza, 1982), 24.

11. Ricardo Senabre, "Sobre el género literaro del *Libro de la vida,*" in *CIT,* 2: 776.

12. Ibid., 773–774; Fernando Lázaro Carreter, "Santa Teresa de Jesús, escritora (El 'Libro de la vida')," in *CIT,* 1: 11–27; Antonio Carreño, "Las paradojas del 'yo' autobiográfico," in *STLMH,* 255–264.

13. Weber, *Teresa of Avila and the Rhetoric of Femininity,* 43 passim; Francisco Márquez Villanueva, "Santa Teresa y el linaje," in *Espiritualidad y literatura en el siglo XVI* (Madrid, Alfaguara, 1968), 141–205; Sol Villacèque, "Rhetorique et pragmatique: La transformation du code dans le *Libro de la vida* de Thérèse d'Avila," *Imprévue* 2 (1985): 21.

14. On the definition of dialogized heteroglossia and its distinction from polyphony and dialogicity, I follow Gary Saul Morson and Caryl Emerson, *Mikhail Bakhtin: Creation of a Prosaics* (Stanford: Stanford University Press, 1990), 142–145.

15. Mikhail M. Bakhtin, *Problems of Dostoevsky's Poetics,* ed. and trans. Caryl Emerson, introd. Wayne C. Booth, Theory and History of Literature, no. 8 (Minneapolis: University of Minnesota Press, 1984), 202.

16. Ibid., 106; Bakhtin, "The Problem of Speech Genres," in *Speech Genres and Other Late Essays,* trans. Vern W. McGee, ed. Caryl Emerson and Michael Holquist (Austin: University of Texas Press, 1986), 60.

17. Mikhail M. Bakhtin, *The Dialogic Imagination: Four Essays,* ed. Michael Holquist, trans. Caryl Emerson and Michael Holquist (Austin: University of Texas Press, 1981), 276. Bakhtin explains the interaction of each word in a text as follows: "The word, directed toward its object, enters a dialogically agitated and tension-filled environment of alien words, value judgments and accents, weaves in and out of complex interrelationships, merges with some, recoils from others, intersects with yet a third group: and all this may crucially shape discourse, may leave a trace in all its semantic layers, may complicate its expression and influence its entire stylistic profile."

18. Many feminist critics have noticed the applicability of Bakhtin's theories to women's writing. See Dale M. Bauer and S. Jaret McKinstry, eds., *Feminism, Bakhtin, and the Dialogic* (Albany: State University of New York Press, 1991). Josephine Donovan points out both the benefits and the limitations of feminist applications of Bakhtin, the most significant drawback being the fact that he does not mention women novelists,

in "Style and Power," in Bauer and McKinstry, *Feminism, Bakhtin, and the Dialogic,* 85–94.

19. Jean Pierre Dedieu, in Gustav Henningsen and John Tedeschi with Charles Amiel, *The Inquisition in Early Modern Europe: Studies on Sources and Methods* (Dekalb: Northern Illinois University Press, 1986), 179.

20. Antonio Gómez-Moriana, "Problemática de la confesión autobiográfica destinada al tribunal inquisitorial," in *L'Autobiographie en Espagne,* Actes du IIe Colloque International de la Baume-les-Aix, 23–24–25 May 1981 (Aix-en-Provence: Université de Provence, 1982), 72; Weber, *Teresa of Avila,* 43 n. 4.

21. Louis Sala-Molins, trans. and ed., *Le Dictionnaire des inquisiteurs: Valence 1494 [Repertorium inquisitorum haereticae pravitatis]* (Paris: Editions Galilée, 1981), 221–222. The *Repertorium* was first published anonymously in Valencia in 1494. Its republication in Venice in 1575 and in Rome in 1578, as well as Peña's references to it in his glosses of Eymerich's *Directorium,* attest to its widespread authority. The prologue states the purpose of the manual as collecting information about the juridical structure of the Inquisition otherwise inconveniently dispersed in many texts. With regard to the organization and logic of the work, Sala-Molins, who in translating the work from the Latin reorganized it according to alphabetization of the words in French, observes, "We are a long way from the meticulous rigor of Eymerich" (47). In his introduction and notes, Sala-Molins provides an appropriately caustic commentary on the *Repertorium,* as, for example, "I hope I have translated the *Repertorium* with enough rigor to render it readable, the nausea notwithstanding" (47).

22. "Quisiera yo que, como me han mandado y dado larga licencia para que escriva el modo de oración y las mercedes que el Señor me ha hecho, me la dieran para que muy por menudo y con claridad dijera mis grandes pecados y ruin vida. Diérame gran consuelo. Mas no han querido, antes atádome mucho en este caso" (*Vida,* prólogo 1).

23. Thomas N. Tentler, *Sin and Confession on the Eve of the Reformation* (Princeton: Princeton University Press, 1977), 86. Although some priests did question confessants, the practice was controversial, particularly on sexual matters, because some claimed that it put new sinful ideas in the confessant's mind.

24. In addition to leading her readers down several generic pathways, Teresa also stratifies her language by social and ideological layers. For example, the reference to her "great sins and wretched life" can be considered a form of what Ernst Robert Curtius calls the "devotional formula," the protestation of sinfulness that amplifies her praise of God, or as a concession of social authority, what Curtius calls the "submission formula" (*European Literature and the Latin Middle Ages,* trans. Willard R. Trask [1953; New York: Harper and Row, 1963], 407–410).

25. "Y por esto pido, por amor del Señor, tenga delante de los ojos quien este discurso de mi vida leyere, que ha sido tan ruin que no he hallado santo, de los que se tornaron a Dios, con quien me consolar. Porque considero que, después que el Señor los llamaba, no le tornaban a ofender. Yo

no sólo tornaba a ser peor, sino que parece traía estudio a resistir las mercedes que Su Majestad me hacía, como quien se vía obligar a servir más, y entendía de sí no podía pagar lo menos de lo que devía.

"Sea bendito por siempre, que tanto me esperó, a quien con todo mi corazón suplico me dé gracia para que con toda claridad y verdad yo haga esta relación que mis confesores me mandan; y aun el Señor sé yo lo quiere muchos días ha, sino que yo no me he atrevido; y que sea para gloria y alabanza suya, y para que de aquí adelante, conociéndome ellos mijor, ayuden a mi flaqueza, para que pueda servir algo de lo que devo al Señor, a quien siempre alaben todas las cosas, amén" (*Vida*, prólogo 1, 2).

26. Kate Greenspan, "The Autohagiographical Tradition in Medieval Women's Devotional Writing," *a/b:Auto/Biography* 6, no. 2 (Fall 1991): 157–168.

27. Bakhtin, *Problems of Dostoevsky's Poetics*, 195.

28. Ibid., 196.

29. Linda H. Peterson, *Victorian Autobiography: The Tradition of Self-Interpretation* (New Haven: Yale University Press, 1986), 3–6. Anne Hunsaker Hawkins's definition of spiritual autobiography implies the reason it depends on biblical typology: "Spiritual autobiography is predicated on the relationship between a particular individual, living in a certain place and in a certain time, and a divine reality that is universal and timeless. This relationship between particular and universal tends to present events in an individual's life in a figurative way as signs of underlying archetypal 'things'" (*Archetypes of Conversion: The Autobiographies of Augustine, Bunyan, and Merton* [Lewisburg, Pa.: Bucknell University Press, 1985], 24).

30. Enrique Llamas Martínez, "Teresa de Jesús y los alumbrados: Hacia una revisión del 'alumbradismo' español del siglo XVI," in *CIT*, 1: 138.

31. Juan de Avila spent about a year (1532–1533) in jail on charges of Illuminist practices and teachings. Although he avoided further prosecution, apparently by conducting his work within the framework of the Church, the Inquisition placed his *Audi, Filia*, a work of spiritual guidance that had been important in Teresa's spiritual development, on the 1559 Index (Kamen, *Inquisition and Society in Spain*, 68–69).

32. Melquíades Andrés Martín explains the shared premises of these movements: "Alumbrados, mystics, and 'Lutherans' invoked experience systematically, a new phenomenon in Spanish culture. Experience, the effort to penetrate into the 'I' and free it from itself, connects the mysticism of in-gathering with the Protestant theory of free inquiry, by way of which man can make immediate contact with God and His word" ("Common Denominator of Alumbrados, Erasmians, 'Lutherans,' and Mystics: The Risk of a More 'Intimate' Spirituality," in Angel Alcalá, ed. and trans., *The Spanish Inquisition and the Inquisitorial Mind*, Atlantic Studies on Society in Change, no. 49 [Boulder: Social Science Monographs; Highland Lakes, N.J.: Atlantic Research and Publications, 1987], 489).

33. Angela Selke also cites Germanic mysticism and Arabic sufism as sources of Illuminism in "El iluminismo de los conversos y la Inquisición: Cristianismo interior de los alumbrados, resentimiento y sublimación," in

Pérez Villanueva, ed., *La Inquisición española*, 617. Also see Antonio Márquez, *Los alumbrados* (Madrid: Taurus, 1972), chaps. 4, 5.

34. The first use of the label "Illuminist" was pejorative. Fray Melchor, the Franciscan who led the development of mental prayer, was described as "illumined [*alumbrado*] by Satan's darkness" (Antonio T. de Nicolás, *Powers of Imagining: Ignatius de Loyola* [Albany: State University of New York Press, 1986], 18; Marcel Bataillon, *Erasmo y España: Estudios sobre la historia espiritual del siglo XVI*, 1: 89).

35. Bernardino Llorca, *La Inquisición española y los alumbrados, 1509–1667* (Salamanca: Universidad Pontífica, 1980), 72–73.

36. Fermín Caballero, *Vida del Ilmo: Melchor Cano* (Madrid, 1871), Appendix 58. Cited in Francisco de Osuna, *Tercer abecedario espiritual*, ed. Melquíades Andrés Martín (Madrid: BAC, 1972), 88. Known for his intellectual and technical approach to questions of faith, Cano played an important role in creating and sustaining the elitist, rationalist bias of the Church.

37. "[El arrobamiento] deja grandes efectos en el alma; esotro [dejamiento] no más que si no pasase, y cansancio en el cuerpo" (*Fundaciones* 6.14).

38. "Sabed, hijas, que no está la falta para ser u no ser oración mental en tener cerrada la boca; si hablando estoy enteramente entendiendo y viendo que hablo con Dios con más advertencia que en la palabras que digo, junto está oración mental y vocal" (*Camino*, Valladolid, 22.1).

39. Cited in Kamen, *Inquisition and Society in Spain*, 120.

40. Selke, "El iluminismo," 621. A profile of the typical Illuminist in the sixteenth century included Jewish ancestry, residence in an urban rather than a rural location, a high level of education achieved largely through self-teaching, and lower-middle-class financial status.

41. Kamen remarks one of the ironies of the automatic association of conversos with Illuminism, that many conversos were "condemned for beliefs that orthodox Judaism would have regarded as heretical" (68).

42. Angel Alcalá, "Inquisitorial Control of Humanists and Writers," in Alcalá, *The Spanish Inquisition*, 326. When it emerged in the course of Luis de León's trial for translating the Song of Songs that his deceased grandfather had cooked "adafinas," the ritual dish prepared on Friday evening, and that he "gestured like a Jew," the Inquisition exhumed his bones and burned them in a public ceremony (Selke, "El iluminismo," 632 n. 22).

43. Archivo Histórico Nacional, *Inquisición leg.* 2.393, cited in Llamas Martínez, *Santa Teresa de Jesús*, 34.

44. While this report seems clearly to specify the order she has in mind as her own Barefoot Carmelites, Teresa's own sentence, which does not name the order, has also been considered to refer to other orders, including the Dominicans and the Jesuits, who disputed the matter for more than two centuries.

45. Eymerich and Peña, *Directorium*, 66.

46. Llamas Martínez, *Santa Teresa de Jesús*, 34.

47. Kamen, *Inquisition and Society in Spain*, 155. The Inquisition did not actually try Ignatius, but ecclesiastical judges repeatedly tried to estab-

lish the Illuminist cast of his theories by repeating a single question about their origin: "What you preach, is it the result of a learned doctrine or of the Holy Spirit?" (Nicolás, *Powers of Imagining*, 17). While there was compelling evidence for the Old Christian lineage of Ignatius, he angered authorities by mandating that Jesuit priests inform only their superior in the order, not the Inquisition, when a person admitted a heretical act or belief in the sacrament of confession.

48. Llamas Martínez, *Santa Teresa de Jesús*, 48.

49. Llamas Martínez, "Teresa de Jesús y los alumbrados," in *CIT*, 1: 141–142.

50. During the beatification process, Báñez testified that he recommended censorship of the *Life* because "it was not appropriate that this book should be made public during her lifetime; but preferable that it be kept in the Inquisition until it could be seen how this woman ended up" (Llamas Martínez, "Teresa de Jesús y los alumbrados," 153). More than one critic has seen misogyny in Báñez's *Judgment*; see, for example, Ulrich Dobhan, "Teresa de Jesús y la emancipación de la mujer," in *CIT*, 1: 127.

51. Báñez's designation of the activity involved in producing the *Life* as "speaking" and his emphasis on sincerity reveals the close link between auricular confession and judicial confession. Oral language lends itself to the assessment of sincerity better than does written, as Walter J. Ong explains: "No matter what pitch of frankness, directness, or authenticity he may strive for, the writer's mask and the reader's are less removable than those of the oral communicator and his hearer. For writing is itself an indirection" (*Interfaces of the Word: Studies in the Evolution of Consciousness and Culture* [Ithaca: Cornell University Press, 1977], 80).

52. These two sentences appear in reverse order: "Yo, como hablava con descuido algunas cosas que ellos tomavan por diferente intención. . . . Preguntávanme algunas cosas; yo respondía con llaneza y descuido" (*Vida* 28.17).

53. Cicero denominated the three levels of style according to their ends: the plain style to teach; the middle style to delight; the grand style to move the emotions. Debora K. Shuger defines this classical plain style as "unadorned, brief, and philosophical," at its best, "clear, urbane, natural, often witty and graceful, and persuasive." "Yet," Shuger continues, "it is suitable only for small, unimportant subjects; it seems commonplace and ordinary, often losing effective strength by seeking meticulous correctness" (*Sacred Rhetoric: The Christian Grand Style in the English Renaissance* [Princeton: Princeton University Press, 1988], 4, 31).

54. Juan de los Angeles, for example, treats plainness as a stylistic choice he makes in accordance with the nature of his audience: "I never tired of communicating good and healthy doctrine . . . sometimes writing in a less rustic and more difficult style for enlightened intellects . . . other times plainer [*llano*] and simpler for the smaller minds" (*Diálogos de la conquista del reino de Dios* [1595], cited in Alberto Porqueras Mayo, *El prólogo en el renacimiento español* [Madrid: CSIC, 1965], 146).

55. Tomás Ramón considers that this plain style requires not an

education in doctrine or rhetoric but perfection of the preacher's own interior life through grace: "[The apostles] received the gift of language, but not so that they might preach with a rhetorical and elegant style, nor so that their listeners might be charmed by their compositions and conclusions, but so that with a plain [*llano*] and ordinary style, they might plainly [*llanamente*] and simply teach the true doctrine of heaven" (*Flores nuevas, cogidas del vergel de las divinas y humanas letras* [Barcelona, 1611–1612], 1: 241, cited in Hilary Dansey Smith, *Preaching in the Spanish Golden Age: A Study of Some Preachers of the Reign of Philip III* [Oxford: Oxford University Press, 1978], 93).

56. Sebastián de Cobarruvias Horozco, comp., *Tesoro de la lengua castellana o española* (1611; Madrid: Turner, 1979), s.v. "llano." Published fewer than thirty years after Teresa's death, this dictionary serves well for establishing public definitions of the words Teresa uses.

57. Cobarruvias, s.v. "llano": "Metafóricamente se toma por la cosa que no tiene estropieço ninguno, sino llaneza y verdad. Hombre llano, el que no tiene altivezes ni cautelas. Confessar de plano, que es lo mesmo que llano, es dezir luego todo lo que passa. Llano es el carnero castrado, a diferencia del cojudo. . . . Allanarse es convencerse y ajustarse a la voluntad del otro."

58. Henry Charles Lea, *A History of the Inquisition of Spain* (1906–1907; New York: American Scholar, 1966), 2: 573–575.

59. *Opus tripartitum*, II, Du Pin, I, 446A, cited in Tentler, *Sin and Confession*, 109.

60. Robert Ricard, "Notas y materiales para el estudio del 'socratismo cristiano' en Santa Teresa y en los espirituales españoles," in *Estudios de literatura religiosa española*, trans. Manuel Muñoz Cortés (Madrid: Editorial Gredos, 1964), 27.

61. Cited in Emilio Orozco Díaz, *Expresión, comunicación y estilo en la obra de Santa Teresa* (Granada: Bolsillo, 1984), 34; E. Allison Peers, "Saint Teresa's Style: A Tentative Appraisal," in *Saint Teresa of Jesus and Other Essays and Addresses* (London: Faber and Faber, 1953), 82.

62. Ramón Menéndez Pidal, "El estilo de Santa Teresa," in *La lengua de Cristóbal Colón y otros estudios sobre el siglo XVI*, 4th ed. (Madrid: Espasa Calpe, 1958), 124; Felicidad Bernabéu Barrachina, "Aspectos vulgares del estilo teresiano y sus posibles razones," *Revista de espiritualidad* 22 (1963): 359–375; Elías Rivers, "The Vernacular Mind of Saint Teresa," in John Sullivan, ed., *Carmelite Studies: Centenary of St. Teresa*, 127; Weber, *Teresa of Avila*, 11 et passim.

63. Thomas Aquinas, *Summa Theologiae*, pt. 1, question 13, art. 4.

64. Paul Tillich, *Systematic Theology* (Chicago: University of Chicago Press, 1951), 1: 239.

65. "Havré de aprovecharme de alguna comparación, aunque yo las quisiera escusar por ser mujer, y escrivir simplemente lo que me mandan; mas este lenguaje de espíritu es tan malo de declarar a los que no saben letras, como yo, que havré de buscar algún modo, y podrá ser las menos

veces acierte a que venga bien la comparación; servirá de dar recreación a vuestra merced de ver tanta torpeza" (*Vida* 11.6).

This apology contrasts markedly with the confidence with which John of the Cross launches into the use of metaphor, here in the prologue to *Spiritual Canticle* [Cántico espiritual]: "Who, finally, can explain the desires He gives them? Certainly, no one can! As a result these persons let something of their experience overflow in figures and similes, and from the abundance of their spirit, pour out secrets and mysteries rather than rational explanations" (Prologue 1).

66. Terence Hawkes, *Metaphor* (London: Methuen, 1972), 2.

67. "Some children complained to their father that they had not eaten, and they cried sadly for something to eat. A neighbor told the father, 'Let those boys have something to eat.' And the father said, 'Why should they eat? I give my word as a gentleman that each one has tripe [*entrañas*, a word meaning the human intestines or a dish made from the stomach lining of a cow] in his body. Truly they always have it, since they live.' The deception, that they had eaten tripe and that they asked to eat out of gluttony not necessity, was believed" (Covarrubias, s.v. "metáphora").

68. Eymerich and Peña, *Directorium*, 126.

69. Ibid., 127.

70. José Rico Verdú, *La retórica española de los siglos XVI y XVII* (Madrid: CSIC, 1973), 268.

71. John Freccero, "Medusa: The Letter and the Spirit," in *Dante: The Poetics of Conversion*, ed. and introd. Rachel Jacoff (Cambridge: Harvard University Press, 1986), 120.

72. Freccero, "Medusa," in *Dante*, 133.

73. Robert Bell, "Metamorphoses of Spiritual Autobiography," *ELH* 44(1977): 108–126.

74. Robert M. Durling, "*The Ascent of Mount Ventoux* and the Crisis of Allegory," *Italian Quarterly* 18(1974): 21.

75. Llamas Martínez, *Santa Teresa de Jesús*, 470, 476.

76. Ibid., 398.

77. Ibid., 400.

78. Bernardino de Laredo, *The Ascent of Mount Sion, being the third book of the treatise of that name* [Subida del Monte Sión, por la vía contemplativa], trans. and introd. E. Allison Peers (London: Faber and Faber, 1950), 14. After ordering revisions of the first edition (1535), the Inquisition permitted several reprintings of the second edition during the sixteenth century: Sevilla, 1538; reprinted in Sevilla, 1540; Medina del Campo, 1542; Valencia, 1590. Teresa's marked copy of the *Ascent* has not been found, but Peers and others consider that she designated parts of the third book, a series of essays on the stages of contemplation leading to mystical union. Fidèle de Ros maintains that she used the second edition in *Le Frère Bernardin de Laredo* (Paris: Librairie Philosophique, 1948), 334.

79. Don Salcedo's wife (Doña Mencía del Aguila) was the daughter of Teresa's uncle, Ruy Sánchez de Cepeda. Although Teresa labels Salcedo a

"pious gentleman" (*caballero santo*), Jodi Bilinkoff speculates that if he did have standing as a gentleman, he held it by legal decree (*hidalgo de ejecutoria*) rather than by hereditary claim. After his wife died in 1570, Salcedo entered the priesthood of Teresa's Barefoot Carmelites (*The Avila of Saint Teresa: Religious Reform in a Sixteenth-Century City* [Ithaca: Cornell University Press, 1989], 66–68).

80. Mary Elizabeth Perry, *Gender and Disorder in Early Modern Seville* (Princeton: Princeton University Press, 1990), 82–83.

81. Ibid., 83.

82. Gaspar Daza, who favored Erasmian educational methods in Spain, gained some renown in Spain for effective preaching, charitable works, and administrative talent. Bilinkoff relates that "little is known of Daza's life" and suggests that he may have been of converso descent (84–86). Daza later supported the foundation at Avila, officiating at the clothing ceremony and reserving the Sacrament, events narrated in *Life* 36.18.

83. Teresa states that she wrote an account of her life, for which she uses the judicial term *discurso de mi vida*, for Cetina (*Life* 23.15). Whatever she wrote in this confession, which does not survive, Cetina judged her experience to derive from God, and he encouraged her to continue in the discipline of prayer.

84. Luis de León called these short works Teresa's "papers" (*papeles*) in his edition of her works, while the title that appears on many copies of the manuscript is "accounts of conscience" (*cuentas de conciencia*). These are addressed to many different audiences, including several priests, confessors, and Inquisitors. In the nineteenth century, they were published under the title *Spiritual Testimonies* (Relaciones espirituales); in this century, Silverio de Santa Teresa divided these accounts into two categories, which he entitled *Relaciones* (Testimonies) and *Mercedes* (Mercies). Contemporary editions use either or both of these designations. I have chosen to use spiritual testimony in English, and in Spanish, cuenta de conciencia. On the spiritual testimonies, see María-Paz Aspe, "Las relaciones espirituales de Teresa de Jesús," in *STLMH*, 291–295.

85. Efrén and Steggink attribute the document to Padre Ibáñez and identify it as a response to *Spiritual Testimony* 1. They do not name the persons who convened to discuss the *Judgment*, except to quote Teresa's niece, who characterized them as "serious and learned men" (*TVST*, 189).

86. "La manera de proceder en la oración que ahora tengo, es la presente: Pocas veces son las que estando en oración puedo tener discurso de entendimiento, porque luego comienza a recogerse el alma y estar en quietud u arrobamiento, de tal manera que ninguna cosa puedo usar de las potencias y sentidos, tanto que, si no es oír—y eso no para entender—, otra cosa no aprovecha" (*Cuenta de conciencia* 1.1).

87. "Estas cosas y razones de tantos santos me esfuerzan cuando trayo estos temores de si no es Dios, siendo yo tan ruin. Mas cuando estoy en oración, y en los días que ando quieta y el pensamiento en Dios, aunque se junten cuantos letrados y santos hay en el mundo y me diesen todos los

tormentos imaginables, y yo quisiere creerlo, no me podrían hacer creer que esto es demonio, porque no puedo" (*Cuenta de conciencia* 1.35).

88. The *Tesoro* gives *clean* the connotation of "the Old Christian, without the race of Moor or Jew" (Covarrubias, s.v. "limpieza").

89. "Havrá como trece años, poco más a menos, que fue allí el obispo de Salamanca, que era inquisidor, creo en Toledo, y lo havía sido aquí. Ella procuró de hablarle para asegurarse más, y diole cuenta de todo. El le dijo que todo esto no era cosa que tocava a su oficio, porque todo lo que vía y entendía siempre la afirmava mas en la fe católica. . . . Dijole—como la vio tan fatigada—que escriviese a el maestro Avila, que era vivo, una larga relación de todo—que era hombre que entendía mucho de oración—, y que con lo que la escriviese se sosegase" (*Cuenta de conciencia* 57a.7).

90. Juan de Avila's letter to Teresa of 12 September 1568 not only assures her about the divine provenance of her experience but also makes editorial suggestions apparently designed to protect the work from the Inquisition: "This book should not get out into the hands of many, because it is necessary to revise some words in some parts; in other parts to clarify or explain them. Other things may be beneficial to you but may not be to others who follow them; because the particular things whereby God carries some persons are not for others. These things, or most of them, I have left noted there, to put them in order when I could (and a way to send them to you will not be lacking)" (Juan de Avila, *Obras completas*, vol. 1, ed. Luis Sala Balust [Madrid: Editorial Católica, 1952], 12 Sept. 1568).

91. "While in St. Joseph's in Avila in the year 1562, the same year in which that monastery was founded, I was ordered by Fr. García de Toledo, a Dominican, who at the time was my confessor, to write of that monastery's foundation, along with many other things; whoever sees that work, if it is published, will learn there of those events" (*Foundations*, Prologue 2).

92. Arthur Darby Nock, *Conversion: The Old and the New Religion from Alexander the Great to Augustine of Hippo* (London: Oxford University Press, 1933), 7.

93. William James, *The Varieties of Religious Experience: A Study in Human Nature*, introd. Reinhold Niebuhr (1902; New York: Macmillan, Collier, 1961), 169.

94. Starobinski, "The Style of Autobiography," in Olney, *Autobiography*, 78.

95. Freccero, "Medusa," in *Dante*, 133.

96. Víctor García de la Concha, *El arte literario de Santa Teresa* (Barcelona: Ariel, 1978), 56; Alberto de la Virgen del Carmen, "Presencia de San Agustín en Sta. Teresa y San Juan de la Cruz," *Revista de espiritualidad* 14 (1955): 175; *TVST*, 147–148. I presented early versions of this section to the International Conference on Patristic, Mediaeval, and Renaissance Studies at Villanova University in 1988 and the Subject of Autobiography conference at the University of Southern Maine in 1989.

97. John Freccero, "Autobiography and Narrative," in *Reconstructing*

Individualism: Autonomy, Individuality, and the Self in Western Thought, ed. Thomas C. Heller, Morton Sosna, and David E. Wellbery (Stanford: Stanford University Press, 1986), 19.

98. Caroline Walker Bynum, *Holy Feast and Holy Fast: The Religious Significance of Food to Medieval Women* (Berkeley, Los Angeles, and London: University of California Press, 1987), 25.

99. James, *Varieties of Religious Experience*, 168.

100. Erich Auerbach, *Mimesis*, trans. Willard R. Trask (1946; Princeton: Princeton University Press, 1953), 43.

101. "Pues ya andava mi alma cansada y, aunque quería, no la dejavan descansar las ruines costumbres que tenía. Acaecióme que, entrando un día en el oratorio, vi una imagen que havían traído allí a guardar, que se havía buscado para cierta fiesta que se hacía en casa. Era de Cristo muy llagado y tan devota, que en mirándola, toda me turbó de verle tal, porque representava bien lo que pasó por nosotros. Fue tanto lo que sentí de lo mal que había agradecido aquellas llagas, que el corazón me parece se me partía, y arrojéme cabe El con grandísimo derramamiento de lágrimas, suplicándole me fortaleciese ya de una vez para no ofenderle.

"Era yo muy devota de la gloriosa Magdalena, y muy muchas veces pensava en su conversión, en especial cuando comulgava; que como savía estava allí cierto el Señor dentro de mí, poníame a sus pies, pareciéndome no eran de desechar mis lágrimas; y no sabía lo que decía (que harto hacía quien por sí me las consentía derramar, pues tan presto se me olvidava aquel sentimiento) y encomendávame a esta gloriosa Santa para que me alcanzase perdón.

"Mas esta postrera vez de esta imagen que digo, me parece me aprovechó más, porque estava ya muy desconfiada de mí y ponía toda mi confianza en Dios. Paréceme le dije entonces, que no me havía de levantar de allí hasta que hiciese lo que le suplicava. Creo cierto me aprovechó, porque fui mejorando mucho desde entonces" (*Vida* 9.1–3).

102. "En este tiempo me dieron las *Confesiones* de San Augustín, que parece el Señor lo ordenó, porque yo no las procuré ni nunca las havía visto. Yo soy muy aficionada a San Augustín, porque el monesterio adonde estuve seglar era de su Orden, y tambián por haver sido pecador, que en los santos que después de serlo el Señor tornó a Sí hallava yo mucho consuelo, pareciéndome en ellos havía de hallar ayuda; y que, como los havía el Señor perdonado, podía hacer a mí; salvo que una cosa me desconsolava, como he dicho, que a ellos sola una vez los había el Señor llamado y no tornavan a caer, y a mí eran ya tantas, que esto me fatigava. Mas considerando en el amor que me tenía, tornava a animarme, que de su misericordia jamás desconfié; de mí, muchas veces. . . .

"Como comencé a leer las *Confesiones*, paréceme me vía yo allí. Comencé a encomendarme mucho a este glorioso Santo. Cuando llegué a su conversión y leí como oyó aquella voz en el huerto, no me parece sino que el Señor me la dio a mí, según sintió mi corazón. Estuve por gran rato que toda me deshacía en lágrimas y entre mí mesma con gran aleción y fatiga" (*Vida* 9.7, 8).

Teresa leaves the circumstances of her introduction to the *Confessions* vague, possibly to emphasize her compliance with restrictions on women's reading, but most editors assume that confessors gave her the 1554 Spanish translation soon after its publication (Salamanca: Portonariis, 1554). The Portuguese Padre Sebastián Toscano dedicated his translation to Doña Leonor de Mascareñas (1503–1584), governess to Philip II and his son Carlos, whom Teresa mentions as a friend in *Foundations* 17.5 (*TVST*, 148).

103. Pierre Courcelle points out that Teresa interprets the voices as interior words spoken by God, but unlike most other commentators, he considers Augustine's message also to be interior (*Les Confessions de Saint Augustin dans la tradition littéraire* [Paris: Etudes Augustiniennes, 1963], 377; also see B. R. Rees, "The Conversion of Saint Augustine," *Trivium* 14 [1979]: 1–17).

104. "'Ya no quiero que tengas conversación con hombres, sino con ángeles.' . . . Desde aquel día yo quedé tan animosa para dejarolo todo por Dios como quien havía querido en aquel memento—que no me parece fue más—dejar otra a su sierva" (*Vida* 24.5, 7).

105. "'No hayas miedo, hija, que yo soy y no te desampararé, no temas'" (*Vida* 25.18). Jane Tylus makes the connection between these words to Teresa and Christ's to Mary Magdalene in *Writing and Vulnerability in the Late Renaissance* (Stanford: Stanford University Press, 1993), 72.

106. *TVST*, 160–161.

Chapter 2

1. Erich Auerbach, "Figura," in *Scenes from the Drama of European Literature*, trans. Ralph Manheim (1944; New York: Meridian, 1957), 53. The Christian tradition of figural interpretation developed as a way of retaining the Old Testament in the scriptural canon, both to allow preservation of Jewish history and to give Christianity the providential nature implied by the Jewish patriarchs' prophecies of the coming of Christ (Joseph A. Mazzeo, "Allegorical Interpretation and History," *Comparative Literature* 30 [Winter 1978]: 15).

2. Thomas Aquinas defines the levels of fourfold allegorical interpretation in "Whether in Holy Scripture a Word May Have Several Senses," tenth article of "The Nature and Domain of Sacred Doctrine": "Therefore that first signification whereby words signify things belongs to the first sense, the historical or literal. That signification whereby things signified by words have themselves also a signification is called the spiritual sense, which is based on the literal, and presupposes it. Now this spiritual sense has a threefold division. For as the Apostle says (Heb. 10:1) the Old Law is a figure of the New Law, and Dionysius says 'the New Law itself is a figure of future glory.' Again, in the New Law, whatever our Head has done is a type of what we ought to do. Therefore, so far as the things of the Old Law signify the things of the New Law, there is the allegorical sense; so far as the things done in Christ, or so far as the things which signify Christ, are signs of what we ought to do, there is the moral sense. But so far as they

signify what relates to eternal glory, there is the anagogical sense" (Thomas, *Summa Theologiae*, pt. 1, question 1, art. 10).

3. John Freccero defines the Incarnation as the "archimedean point" in history: "The Christ event was the end term of an historical process, the 'fullness of time,' from the perspective of which the history of the world might be read and judged according to a meaning which perhaps even the participants in that history could not perceive. The 'then' and 'now,' the Old Testament and the New, were . . . the letter and the spirit respectively of God's revelation" ("Medusa," in *Dante: The Poetics of Conversion*, ed. and introd. Rachel Jacoff [Cambridge: Harvard University Press, 1986], 132–133).

4. The mnemonic jingle goes this way: "Littera gesta docet, / quid credas allegoria, / moralis quid agas, / quo tendas anagogia."

5. Lawrence Rothfield, "Autobiography and Perspective in *The Confessions* of St. Augustine," *Comparative Literature* 33 (Summer 1981): 221–222.

6. Henri de Lubac, *Exégèse médiévale: Les quatre sens de l'écriture* (Paris: Aubier, 1959), 1: 553–554; Ann W. Astell, *The Song of Songs in the Middle Ages* (Ithaca: Cornell University Press, 1990), 7.

7. Alan Clifford Charity, *Events and Their Afterlife: The Dialectics of Christian Typology in the Bible and Dante* (Cambridge: Cambridge University Press, 1966), 160.

8. Ibid.

9. Northrop Frye, *The Great Code: The Bible and Literature* (New York: Harcourt Brace Jovanovich, 1982), 81.

10. Joel Sangnieux, "Santa Teresa y los libros," in *CIT*, 2: 753.

11. Teresa occasionally switches languages in the middle of a quotation, here from Latin to Spanish in a typically free citation of Psalm 119: 137 ("How just thou art, O Lord! How straight and true are thy decrees!"): "One time, praying the Hours . . . I came to the verse that says: *Justus es, Domine, y tus juicios* ["judgments" in Spanish]" (*Life* 19.9).

12. Melquíades Andrés Martín, *La teología española en el siglo XVI* (Madrid: BAC, 1977), 1: 322. The 1559 Index banned "the Bible in our vernacular or in any other, wholly or in part, unless it be in Hebrew, Chaldean, Greek or Latin" (E. M. Wilson, "Spanish Versions," in S. L. Greenslade, ed., *The West from the Reformation to the Present Day*, vol. 3 of *The Cambridge History of the Bible* [Cambridge: Cambridge University Press, 1963], 125). These restrictions were part of wide-ranging censorship designed to consolidate the power of the Catholic kings (Virgilio Pinto Crespo, *Inquisición y control ideológico en la España del siglo XVI* [Madrid: Taurus, 1983], 25).

13. "Estando en esta quietud, con no entender casi cosa que rece en latín, en especial del Salterio, no sólo entender el verso en romance, sino pasar adelante en regalarme de ver lo que el romance quiere decir" (*Vida* 15.7).

14. "Cuando se quitaron muchos libros de romance, que no se leyesen, yo sentí mucho, porque algunos me dava recreación leerlos, y yo no podía

ya, por dejarlos en latín; me dijo el Señor: 'No tengas pena, que yo te daré un libro vivo.' . . . Su Majestad ha sido el libro verdadero adonde he visto las verdades" (*Vida* 26.6).

15. "¡Bendito sea tal libro, que deja imprimido lo que se ha de leer y hacer de manera que no se puede olvidar! ¿Quién ve a el Señor cubierto de llagas y afligido con persecuciones que no las abrace y las ame y las desee?" (*Vida* 26.6).

16. "Que no hagamos cosa que valga nada por Vos en público, ni osemos hablar algunas verdades que lloramos en secreto, sino que no nos habíades de oír petición tan justa. No lo creo yo, Señor, de vuestra bondad y justicia, que sois justo juez y no como los jueces del mundo que—como son hijos de Adán, y, en fin, todos varones—no hay virtud de mujer que no tengan por sospechosa. . . . [V]eo los tiempos de manera que no es razón desechar ánimos virtuosos y fuertes, aunque sean de mujeres" (*Camino*, Escorial, 4.1).

17. Augustine of Hippo, *Exposition on the Book of Psalms*, trans. H. M. Wilkins (Oxford: John Henry Parker, 1853), 272–282. I have modernized the translation.

18. Michael Walzer, *Exodus and Revolution* (New York: Basic Books, 1985), 14–17.

19. "Por otra parte, se querría meter en mitad del mundo, por ver si pudiese ser parte para que un alma alabase más a Dios; y si es mujer, se aflige del atamiento que le hace su natural, porque no puede hacer esto, y ha gran envidia, a los que tienen libertad para dar voces, publicando quién es este gran Dios de las cavallerías.

"¡Oh pobre mariposilla, atada con tantas cadenas que no te dejan volar lo que querrías! ¡Havedla lástima, mi Dios; ordenad ya de manera que ella pueda cumplir en algo sus deseos para vuestra honra y gloria. No os acordéis de lo poco que lo merece y de su bajo natural. Poderoso sois Vos, Señor, para que la gran mar se retire y el gran Jordán, y dejen pasar los hijos de Israel; no la hayáis lástima, que con vuestra fortaleza ayudada puede pasar muchos trabajos. Ella está determinada a ello, y los desea padecer; alargad, Señor, vuestro poderoso brazo, no se le pase la vida en cosas tan bajas; parézcase vuestra grandeza en cosa tan feminil y baja, para que, entendiendo el mundo que no es nada de ella, os alaben a Vos" (*Moradas* 6.6.3–4).

20. James Samuel Preus, *From Shadow to Promise: Old Testament Interpretation from Augustine to the Young Luther* (Cambridge: Harvard University Press, 1969), 59.

21. Luis de León, *Obras completas*, ed. Félix García (Madrid: BAC, 1944), 1: 930.

22. "'Diles que no se sigan por sola una parte de la Escritura, que miren otras'" (*Cuenta de conciencia* 16).

23. Sanford Shepard, *Lost Lexicon: Secret Meanings in the Vocabulary of Spanish Literature During the Inquisition* (Miami: Ediciones Universal, 1982), 46.

24. Sala-Molins, *Repertorium*, 251.

25. *Cathólica impugnación del herético libelo maldito e descomulgado*

que el año pasado, chap. 26, 135–137, cited in Andrés Martín, *La teología española en el siglo XVI,* 1: 318.

26. Sala-Molins, *Repertorium,* 129.

27. A. M. Honeyman, "Matthew V.18 and the Validity of the Law," *New Testament Studies* 1 (1954–1955): 142.

28. "En esta majestad se me dio a entender una verdad, que es cumplimiento de todas las verdades; no sé yo decir cómo, porque no vi nada. Dijéronme, sin ver quién, mas bien entendí ser la mesma Verdad: 'No es poco esto que hago por ti, que una de las cosas es en que mucho me deves; porque todo el daño que viene al mundo es de no conocer las verdades de la Escritura con clara verdad; no faltará una tilde de ella.' . . . [M]as quedé de una suerte que tampoco sé decir, con grandísima fortaleza y muy de veras para cumplir con todas mis fuerzas la más pequeña parte de la Escritura divina" (*Vida* 40.1,2).

29. "Que con ella [Jacob] devía de entender otros secretos, que no los supo decir; que sólo ver una escala que bajavan y subían ángeles, si no huviera más luz interior, no entendiera tan grandes misterios" (*Moradas* 6.4.6).

30. Cited in Efrén and Steggink, eds., *Santa Teresa de Jesús,* 579.

31. Manuel Durán, *Luis de Léon* (New York: Twayne, 1971), 31–33.

32. Origen, *The Song of Songs: Commentary and Homilies,* trans. R. P. Lawson, Ancient Christian Writers Series, no. 26 (London: Longmans, 1957), 21–22.

33. Bynum attributes Bernard's emphasis on the development of qualities considered feminine to the Cistercian attempts to define authority in the monastic context (*Jesus as Mother,* 147).

34. Astell, *The Song of Songs in the Middle Ages,* 8.

35. Critics have defined the genre of the *Meditations* in various ways: Efrén and Steggink assert "it is neither a commentary nor an analysis of the Song of Songs" but rather "personal reflections suggested by phrases from the Song" (*Obras completas,* 421). Guido Mancini describes the *Meditations* as "a mixture of interpretative intuitions, extreme lyrical flights, and practical applications to convent life" ("Tradición y originalidad en el lenguaje coloquial teresiano," in *CIT,* 2: 484).

36. Giovanni M. Bertini, "Interpretación de *Conceptos del amor de Dios* de Teresa de Jesús," in *CIT,* 2: 548; Jean Vilnet, *Bible et mystique chez Saint Jean de la Croix* (Belgium: Desclée de Brouwer, 1949), 16.

37. "Bien sabe Su Majestad que, aunque algunas veces he oído esposición de algunas palabras de éstas y me la han dicho pidiéndolo yo—son pocas—, que poco ni mucho no se me acuerda, porque tengo muy mala memoria, y ansí no podré decir sino lo que el Señor me enseñare y fuere a mi propósito" (*Meditaciones* 1.10).

38. Elizabeth Theresa Howe identifies Bernard as the doctor to whom Teresa refers ("The Mystical Kiss and the Canticle of Canticles: Three Interpretations," *American Benedictine Review* 33 (1982): 304. No evidence exists that Teresa read Bernard's sermons on the Song, but because

Francisco de Osuna cites them often in *Tercer abecedario espiritual*, a work Teresa studied carefully, she can be said to have known Bernard at least indirectly.

39. Marvin H. Pope, ed., *Song of Songs: A New Translation with Introduction and Commentary*, Anchor Bible (London: Sheed and Ward, 1946), 297.

40. "Esto no entiendo cómo es, y no entenderlo me hace gran regalo" (*Meditaciones* 1.1).

41. "Conoció que es posible pasar el alma enamorada por su Esposo todos esos regalos y desmayos y muertes y afliciones y deleites y gozos con El" (*Meditaciones* 1.6).

42. Origen, *Song of Songs*, 23.

43. "Dirán que soy una necia, que no quiere decir esto, que tiene muchas significaciones, que está claro que no havíamos de decir esta palabra a Dios, que por eso es bien estas cosas no las lean gentes simples. Yo lo confieso, que tiene muchos entendimientos; mas el alma que está abrasada de amor que la desatina, no quiere ninguno sino decir estas palabras; sí, que no se lo quita el Señor" (*Meditaciones* 1.11).

44. "Tengo por cierto no le pesa que nos consolemos y deleitemos en sus palabras y obras: como se holgaría y gustaría el rey, si a un pastorcillo amase y le cayese en gracia, y le viese embovado mirando el brocado y pensando qué es aquello y cómo se hizo" (*Meditaciones* 1.9).

45. "¿Qué más era menester para encendernos en amor suyo y pensar que tomó este estilo no sin gran causa?" (*Meditaciones* 1.4).

46. Henri de Lubac remarks the absence of the allegorical sense in the *Meditations*: "In St. Teresa's commentary on the Song of Songs, no trace of the ecclesial meaning, which had been so much emphasized by a St. Bernard, a Gilbert of Holland, and even a Luis de León, will remain" (*The Sources of Revelation*, trans. Luke O'Neill [New York: Herder and Herder, 1968], 53, n. 34). In their *Introductio specialis in Vetus Testamentum* (Rome, 1946), A. Miller and A. Metzinger make the charge often leveled against biblical commentaries by mystics: "[The works of] St. Francis of Sales, St. John of the Cross, and St. Teresa [are] not exegetical works, but purely ascetical-mystical. In these works, in fact, the union of the soul with Christ is not considered primarily insofar as the soul is ecclesiastical because a member of the mystical Body of Christ, but rather as a private and individual mystical life" (cited in Pietro della Madre di Dio, "La sacra scrittura nelle opere di S. Teresa," *Rivista di vita spirituale* 18 [1964]: 96–97).

47. "¡Oh, hijas mías, qué secretos tan grandes hay en estas palabras! Dénoslo nuestro Señor a sentir, que harto mal se pueden decir" (*Meditaciones* 4.1).

48. "No como algunos letrados, que no les lleva el Señor por este modo de oración ni tienen principio de espíritu, que quieren llevar las cosas por tanta razón y tan medidas por sus entendimientos, que no parece sino que han ellos con sus letras de comprender todas las grandezas de Dios" (*Meditaciones* 6.7).

49. "Como quien tenía gran fe y sabiduría, entendió luego que, entreviniendo estas dos cosas, no havía más que saber ni dudar" (*Meditaciones* 6.7).

50. "Torno a decir, Dios mío, y a suplicaros, por la sangre de vuestro Hijo, que me hagáis esta merced: 'béseme con beso de su boca,' que sin Vos, ¿qué soy yo, Señor?" (*Meditaciones* 4.7).

51. "Déos nuestro Señor a entender—u por mejor decir, a gustar—qué es del gozo del alma cuando está ansí" (*Meditaciones* 4.5).

52. "Entiendo yo aquí que pide hacer grandes obras en servicio de nuestro Señor y del prójimo, y por esto huelga de perder aquel deleite y contento" (*Meditaciones* 7.3).

53. "Acuérdome ahora lo que muchas veces he pensado de aquella santa Samaritana, qué herida devía de estar de esta yerva y cuán bien havía comprendido en su corazón las palabras del Señor, pues deja al mesmo Señor porque ganen y aprovechen los de su pueblo; que da bien a entender lo que voy diciendo; y en pago de esta tan gran caridad, mereció ser creída y ver el gran bien que hizo nuestro Señor en aquel pueblo" (*Meditaciones* 7.5).

54. On the *Vejamen*, see Juan de Dios Martín Velasco, "'Búscame en ti-búscate in mi': La correlación entre el descubrimiento del hombre y el descubrimiento de Dios en Santa Teresa," in *CIT*, 2: 809–834.

55. "Caro costaría si no pudiésemos buscar a Dios sino cuando estuviésemos muertos al mundo. No lo estava la Madalena, ni la Samaritana, ni la Cananea, cuando le hallaron" (*Vejamen* 6). Teresa's sarcastic rejection of Juan de la Cruz's emphasis on "perfect contemplation" refers to a long-standing dialogue with him about the nature and goal of spiritual experience. Juan counseled her to follow a contemplative life detached from the world with serene union unmarked by raptures, visions, or locutions from God.

56. J. L. Austin, *Philosophical Papers*, ed. J. O. Urmson and G. J. Warnock (Oxford: Clarendon, 1961), 220.

57. "Heme acordado que esta salutación del Señor devía ser mucho más de lo que suena, y el decir a la gloriosa Magdalena que se fuese en paz; porque como las palabras del Señor son hechas como obras en nosotros, de tal manera devían hacer la operación en aquellas almas que estavan ya dispuestas, que apartase en ellos todo lo que es corpóreo en el alma y la dejase en puro espíritu, para que se pudiese juntar en esta unión celestial con el espíritu increado" (*Moradas* 7.2.9).

58. "Si una labradora se casase con el rey y tuviese hijos, ¿ya no quedan de sangre real? Pues si a un alma nuestro Señor hace tanta merced, que tan sin división se junte con ella, ¡qué deseos, qué efectos, qué hijos de obras heroicas podrán nacer de allí, si no fuere por su culpa!" (*Meditaciones* 3.8).

59. "Como lo hizo con la Magdalena, con brevedad, hácelo en otras personas, conforme a lo que ellas hacen en dejar a Su Majestad hacer" (*Vida* 22.15).

60. Teresa might have read either of two current editions: *Legenda seu Flos Sanctorum in lingua hispanica cum suis figuris depictis, in cuius*

principio est prologus Gamberti (Toledo, 1511) or, Pedro de la Vega, *Flos Sanctorum: La Vida de nuestro señor Jesu Christo, de su sanctissima Madre y de los otros sanctos segund el orden de sus fiestas*, 1521, 1541, 1578 (*TVST*, 35). On the figure of Mary Magdalene in Christian mythology, see Marina Warner, *Alone of All Her Sex: The Myth and the Cult of the Virgin Mary* (1976; New York: Random House, Vintage, 1983), 224–235.

61. Victor Saxer, *Le Culte de Marie Magdeleine en Occident des origines à la fin du moyen age* (Paris: Clavreuil, 1959), 6.

62. Alicia Ostriker, "The Thieves of Language: Women Poets and Revisionary Mythmaking," in Elaine Showalter, ed., *The New Feminist Criticism: Essays on Women, Literature, and Theory* (New York: Pantheon, 1985), 317–318.

63. Mary Elizabeth Perry, *Gender and Disorder in Early Modern Seville* (Princeton: Princeton University Press, 1990), 146.

64. Luke 8.3 also provides that Mary Magdalene was one of Jesus' followers who had her "own resources."

65. "Y ¿pensáis que le sería poca mortificación a una señora como ella era irse por esas calles—y por ventura sola, porque no llevava hervor para entender cómo iva—y entrar a donde nunca havía entrado, y después sufrir la mormuración del fariseo, y otras muy muchas que devía sufrir?" (*Moradas* 7.4.15).

66. "Porque ver en el pueblo una mujer como ella hacer tanta mudanza, y—como sabemos—entre tan mala gente, que bastava ver que tenía amistad con el Señor—a quien ellos tenían tan aborrecido—para traer a la memoria la vida que havía hecho, y que se quería ahora hacer santa (porque está claro que luego mudaría vestido y todo lo demás); pues ahora se dice a personas que no son tan nombradas, ¿qué sería entonces?" (*Moradas* 7.4.15).

67. "Y pensáis que aunque vos, hijas, no os disculpéis, ha de faltar quien torne por vos? Mirad como respondió el Señor por la Magdalena en casa del Fariseo, y cuando su hermana la culpava" (*Camino*, Valladolid 15.7; also see *Castle* 6.11.12).

68. "Considerávase a sus pies y llorava con la Magdalena, ni más ni menos que si con los ojos corporales le viera en casa del fariseo" (*Camino*, Valladolid 34.8).

69. "Mirad un san Pablo, una Magdalena: en tres días el uno comenzó a entenderse que estava enfermo de amor; éste fue san Pablo. La Magdalena desde el primer día, ¡y cuán bien entendido!" (*Camino*, Valladolid 40.3).

70. "¡Oh, qué de veces me acuerdo del agua viva que dijo el Señor a la Samaritana!" (*Vida* 30.19; also see *Road* 19.2; *Castle* 6.6.5; *Foundations* 31.46).

71. In *Writing and Vulnerability in the Late Renaissance*, Jane Tylus points out the apostolic facet of Teresa's version of Mary Magdalene (Stanford: Stanford University Press, 1993), 72–74.

72. Marjorie M. Malvern, *Venus in Sackcloth: The Magdalen's Origins and Metamorphoses* (Carbondale: Southern Illinois University Press, 1975), 76–77.

73. "Imite a la Magdalena, que de que esté fuerte, Dios la llevará a el desierto" (*Vida* 22.12).

74. "Mas ¡qué devía pasar la gloriosa Virgen y esta bendita santa!, ¡qué de amenazas, qué de malas palabras, y qué de encontrones, y qué descomedidas! Pues ¡con qué gente lo havían tan cortesana! Sí, lo era del infierno, que eran ministros del demonio" (*Camino*, 26.8).

75. "¡Qué devía de pasar san Pablo y la Magdalena y otros semejantes, en quien tan crecido estava este fuego de amor de Dios?" (*Vida* 21.7).

76. An abbreviated version of the story appears in Mark 16:9–11.

77. Jacobus de Voragine, *The Golden Legend*, trans. Granger Ryan and Helmut Ripperger (London: Longmans, Green, 1941), 2: 392–393.

78. "Creedme que Marta y María han de andar juntas para hospedar al Señor y tenerle siempre consigo, y no le hacer mal hospedaje, no le dando de comer. ¿Cómo se lo diera María, sentada siempre a los pies, si su hermana no se ayudara? Su manjar es que de todas las maneras que pudiéremos lleguemos almas para que se salven y siempre le alaben" (*Moradas* 7.4.14; also see *Road* 17.5).

79. "La otra, que no podéis vosotras ni tenéis cómo allegar almas a Dios, que lo haríades de buena gana, mas que no haviendo de enseñar ni de predicar, como hacían los Apóstoles, que no sabéis cómo" (*Moradas* 7.4.16).

Chapter 3

1. Both Teresa and Augustine echo New Testament descriptions of Christian conversion, 2 Corinthians 5:7 and Romans 5:4, for example.

2. Gari Laguardia, "Santa Teresa and the Problem of Desire," *Hispania* 63 (Sept. 1980): 523; also see Weber, *Teresa of Avila and the Rhetoric of Femininity*, 51.

3. Laguardia, "Santa Teresa and the Problem of Desire," 524.

4. Weber, *Teresa of Avila*, 51, 64.

5. J. J. O'Meara explains that "the *Confessions* is no autobiography, and not even a partial autobiography. It is the use of Augustine's life and confession of faith in God as an illustration of his theory of man" (*The Young Augustine: The Growth of St. Augustine's Mind up to His Conversion* [London: Longmans, 1954], 18).

6. "Eramos tres hermanas y nueve hermanos. Todos parecieron a sus padres—por la bondad de Dios—en ser virtuosos, si no fui yo, aungue era la más querida de mi padre" (*Vida* 1.4). The children Teresa (b. 1515) refers to here are two half-siblings by her father's first wife, María (b. 1505) and Juan de Cepeda (b. 1507), and her full siblings, Hernando (b. 1510), Rodrigo (b. 1511), Juan de Ahumada (b. 1517), Lorenzo (b. 1519), Antonio (b. 1520), Pedro (b. 1521), Jerónimo (b. 1522), Augustín (b. 1527), and Juana (b. 1528).

7. *TVST*, 39.

8. Victoria Lincoln, *Teresa, A Woman: A Biography of Teresa of Avila*, ed. Elias Rivers and Antonio T. de Nicolás (New York: Paragon, 1984), 34–35.

9. Jean Pierre Dedieu, "The Archives of the Holy Office of Toledo as a Source of Historical Anthropology," trans. E. W. Monter, in Henningsen and Tedeschi with Amiel, eds., *The Inquisition in Early Modern Europe*, 166.

10. Eymerich and Peña, *Directorium*, 121.

11. Ibid., 122–123.

12. Lea, *A History of the Inquisition of Spain*, 2: 459.

13. Adrienne Schizzano Mandel, "Le procès Inquisitorial comme acte autobiographique: Le cas de Sor María de San Jerónimo," in *L'Autobiographie dans le monde hispanique*, Actes du colloque international de la Baum-les-Aix, 11–13 mai 1979 (Aix-en-Provence: Université de Provence, 1980), 163; Perry, *Gender and Disorder in Early Modern Seville*, 120.

14. Perry, *Gender and Disorder in Early Modern Seville*, 119–120.

15. "El tener padres virtuosos y temerosos de Dios me bastara, si yo no fuera tan ruin, con lo que el Señor me favorecía para ser buena" (*Vida* 1.1).

16. Alfonso de Villegas, *Flos Sanctorum* [The Lives of the Saints], trans. W. and E. K[insman] B[rothers] from Italian, 4th ed. (Rouen: J. Cousturier, 1636), 47. University Microfilms HN434407.

17. Márquez Villanueva, "Santa Teresa y el linaje," 151.

18. Teresa's paternal grandmother, Inés, came from an Old Christian family. Her brother, Pedro de Cepeda, and Enrique de Hamusco, a teacher of theology and a prebendary in the Church, made declarations against Teresa's father (*TVST*, 4).

19. *TVST*, 4–5.

20. Ibid., 5.

21. Kamen, *Inquisition and Society in Spain*, 162.

22. Ibid., 122.

23. Juan Ignacio Gutiérrez Nieto, "El proceso de encastamiento social de la Castilla del siglo XVI: La respuesta conversa," in *CIT*, 1: 104.

24. Cited in Gutiérrez Nieto, "El proceso," 104.

25. Américo Castro, *Teresa la santa y otros ensayos* (Madrid: Alianza, 1982), 18. Sanford Shepard conjures a melodramatic scenario: "The social inability that former Judaism carried, the repugnance the convert inspired in simple minds manipulated by fanatical clergy, the infamy of having been penanced, the shame of falling [*sic*] from father to children and grandchildren, the need to lie about ancestry and the fear of discovery must have oppressed the saint by day and by night. The shame of her ancestors must have lain in ambush to snag her and expose her to the ridicule of the world. The degradation of her line must have tracked her to the very door of her interior castle" (*Lost Lexicon: Secret Meanings in the Vocabulary of Spanish Literature During the Inquisition* [Miami: Ediciones Universal, 1982], 125).

26. Diego de Yepes, *Vida de Santa Teresa de Jesús*, Tesoro de escritores místicos españoles, vol. 1. (1587; Paris: Garnier, 1847), 6.

27. Francisco de Ribera, *La Vida de la Madre Teresa de Jesús, fundadora de las Descalças y Descalços*, ed. and introd. Jaime Pons (1590; Barcelona: Gustavo Gili, 1908), 94.

28. Silverio de Santa Teresa, *Procesos,* 1: 6, 276.

29. Ibid., 2: 278.

30. "Pues no sería por ser de sangre ilustre el hacerme honra" (*Fundaciones* 27.12).

31. Narciso Alonso Cortés, "Pleitos de los Cepeda," *Boletín de la Real Academia Española* 25 (1964): 85–110.

32. *TVST,* 4 n. 11; mentioned but not identified in Márquez Villanueva, "Santa Teresa y el linaje," 146 n. 8.

33. "Era mi padre aficionado a leer buenos libros, y ansí los tenía de romance para que leyesen sus hijos, éstos. Con el cuidado que mi madre tenía de hacernos rezar y ponernos en ser devotos de nuestra Señora y de algunos santos, comenzó a despertarme, de edad—a mi parecer—de seis u siete años" (*Vida* 1.1).

34. Víctor García de la Concha, *El arte literario de Santa Teresa* (Barcelona: Ariel, 1978), 17. The books in his library ranged beyond those of the typical merchant (Sangnieux, "Santa Teresa y los libros," 751).

35. "Era aficionada a libros de cavallerías, y no tan mal tomava este pasatiempo como yo le tomé para mí, porque no perdía su lavor, sino desenvolvíemenos para leer en ellos. . . . De esto le pesava tanto a mi padre, que se havía de tener aviso a que no lo viese. Yo comencé a quedarme en costumbre de leerlos, y aquella pequeña falta que en ella vi, me comenzó a enfriar los deseos y comenzar a faltar en los demás" (*Vida* 2.1).

36. "Era tan estremo lo que en esto me embevía, que si no tenía libro nuevo, no me parece tenía contento. Comencé a traer galas y a desear contentar en parecer bien, con mucho cuidado de manos y cavello, y olores y todas las vanidades que en esto podía tener" (*Vida* 2.1, 2).

37. When the marriage was annulled because Alonso's first wife had been a fourth cousin to Beatriz, Alonso had to provide an increased dowry and buy a dispensation to marry her legally. Within fifteen months of their marriage on 17 October 1509, she had borne two children.

38. "Como yo comencé a entender lo que havía perdido, afligida fuime a una imagen de Nuestra Señora y supliquéla fuese mi madre, con muchas lágrimas" (*Vida* 1.7).

39. "Cuando voy a quejarme de mis padres, tampoco puedo; porque no vía en ellos sino todo bien y cuidado de mi bien" (*Vida* 1.8).

40. Eymerich and Peña, *Directorium,* 123.

41. "Yo a hacer obras para descubrir la que era, y el Señor encubrir los males y descubrir alguna pequeña virtud, si tenía, y hacerla grande en los ojos de todos, de manera que siempre me tenían en mucho" (*Vida* 7.18).

42. "Para caer, havía muchos amigos que me ayudasen; para levantarme, hallávame tan sola, que ahora me espanto cómo no me estava siempre caída" (*Vida* 7.22).

43. "No sé cómo he de pasar de aquí, cuando me acuerdo la manera de mi profesión y la gran determinación y contento con que la hice y el desposorio que hice con Vos. Esto no lo puedo decir sin lágrimas, y havían de ser lágrimas de sangre y quebrárseme el corazón, y no era mucho sentimiento para lo que después os ofendí" (*Vida* 4.3).

44. Ribera, *La Vida*, 115–119.
45. Ricardo García Cárcel, *Herejía y sociedad en el siglo XVI: La Inquisición en Valencia, 1530–1609*, 2d ed. (1976; Barcelona: Península, 1980), 251–257.
46. Jeremy Tambling reads the episode as a comment on the physical separation between confessor and confessant mandated by the Council of Trent and represented architecturally by the confessional box (*Confession: Sexuality, Sin, and the Subject* [New York: St. Martin's Press, 1990], 69–70).
47. "He visto por espiriencia que es mijor—siendo virtuosos y de santas costumbres—no tener ningunas [letras]; porque ni ellos se fían de sí, sin preguntar a quien las tenga buenas, ni yo me fiara; y buen letrado nunca me engañó. Estotros tampoco me devían de querer engañar, sino no sabían más. Yo pensava que sí, y que no era obligada a más de creerlos, como era cosa ancha lo que me decían y de más libertad; que si fuera apretada, yo soy tan ruin que buscara otros. Lo que era pecado venial decíanme que no era ninguno; lo que era gravísimo mortal, que era venial" (*Vida* 5.3).
48. Lincoln, *Teresa, A Woman*, 24; *TVST*, 137.
49. "Y ansí no es de culpar a la casa adonde estava . . . a mí me hizo harto daño no estar en monesterio encerrado" (*Vida* 7.1, 3).
50. "No sé para qué he dicho esto" (*Vida* 7.16).
51. "Como él no decía mentira, y ya, conforme a lo que yo tratava con él, no la havía yo de decir" (*Vida* 7.12).
52. Laguardia, "Santa Teresa and the Problem of Desire," 524.
53. Efrén and Steggink attribute his pain to a lung infection (*TVST*, 39–40).
54. Hawkins, *Archetypes of Conversion*, 33. On Augustine's reference to the parable of the prodigal son in his writings, see Leo Charles Ferrari, "The Theme of the Prodigal Son in Augustine's *Confessions*," *Recherches Augustiniennes* 12 (1977): 105–118.
55. Etienne Gilson, *Reason and Revelation in the Middle Ages* (New York: Scribner's, 1938), 17.
56. Alain Boureau, "Les structures narratives de *La Legenda aurea*: De la variation au grand chant sacré," in *"Legenda aurea": Sept siècles de diffusion*, Actes du colloque international sur la *Legenda aurea*: Texte latin et branches vernaculaires, Université de Quebec, Montreal, 11–12 May 1983 (Montreal: Bellarmin, 1986), 68–70.
57. Ibid., 70–73. Among the defenders of the faith, Boureau includes Augustine and Jerome, and as examples of the preachers he cites Mary Magdalene, Luke, and Gregory.
58. "Como vía los martirios que por Dios las santas pasavan, parecíamen compravan muy barato el ir a gozar de Dios, y deseava yo mucho morir ansí" (*Vida* 1.5).
59. Jacobus, *The Golden Legend*, 2: 708–716.
60. Alison Goddard Elliott, *Roads to Paradise: Reading the Lives of the Early Saints* (Hanover: University Press of New England, 1987), 22.
61. "El tener padres nos parecía el mayor embarazo" (*Vida* 1.5).

62. Charles F. Altman, "Two Types of Opposition and the Structure of Latin Saints' Lives," *Medievalia et Humanistica* 6 (1975): 1–11.

63. "Gustava mucho, cuando jugava con otras niñas, hacer monesterios, como que éramos monjas; y yo me parece deseava serlo, aunque no tanto como las cosas que he dicho" (*Vida* 1.6).

64. "Cuando salí de casa de mi padres, no creo será más el sentimiento cuando me muera; porque me parece cada hueso se me apartava por sí" (*Vida* 4.1).

65. The physical symptoms Teresa describes include aches in her jaw and teeth; pains and noises in her head; backaches; attacks of nerves; hayfever; colds; fevers and quartan fevers; heart trouble; pains in her liver, kidneys, and uterus; paralysis; palsy; and daily vomiting. Requested by Efrén and Steggink to diagnose the symptoms, Dr. Emilio Vicente concludes that "we can affirm that the major part of the illnesses the Saint suffered in the course of her life were of neurotic origin," but he does not exclude the possibility of physical illness. Although he labels her paralysis neurotic in origin, he speculates that dehydration caused by the attempted cure caused spasms resembling those of cholera. While also maintaining the ultimate importance of psychological causes, Efrén and Steggink propose that she might have had a hyperthyroid condition; Juan Rof Carballo diagnoses all of her symptoms as cerebral meningitis; René Fülop Miller designates her illness as hysterical epilepsy. In addition, Teresa probably had at least one case of pneumonia, numerous chronic infections, and cyclical pain associated with an abnormal menstrual cycle. From the blood stains found on her deathbed, as well as her prior complaints of backaches, Vicente judges that she died of uterine cancer that had metastasized through the vertebrae (*TVST*, 129–134).

66. Josef Breuer and Sigmund Freud, *Studies on Hysteria*, trans. and ed. James Strachey with Anna Freud, Alix Strachey, and Alan Tyson (1955; New York: Basic Books, 1957), 232.

67. "Y ansí me acaece, que cuando en las vidas de los santos leemos que convertieron almas, mucha más devoción me hace y más ternura y más envidia que todos los martirios que padecen" (*Fundaciones* 1.7).

Chapter 4

1. William James lists ineffability along with noetic quality, transiency, and passivity as the essential characteristics of mystical experience (*The Varieties of Religious Experience*, 299–300).

2. For an example of the many treatments of the *Life* as allegory, see Joseph Chorpenning, "St. Teresa of Avila as Allegorist: Chapters 11–22 of the *Libro de la vida*," *Studia Mystica* 9 (1986): 3–22; and E. W. Trueman Dicken, *The Crucible of Love: A Study of the Mysticism of St. Teresa of Avila and St. John of the Cross* (New York: Sheed and Ward, 1963), 188. On the *Interior Castle*, see Weber, *Teresa of Avila and the Rhetoric of Femininity*, 98; Concha, *El arte literario de Santa Teresa*, 272.

3. Michel de Certeau, "Mystic Speech," in *Heterologies: Discourse on*

the Other, trans. Brian Massumi, introd. Wlad Godzich, Theory and History of Literature, vol. 17 (Minneapolis: University of Minnesota Press, 1986), 97.

4. Bruce Bubacz, *St. Augustine's Theory of Knowledge*, Texts and Studies in Religion, no. 11 (New York: Edward Mellen, 1981), 61–62.

5. "Me parece que sentir las muertes y travajos de él [el mundo] es desatino, a lo menos que dure mucho el dolor u el amor de los parientes, amigos, etc." (*Cuenta de conciencia* 1.25).

6. "Esto me aprovechó mucho, y lo que dice san Agustín: 'Dame, Señor, lo que me mandas, y manda lo que quisieres'" (*Vida* 13.3).

7. Possible sources for the analogy of the garden include the Song of Songs (Concha, *El arte literario de Santa Teresa*, 245–246); the garden of Mt. Carmel and the convents in the Carmelite order (Chorpenning, "St. Teresa of Avila as Allegorist," 13–14); Osuna's *Third Spiritual Alphabet* (Alberto Barrientos et al., eds., *Santa Teresa de Jesús: Obras completas* [Madrid: Espiritualidad, 1984], 63 n. 4).

8. "Era tan recio mi corazón en este caso que, si leyera toda la Pasión, no llorara un lágrima" (*Vida* 3.1).

9. Also see *Life* 11.10: "There is nothing but dryness, distaste, vapidness" (*sequedad y desgusto y desabor*).

10. "Llamo 'agua' aquí las lágrimas y, aunque no las hayas, la ternura y sentimiento interior de devoción" (*Vida* 11.9).

11. "Dale gran deleite ver aplacado aquel ímpetu de el fuego con agua que le hacer más crecer. Parece esto algaravía y pasa ansí" (*Vida* 19.1).

12. Dicken, *Crucible of Love*, 178–187.

13. "Paréceme a mí que se puede regar de cuatro maneras: u con sacar el agua de un pozo, que es a nuestro gran travajo; u con noria y arcaduces, que se saca con un torno—yo lo he sacado algunas veces—: es a menos travajo que estotro, y sácase más agua; u de un río u arroyo: esto se riega muy mijor, que queda más harta la tierra de agua y no se ha menester regar tan a menudo, y es a menos travajo mucho el hortolano; u con llover mucho, que lo riega el Señor sin travajo ninguno nuestro, y es muy sin comparación mijor que todo lo que queda dicho" (*Vida* 11.7).

14. "Es, pues, esta oración una centellica que comienza el Señor a encender en el alma del verdadero amor suyo, y quiere que el alma vaya entendiendo qué cosa es este amor con regalo. . . . [P]or mucho que quiera comenzar a hacer arder el fuego para alcanzar este gusto, no parece sino que le echa agua para matarle . . . y si no la mata por su culpa, ésta es la que comienza a encender el gran fuego que echa llamas de sí, como diré en su lugar" (*Vida* 15.4).

15. "Sola la voluntad se ocupa de manera que—sin saber cómo—se cautiva; sólo da consentimiento para que la encarcele Dios, como quien bian [*sic*] sabe ser cautivo de quien ama. ¡Oh Jesús y Señor mío, qué nos vale aquí vuestro amor!, porque éste tiene al nuestro tan atado que no deja libertad para amar en aquel punto a otra cosa sino a Vos" (*Vida* 14.2).

16. See *Life* 15.6 and 26.2 for additional explanations of the role of memory.

17. "Esto, aunque parece todo uno, es diferente de la oración de quietud que dije; en parte, porque allí está el alma que no se querría bullir ni menear, gozando en aquel ocio santo de María; en esta oración puede también ser Marta (ansí que está casi obrando juntamente en vida activa y contemplativa)" (*Vida* 17.4).

18. "'¿Cuándo, mi dios, ha de estar ya toda junta mi alma en vuestra alabanza, y no hecha pedazos, sin poder valerse a sí?'" (*Vida* 17.5).

19. "A mi entender es diferente la unión del levantamiento en esta misma unión . . . obra el Señor de diferente manera" (*Vida* 18.7).

20. "Ansí que a esta mariposilla importuna de la memoria aquí se le queman las alas: ya no puede más bullir. La voluntad deve estar bien ocupada en amar, mas no entiende cómo ama. El entendimiento, si entiende, no se entiende cómo entiende; al menos no puede comprehender nada de lo que entiende" (*Vida* 18.14).

21. "La voluntad es la que mantiene la tela, mas las otras dos potencias presto tornan a importunar" (*Vida* 18.12).

22. "Se entiende hay diferencia en alguna manera, y muy conocida, del alma a el espíritu, aunque más sea todo una. Conócese una división tan delicada, que algunas veces parece obra de diferente manera lo uno de lo otros, como el sabor que les quiere dar el Señor" (*Moradas* 7.1.12).

23. "Ni sé entender que es mente, ni qué diferencia tenga del alma u espíritu" (*Vida* 18.2).

24. "Bien que el alma alguna vez sale de sí mesma, a manera de un fuego que está ardiendo y hecho llama, y algunas veces crece este fuego con ímpetu; esta llama sube muy arriba del fuego, mas no por eso es cosa diferente, si no la mesma llama que está en el fuego" (*Vida* 18.2).

25. "No sé si la comparación cuadra, mas en hecho de verdad ello pasa ansí" (*Vida* 20.2).

26. "Mas un fuego pequeño también es fuego como un grande, y ya se ve la diferencia que hay de lo uno a lo otro: en un fuego pequeño, primero que un hierro pequeño se hace ascua, pasa mucho espacio; mas si el fuego es grande, aunque sea mayor el hierro, en muy poquito pierde del todo su ser, al parecer" (*Vida* 18.7).

27. "Buscar remedio para vivir muy contra voluntad de el espíritu, u de lo superior de el alma, que no querría salir de esta pena" (*Vida* 20.14).

28. "Víale en las manos un dardo de oro largo, y al fin de el hierro me parecía tener un poco de fuego; éste me parecía meter por el corazón algunas veces y que me llegava a las entrañas. Al sacarle, me parecía las llevava consigo, y me dejava abrasada en amor grande de Dios" (*Vida* 29.13).

29. "Creo deve ser la causa que, como en la meditación es todo buscar a Dios, como una vez se halla y queda el alma acostumbrada por obra de la voluntad a tornarle a buscar, no quiere cansarse con el entendimiento; y también me parece que, como la voluntad esté ya encendida, no quiere esta potencia generosa aprovecharse de estotra si pudiese; y no hace mal, mas será imposible—en especial hasta que lleve a estas otras postreras moradas—y perderá tiempo" (*Moradas* 6.7.7).

30. Scholars have located a number of antecedents and possible sources

of Teresa's analogy of the castle: Gaston Etchegoyen points out castle imagery in several works Teresa knew—Ludolph of Saxony's *Vita Christi,* Osuna's *Tercer abecedario espiritual,* and Laredo's *Subida del monte Sión;* Javier Herrero links the castle to the setting of the novels of chivalry; Chorpenning relates Teresa's use of the castle to the tradition of using architectural symbols as mnemonic and organizational devices in theological works; Swietlicki finds an analogue in the jeweled castle of the Cabala, the *Zohar* in particular; Márquez Villanueva suggests as a source Luis Lobera's 1546 medical treatise comparing the human body to a fortified tower: Gaston Etchegoyen, *L'amour divin: Essai sur les sources de Sainte Thérèse* (Paris: Féret, 1923), 331–336; Javier Herrero, "The Knight and the Mystical Castle," *Studies in Formative Spirituality* 4 (1983): 393–407; Joseph Chorpenning, "The Literary and Theological Method of *The Interior Castle,*" *Journal of Hispanic Philology* 3 (1979): 121–133; Catherine Swietlicki, *Spanish Christian Cabala: The Works of Luis de León, Santa Teresa de Jesús, and San Juan de la Cruz* (Columbia: University of Missouri Press, 1986), 50–51; Francisco Márquez Villanueva, "El símil del castillo interior: Sentido y génesis," in *CIT,* 2: 495–522.

Given that some early copies of the *Interior Castle* carry the subtitle *Castillo de Magdalón,* I add to these possibilities the castle "called Magdalene," which the *Golden Legend* relates Mary inherited at the early death of her parents. At the same time, I agree with Márquez Villanueva's surmise that Teresa probably did not think of the analogy as having any particular source: "It is likely that not even she herself, always complaining about her weak memory, could ascribe the simile to any specific memory among those that had become an integral part of her person" ("El símil del castillo interior," 499).

31. Helmut A. Hatzfeld, *Santa Teresa de Avila* (New York: Twayne, 1969), 23, 39.

32. Swietlicki, *Spanish Christian Cabala,* 51.

33. Weber, *Teresa of Avila and the Rhetoric of Femininity,* 109.

34. "Estando hoy suplicando a nuestro Señor hablase por mí—porque yo no atinava a cosa que decir ni cómo comenzar a cumplir esta obediencia—se me ofreció lo que ahora diré para comenzar con algún fundamento, que es considerar nuestra alma como un castillo todo de un diamante u muy claro cristal, adonde hay muchos aposentos, ansí como en el cielo hay muchas moradas. Que si bien lo consideramos, hermanas, no es otra cosa el alma del justo sino un paraíso adonde dice El tiene sus deleites" (*Moradas* 1.1.1).

35. Michel de Certeau, *The Mystic Fable: The Sixteenth and Seventeenth Centuries,* trans. Michael B. Smith (1982; Chicago: University of Chicago Press, 1992), 1: 189.

36. "No hallo yo cosa con qué comparar la gran hermosura de un alma y la gran capacidad, y verdaderamente apenas deven llegar nuestros entendimientos—por agudos que fuesen—a comprehenderla" (*Moradas* 1.1.1).

37. "No es pequeña lástima y confusión que por nuestra culpa no entendamos a nosotros mesmos ni sepamos quién somos. ¿No sería gran

ignorancia, hijas mías, que preguntasen a uno quién es y no se conociese ni supiese quién fue su padre, ni su madre, ni de qué tierra?" [*Moradas* 1.1.2].

38. "Y a mi parecer jamás nos acabamos de conocer, si no procuramos conocer a Dios; mirando su grandeza, acudamos a nuestra bajeza, y mirando su limpieza, veremos nuestra suciedad" [*Moradas* 1.2.9].

39. "Pongamos los ojos en Cristo nuestro bien y allí deprenderemos la verdadera humildad, y en sus santos, y ennoblecerse ha el entendimiento" [*Moradas* 1.2.11].

40. "Luego el entendimiento acude con darle a entender que no puede cobrar mejor amigo, aunque viva muchos años; que todo el mundo está lleno de falsedad y estos contentos que le pone el demonio, de trabajos y cuidados y contradiciones, y le dice que esté cierto que fuera de este castillo no hallará seguridad ni paz; que se deje de andar por casas ajenas, pues la suya es tan llena de bienes si la quiere gozar; que quién hay que halle todo lo que ha menester como en su casa, en especial tiniendo tal huésped que le haría señor de todos los bienes, si él quiere no andar perdido, como el hijo pródigo, comiendo manjar de puercos" [*Moradas* 2.1.4].

41. Dicken observes that in the *Interior Castle* she separates the prayer of recollection from the prayer of quiet, while in the *Life* she conflates them (180).

42. "¡Oh, Señor, tomad en cuenta lo mucho que pasamos en este camino por falta de saber! Y es el mal, que como no pensamos que hay que saber más de pensar en Vos, aun no sabemos preguntar a los que saben ni entendemos qué hay que preguntar" [*Moradas* 4.1.9].

43. "Queda una certidumbre grandísima, de manera que, aunque algunas veces en cosas muy imposibles a el parecer, no deja de venirle duda si será u no será, y andan con algunas vacilaciones el entendimiento, en la mesma alma está una seguridad, que no se puede rendir, aunque le parezca que vaya todo al contrario de lo que entendió, y pasan años, no se le quita aquel pensar que Dios buscará otros medios que los hombres no entienden" [*Moradas* 6.3.7].

44. "La cera no se le imprime a sí; sólo está dispuesta" [*Moradas* 5.2.12].

45. "Vine a entender por espiriencia que el pensamiento o imaginativa, por que mejor se entienda, no es el entendimiento" [*Moradas* 4.1.8].

46. "Escriviendo esto estoy considerando lo que pasa en mi cabeza del gran ruido de ella, que dije al principio, por donde se me hizo casi imposible poder hacer lo que me mandavan de escrivir. No parece sino que están en ella muchos ríos caudalosos y por otra parte que estas aguas se despeñan, muchos pajarillos y silbos, y no en los oídos, sino en lo superior de la cabeza, adonde dicen que está lo superior del alma . . . y no será mucho que haya querido el Señor darme este mal de cabeza para entenderlo mejor" [*Moradas* 4.1.10].

47. "Ya havréis oído sus maravillas en cómo se cría la seda, que sólo El pudo hacer semejante invención, y cómo de una simiente que es a manera de granos de pimienta pequeños (que yo nunca la he visto, sino oído, y ansí, si algo fuere torcido, no es mía la culpa), con el calor, en comenzando

a haver hoja en los morales, comienza esta simiente a vivir; que hasta que hay este mantenimiento de que se sustentan se está muerta" (*Moradas* 5.2.2).

48. "La mesma alma no se conoce a sí" (*Moradas* 5.2.7).

49. "Queda imprimido en la memoria, que nunca jamás se olvida" (6.4.5).

50. This vision may include locutions, which the soul can identify as divine by their power and by its immediate need for them at the particular time they are given.

51. "En lo muy interior del alma quedan bien escritas y jamás se olvidan" (*Moradas* 6.4.6).

52. "Se entiende hay diferencia en alguna manera, y muy conocida, del alma a el espíritu, aunque más sea todo una. Conócese una división tan delicada, que algunas veces parece obra de diferente manera lo uno de lo otro, como el sabor que les quiere dar el Señor" (*Moradas* 7.1.12).

53. "Queda el alma, digo el espíritu de esta alma, hecho una cosa con Dios" (*Moradas* 7.2.4).

54. "Acá es como si cayendo agua del cielo en un río u fuente, adonde queda hecho todo agua, que no podrán ya dividir ni apartar cuál es el agua del río u lo que cayó del cielo; o como si un arroíco pequeño entra en la mar, no havrá remedio de apartarse" (*Moradas* 7.2.6).

55. "Quizá es esto lo que dice san Pablo: 'El que se arrima y allega a Dios, hácese un espíritu con El,' tocando este soberano matrimonio, que presupone haverse llegado Su Majestad a el alma por unión" (*Moradas* 7.2.6).

56. "Ansí me parece puede decir aquí el alma, porque es adonde la mariposilla, que hemos dicho, muere, y con grandísimo gozo, porque su vida es ya Cristo" (*Moradas* 7.2.6).

57. "Estos efectos—con todos los demás que hemos dicho que sean buenos en los grados de oración que quedan dichos—da Dios cuando llega el alma a Sí, con este ósculo que pedía la esposa, que yo entiendo aquí se le cumple esta petición. Aquí se dan las aguas a esta cierva que va herida, en abundancia. Aquí se deleita en el tabernáculo de Dios. Aquí halla la paloma que envió Noé a ver si era acabada la tempestad, la oliva, por señal que ha hallado tierra firme dentro en las aguas y tempestades de este mundo" (*Moradas* 7.3.13).

Chapter 5

1. Ribera, *La Vida*, 375, 216; Jodi Bilinkoff, *The Avila of Saint Teresa*, 134.

2. "Sería recia cosa que nos estuviese claramente diciendo Dios que fuésemos a alguna cosa que le importa y no quisiésemos sino estarle mirando, porque estamos a nuestro placer" (*Fundaciones* 5.5).

3. "Sino que ninguna fundación ha querido el Señor que se haga sin mucho trabajo mío" (*Fundaciones* 24.15). Unless otherwise specified, all parenthetical citations in this chapter and its notes refer to the *Foundations*.

4. Maureen Quilligan, *The Allegory of Female Authority: Christine de Pizan's "Cité des Dames"* (Ithaca: Cornell University Press, 1991).

5. See, for example, Etienne Balibar, "The Nation Form: History and Ideology," trans. Chris Turner, in Etienne Balibar and Immanuel Wallerstein, eds., *Race, Nation, Class: Ambiguous Identities* (1988; London: Verso, 1991), 102.

6. Teófanes Egido Martínez, "Santa Teresa y su circunstancia," in Teófanes Egido Martínez, ed., *Teresa de Jesús: Mujer, cristiana, maestra* (Madrid: Espiritualidad, 1982), 19.

7. "Haviendo un día comulgado, mandóme mucho Su Majestad lo procurase con todas mis fuerzas, haciéndome grandes promesas de que no se dejaría de hacer el monesterio, y que se serviría mucho en él, y que se llamase San Josef" (*Vida* 32.11).

8. Bilinkoff, *The Avila of Saint Teresa*, 137–145.

9. Edward Said, *Beginnings: Intention and Method* (Baltimore: Johns Hopkins University Press, 1975), 12.

10. "Alegróse de ver la manera de vivir y un retrato—aunque imperfecto—del principio de nuestra Orden" (*Fundaciones* 2.3).

11. "En viendo yo la gran voluntad de nuestro reverendísimo general para que hiciese más monesterios, me pareció los vía hechos" (*Fundaciones* 2.4).

12. "Este [Alonso Maldonado] venía de las Indias poco havía. Comenzóme a contar de los muchos millones de almas que allí se perdían por falta de doctrina, y hízonos un sermón y plática animando a la penitencia, y fuese. Yo quedé tan lastimada de la perdición de tantas alma, que no cabía en mí. Fuime a una ermita con hartas lágrimas; clamava a nuestro Señor, suplicándole diese medio cómo yo pudiese algo para ganar algún alma para su servicio, pues tantas llevaba el demonio, y que pudiese mi oración algo, ya que yo no era para más" (*Fundaciones* 1.7).

13. "Acordándome de las palabras que nuestro Señor me havía dicho, vía ya algún principio de lo que antes no podía entender" (*Fundaciones* 2.4).

14. James V. Mirollo, "The Lives of Saints Teresa of Avila and Benvenuto of Florence," *Texas Studies in Literature and Language* 29 (1987): 54–73.

15. Etchegoyen, *L'amour divin*, cited in Denis de Rougemont, *Love in the Western World*, trans. Montgomery Belgion (1940; New York: Schocken, 1983), 162.

16. On the New World chronicles, see René Jara and Nicholas Spadaccini, eds., *1492–1992: Re/Discovering Colonial Writing*, Hispanic Issues, no. 4 (Minneapolis: Prisma, 1989).

17. J. H. Elliott, introduction to Hernán Cortés, *Hernán Cortés: Letters from Mexico*, ed. and trans. Anthony Pagden (New Haven: Yale University Press, 1986), xliv.

18. Mario Hernández Sánchez-Barba, introduction to *Hernán Cortés: Cartas y documentos* (Mexico: Porrúa, 1963), xix.

19. "¡Oh, válame Dios, cuán diferente entenderemos estas ignorancias

en el diá adonde se entenderá la verdad de todas las cosas, y cuántos padres se verán ir al infierno por haver tenido hijos—y cuántas madres—y también se verán en el cielo por medio de sus hijas!" (*Fundaciones* 20.3).

20. Hernán Cortés, Fifth Letter, in *Hernán Cortés*, 350–351.

21. Weber, *Teresa of Avila and the Rhetoric of Femininity*, 133.

22. Ibid., 128.

23. Cortés, Third Letter, in *Hernán Cortés*, 167.

24. Bilinkoff, *The Avila of Saint Teresa*, 137–147; Weber, *Teresa of Avila and the Rhetoric of Femininity*, 125–126.

25. Weber, *Teresa of Avila and the Rhetoric of Femininity*, 133.

26. *TVST*, 335–338.

27. Ribera, *La Vida*, 351.

28. Teófanes Egido Martínez, "Tratamiento historiográfico de Sta. Teresa," in Teófanes Egido Martínez et al., eds., *Perfil histórico de Santa Teresa* (Madrid: Espiritualidad, 1981), 30–31.

29. José Antonio Alvarez Vázquez, "Financiación de las fundaciones teresianas," in *CIT*, 1: 280.

30. An unusual feature of the contract, a clause requiring that the purchaser pay a sales tax, forced Lorenzo into hiding to avoid arrest until he could come up with the additional money.

31. Weber, *Teresa of Avila and the Rhetoric of Femininity*, 122, 156–157.

32. Said, *Beginnings*, 48.

33. "Que cada una haga cuenta de las que vinieren, que en ella torna a comenzar esta primera regla de la Orden de la Virgen nuestra Señora, y en ninguna manera se consienta en nada relajación" (*Fundaciones* 27.11).

34. "Que parece las escogía el Señor—, cuales convenía para el cimiento de semejante edificio" (*Fundaciones* 9.1).

35. Christine de Pizan, *Book of the City of Ladies*, trans. Earl Jeffrey Richards (New York: Persea, 1982), 11.

36. Weber, *Teresa of Avila and the Rhetoric of Femininity*, 150.

37. Claire Guilhem, "L'Inquisition et la dévaluation des discours féminins," in Bartolomé Bennassar, ed., *L'Inquisition espagnole: XV–XIX siècle* (Paris: Hachette, 1979), 215.

38. Gerda Lerner, *The Creation of Feminist Consciousness* (New York: Oxford University Press, 1993), 221.

39. "Porque ella havía estado pensando en un casamiento que la traían, que le estava demasiado de bien, y diciendo entre sí: ¡Con qué poco se contenta mi padre, con que tenga un mayorazgo, y pienso yo que ha de comenzar mi linaje en mí!" (*Fundaciones* 22.5).

40. Kieran Kavanaugh and Otilio Rodríguez, trans. and eds., *The Collected Works of St. Teresa of Avila* (Washington, D.C.: Institute of Carmelite Studies, 1976–1985), 3: 437 nn. 19, 20.

41. "Yo me consolé muy mucho lo que allí estuvo, aunque con harta confusión, y me dura; porque vía que la que había hecho allí la penitencia tan áspera, era mujer como yo y más delicada, por ser quien era, y no tan gran pecadora como yo soy—que en esto de la una a la otra no se sufre

comparación—, y he recibido muy mayores mercedes de nuestro Señor de muchas maneras, y no me tener ya en el infierno, según mis grandes pecados, es grandísima. Sólo el deseo de remedarla, si pudiera, me consolava, mas no mucho; porque toda mi vida se me ha ido en deseos y las obras no las hago" *(Fundaciones* 28.35).

42. Alvarez Vázquez, "Financiación," 253.

Chapter 6

1. Ribera, *La Vida*, 528.
2. Quoted in Llamas Martínez, *Santa Teresa de Jesús*, 397.
3. Silverio de Santa Teresa, *Procesos de beatificación y canonización de Santa Teresa de Jesús*, 3 vols. (Burgos: Monte Carmelo, 1934–1935), 1: 3.
4. Ibid., 1: vi–xxviii.
5. Ibid., 3: lxx.
6. Ibid., 1: 451, 484; 2: 151; 1: 273.
7. Ibid., 2: 596.
8. Ibid., 61.
9. Ibid., 3: 308.
10. Ibid., 304.
11. Ibid., 1: 232.
12. Ibid., 3: xii.
13. Ibid., 142.
14. Ibid., 2: 232.
15. Ibid., 3: xi–xv.

Chapter 7

1. George Eliot, *Middlemarch: A Study of Provincial Life*, introd. W. J. Harvey (Harmondsworth, England: Penguin, 1965), 25.
2. Critics have made this point in various contexts: from a literary and historical perspective, Catherine Swietlicki observes that "the problem with an exclusively psychoanalytic approach to a female writer's texts is that it constructs the psyche transhistorically, without considering how the psycholinguistic aspects of her writing are socially and culturally articulated," in "Writing 'Femystic' Space: In the Margins of Saint Teresa's *Castillo interior*," *Journal of Hispanic Philology* 13 (1989 [1990]): 274; from a political perspective, Jean Franco argues that "in decontextualizing mystical experience and the Virgin Mother in order to align them with the antirational and anti-authoritarian arguments of contemporary criticism, they ignore the very aspects of mysticism that allow it to be successfully recuperated by patriarchy" *(Plotting Women: Gender and Representation in Mexico* [New York: Columbia University Press, 1989], xvi).
3. Juliet Mitchell, ed., and Jacqueline Rose, trans. and ed., *Feminine Sexuality: Jacques Lacan and the "école freudienne"* (New York: Norton, 1985), 47.
4. Ibid., 146.

5. Luce Irigaray, *This Sex Which Is Not One*, trans. Catherine Porter with Carolyn Burke (Ithaca: Cornell University Press, 1985), 91.

6. Luce Irigaray, *Speculum of the Other Woman*, trans. Gillian C. Gill (1974; Ithaca: Cornell University Press, 1985), 191. Quotations from Ruysbroeck, Meister Eckhart, and Angela of Foligno serve as epigraphs to "La mystérique," and allusions to Teresa of Avila, John of the Cross, and, most likely, many other mystics as well, appear in the text of the chapter.

7. At about this point in the chapter, having subdued the male philosopher with sarcasm, Irigaray turns her mockery against the mystic herself. I thoroughly agree with Grosz's view of the problematic nature of Irigaray's texts: "Irigaray's writings are extremely difficult to write about. They are exceptionally elusive, fluid and ambiguous—the moment one feels relatively confident about what she means in one context, one loses grasp of other related passages which seemed comprehensible when they were read" (*Sexual Subversions: Three French Feminists* [Sydney: Allen & Unwin, 1989], 101).

8. Grosz, *Sexual Subversions*, xvi.

9. Luce Irigaray, *Ethique de la différence sexuelle* (Paris: Minuit, 1984), 69.

10. Irigaray, *This Sex*, 209, 207.

11. Ibid., 213–214.

12. Grosz, *Sexual Subversions*, xvii.

13. Irigaray, *Ethique*, 19–20.

14. Irigaray, *Speculum*, 196–197.

15. Irigaray does not identify the source of this or the other epigraphs to "La mystérique," but the sentence can be found in a document known as Angela of Foligno's "last letter," which appears in the compendium of her writings entitled in Latin *Liber de Vere Fidelium Experientia*, in English *The Book of Divine Consolation of the Blessed Angela of Foligno*, trans. Mary G. Steegmann, introd. Algar Thorold (New York: Cooper Square, 1966).

16. Irigaray, *Ethique*, 73. Angela of Foligno also affirms the dualism of self and God. The sentence Irigaray takes as epigraph reads in its entirety, "Oh incomprehensible Charity; there is no greater charity than this, through which my God was made flesh in order to make me God." In separating this clause from the complete sentence, Irigaray loses the implication of difference, stated here between God's Charity and human charity and elsewhere in Angela's works between Uncreated and created.

17. Paul Julian Smith labels this passage a description of the "love of non-difference" of infantile jouissance in "Writing Women in Golden Age Spain: Saint Teresa and María de Zayas," *MLN* 102 (1987): 232–233.

18. The poem, probably written as a carol (villancico), goes by the title "Búscate en Mí": "Fuiste por amor criada / Hermosa, bella, y ansí / En mis entrañas pintada, / Si te perdieres, mi amada, / *Alma, buscarte has en Mí.* / Que Yo sí que te hallarás / En mi pecho retratada / Y tan al vivo sacada, / Que si te ves te holgarás / Viéndote tan bien pintada" (*Líricas* 4).

19. Juliana Schiesari, *The Gendering of Melancholy: Feminism, Psycho-*

analysis, and the Symbolics of Loss in Renaissance Literature (Ithaca: Cornell University Press, 1992), 88–93.

20. Julia Kristeva, *Black Sun: Depression and Melancholia*, trans. Leon S. Roudiez (1987; New York: Columbia University Press, 1989), 14. Kristeva generally uses the term "melancholia" for the "melancholy/depressive composite."

21. Julia Kristeva, *Revolution in Poetic Language*, trans. Margaret Waller, introd. Leon S. Roudiez (1974; New York: Columbia University Press, 1984), 25. Kristeva explains her concept of the *chora* in *In the Beginning Was Love: Psychoanalysis and Faith*: "At the very beginning of philosophy, before thought was constricted by the notion that language must reflect ideas, Plato, recalling the work of the atomists, spoke in the *Timaeus* of the *chora*, an ancient, mobile, unstable receptable, prior to the One, to the father, and even to the syllable, metaphorically suggesting something nourishing and maternal" (trans. Arthur Goldhammer [1985; New York: Columbia University Press, 1987], 5).

22. Cynthia Chase, "Desire and Identification in Lacan and Kristeva," in Richard Feldstein and Judith Roof, eds., *Feminism and Psychoanalysis* (Ithaca: Cornell University Press, 1989), 81.

23. Kristeva, *Black Sun*, 40.

24. Ibid., 54.

25. Ibid., 28–29.

26. Sebastián Cobarruvias Horozco, comp., *Tesoro de la lengua castellana o española* (1611; Madrid: Turner, 1979), s.v. "tristeza."

27. Kristeva, *Black Sun*, 61.

28. Ibid., 78.

29. Anna Burr Jameson, *Legends of the Monastic Orders as Represented in the Fine Arts*, 4th ed. (London: Longmans, Green, 1867), 415.

30. Eliot, *Middlemarch*, 896.

31. Cited in Aldous Huxley, *The Perennial Philosophy* (1944; New York: Harper Colophon, 1970), 52.

BIBLIOGRAPHY

Primary Works

Spanish editions

Efrén de la Madre de Dios and Otger Steggink, eds. *Santa Teresa de Jesús: Obras completas*. Madrid: BAC, 1954.

Barrientos, Alberto et al., eds. *Santa Teresa de Jesús: Obras completas*. Madrid: Espiritualidad, 1984.

English translations

Kavanaugh, Kieran, and Otilio Rodríguez, trans. and eds. *The Collected Works of St. Teresa of Avila*. 3 vols. Washington, D.C.: Institute of Carmelite Studies, 1976–1985.

Peers, E. Allison, trans. and ed. *The Complete Works of Teresa of Avila*. 3 vols. London: Sheed and Ward, 1944–1946.

Secondary Works

Alberto de la Virgen del Carmen. "Presencia de San Agustín en Sta. Teresa y San Juan de la Cruz." *Revista de espiritualidad* 14 (1955): 170–184.

Alcalá, Angel. "Inquisitorial Control of Humanists and Writers." In Angel Alcalá, ed. and trans., *The Spanish Inquisition and the Inquisitorial Mind*, 321–360.

Alcalá, Angel, ed. and trans. *The Spanish Inquisition and the Inquisitorial Mind*. Atlantic Studies on Society in Change, no. 49. Boulder: Social Science Monographs; Highland Lakes, N.J.: Atlantic Research and Publications, 1987.

Altman, Charles F. "Two Types of Opposition and the Structure of Latin Saints' Lives." *Medievalia et Humanistica* 6 (1975): 1–11.

Alvarez Vázquez, José Antonio. "Financiación de las fundaciones teresianas." In Teófanes Egido Martínez et al., eds., *CIT*, 1: 249–285.

Andrés Martín, Melquíades. "Common Denominator of Alumbrados, Erasmians, 'Lutherans,' and Mystics: The Risk of a More 'Intimate' Spirituality." In Angel Alcalá, ed. and trans., *The Spanish Inquisition and the Inquisitorial Mind*, 457–492.

———. *La teología española en el siglo XVI.* 2 vols. Madrid: BAC, 1977.

Angela of Foligno. *The Book of Divine Consolation of the Blessed Angela of Foligno.* Trans. Mary G. Steegmann, introd. Algar Thorold. New York: Cooper Square, 1966.

Aquinas, Thomas. *Summa Theologiae.* 3 vols. Trans. Fathers of the English Dominican Province. New York: Benziger, 1947.

Aspe, María-Paz. "Las relaciones espirituales de Teresa de Jesús." In Manuel Criado de Val, ed., *Santa Teresa y la literatura mística hispánica*, 291–295.

Astell, Ann W. *The Song of Songs in the Middle Ages.* Ithaca: Cornell University Press, 1990.

Auerbach, Erich. "Figura." In *Scenes from the Drama of European Literature*, 11–76. Trans. Ralph Manheim. 1944; New York: Meridian, 1957.

———. *Mimesis.* Trans. Willard R. Trask. 1946; Princeton: Princeton University Press, 1953.

Augustine of Hippo. *Confessions.* Trans. R. S. Pine-Coffin. Harmondsworth, England: Penguin, 1961.

———. *Exposition on the Book of Psalms.* Trans. H. M. Wilkins. Oxford: John Henry Parker, 1853.

Austin, J. L. *Philosophical Papers.* Ed. J. O. Urmson and G. J. Warnock. Oxford: Clarendon, 1961.

L'Autobiographie en Espagne. Actes du IIe Colloque International de la Baume-les-Aix, 23–25 May 1981. Aix-en-Provence: Université de Provence, 1982.

Bakhtin, Mikhail M. *The Dialogic Imagination: Four Essays.* Ed. Michael Holquist, trans. Caryl Emerson and Michael Holquist. Austin: University of Texas Press, 1981.

———. *Problems of Dostoevsky's Poetics.* Ed. and trans. Caryl Emerson, introd. Wayne C. Booth. Theory and History of Literature, no. 8. Minneapolis: University of Minnesota Press, 1984.

———. "The Problem of Speech Genres." In *Speech Genres and Other Late Essays*, trans. Vern W. McGee, ed. Caryl Emerson and Michael Holquist, 60–102. Austin: University of Texas Press, 1986.

Balibar, Etienne. "The Nation Form: History and Ideology." Trans. Chris Turner. In Etienne Balibar and Immanuel Wallerstein, eds., *Race, Nation, Class: Ambiguous Identities*, 86–106. 1988; London: Verso, 1991.

Bataillon, Marcel. *Erasmo y España: Estudios sobre la historia espiritual del siglo XVI.* Trans. Antonio Alatorre. 2 vols. 1937; Mexico City: Fondo de Cultura Económica, 1950.

Bauer, Dale M., and S. Jaret McKinstry, eds. *Feminism, Bakhtin, and the Dialogic*. Albany: State University of New York Press, 1991.

Bell, Robert. "Metamorphoses of Spiritual Autobiography." *ELH* 44 (1977): 108–126.

Bennassar, Bartolomé, ed. *L'Inquisition espagnole: XV–XIX siècle*. Paris: Hachette, 1979.

Bernabéu Barrachina, Felicidad. "Aspectos vulgares del estilo teresiano y sus posibles razones." *Revista de espiritualidad* 22 (1963): 359–375.

Bernard of Clairvaux. *Bernard of Clairvaux: On the Song of Songs*. Trans. Kilian Walsh and Irene Edmunds, introd. M. Corneille Halflants. 4 vols. Spencer, Mass.: Cistercian, 1971–1980.

Bertini, Giovanni M. "Interpretación de *Conceptos del amor de Dios* de Teresa de Jesús." In Teófanes Egido Martínez et al., eds., *CIT*, 2: 545–556.

Bilinkoff, Jodi. *The Avila of Saint Teresa: Religious Reform in a Sixteenth-Century City*. Ithaca: Cornell University Press, 1989.

Boureau, Alain. "Les structures narratives de *La Legenda aurea*: De la variation au grand chant sacré." In *"Legenda aurea": Sept siècles de diffusion*, Actes du colloque international sur la *Legenda aurea*: Texte latin et branches vernaculaires. Université de Québec, Montréal, 11–12 May 1983, 57–76. Montreal: Bellarmin, 1986.

Breuer, Josef, and Sigmund Freud. *Studies on Hysteria*. Trans. and ed. James Strachey with Anna Freud, Alix Strachey, and Alan Tyson. 1955; New York: Basic Books, 1957.

Bruss, Elizabeth W. *Autobiographical Acts: The Changing Situation of a Literary Genre*. Baltimore: Johns Hopkins University Press, 1976.

Bubacz, Bruce. *St. Augustine's Theory of Knowledge*. Texts and Studies in Religion, no. 11. New York: Edward Mellen, 1981.

Bynum, Caroline Walker. *Holy Feast and Holy Fast: The Religious Significance of Food to Medieval Women*. Berkeley, Los Angeles, and London: University of California Press, 1987.

———. *Jesus as Mother: Studies in the Spirituality of the High Middle Ages*. Berkeley, Los Angeles, and London: University of California Press, 1982.

Carreño, Antonio. "Las paradojas del 'yo' autobiográfico." In Manuel Criado de Val, ed., *Santa Teresa y la literatura mística hispánica*, 255–264.

Castro, Américo. *Teresa la santa y otros ensayos*. Madrid: Alianza, 1982.

Certeau, Michel de. *The Mystic Fable: The Sixteenth and Seventeenth Centuries*. Trans. Michael B. Smith. 1982; Chicago: University of Chicago Press, 1992.

———. "Mystic Speech." In *Heterologies: Discourse on the Other*, trans. Brian Massumi, introd. Wlad Godzich, 80–100. Theory and History of Literature, vol. 17. Minneapolis: University of Minnesota Press, 1986.

Charity, Alan Clifford. *Events and Their Afterlife: The Dialectics of Christian Typology in the Bible and Dante*. Cambridge: Cambridge University Press, 1966.

Chase, Cynthia. "Desire and Identification in Lacan and Kristeva." In

Richard Feldstein and Judith Roof, eds., *Feminism and Psychoanalysis*, 80–90. Ithaca: Cornell University Press, 1989.

Chorpenning, Joseph. "The Literary and Theological Method of *The Interior Castle*." *Journal of Hispanic Philology* 3 (1979): 121–133.

———. "St. Teresa of Avila as Allegorist: Chapters 11–22 of the *Libro de la vida*." *Studia Mystica* 9 (1986): 3–22.

Concha, Víctor García de la. *El arte literario de Santa Teresa.* Barcelona: Ariel, 1978.

Contreras, Jaime. "The Impact of Protestantism in Spain: 1520–1600." In Stephen Haliczer, ed. and trans., *Inquisition and Society in Early Modern Europe*, 47–63.

Cortés, Hernán. *Hernán Cortés: Letters from Mexico.* Ed. and trans. Anthony Pagden, introd. J. H. Elliott. New Haven: Yale University Press, 1986.

Cortés, Narciso Alonso. "Pleitos de los Cepeda." *Boletín de la Real Academia Española* 25 (1964): 85–110.

Courcelle, Pierre. *Les Confessions de Saint Augustin dans la tradition littéraire.* Paris: Etudes Augustiniennes, 1963.

Cobarruvias Horozco, Sebastián de, comp. *Tesoro de la lengua castellana o española.* 1611; Madrid: Turner, 1979.

Criado de Val, Manuel, *Santa Teresa y la literatura mística hispánica.* Actas del I congreso internacional sobre Santa Teresa y la mística hispánica. Madrid: EDI, 1984.

Curtius, Ernst Robert. *European Literature and the Latin Middle Ages.* Trans. Willard R. Trask. 1953; New York: Harper and Row, 1963.

Dedieu, Jean Pierre. "The Archives of the Holy Office of Toledo as a Source of Historical Anthropology." Trans. E. W. Monter. In Gustav Henningsen and John Tedeschi with Charles Amiel, eds., *The Inquisition in Early Modern Europe: Studies on Sources and Methods*, 175–185.

de Lauretis, Teresa. *Technologies of Gender: Essays on Theory, Film, and Fiction.* Bloomington: Indiana University Press, 1987.

Dicken, E. W. Trueman. *The Crucible of Love: A Study of the Mysticism of St. Teresa of Avila and St. John of the Cross.* New York: Sheed and Ward, 1963.

Dobhan, Ulrich. "Teresa de Jesús y la emancipación de la mujer." In Teófanes Egido Martínez et al., eds., *CIT*, 1: 121–136.

Donovan, Josephine. "Style and Power." In Dale M. Bauer and S. Jaret McKinstry, eds., *Feminism, Bakhtin, and the Dialogic*, 85–94.

Durán, Manuel. *Luis de León.* New York: Twayne, 1971.

Durling, Robert M. "*The Ascent of Mount Ventoux* and the Crisis of Allegory." *Italian Quarterly* 18 (1974): 7–28.

Efrén de la Madre de Dios, and Otger Steggink. *Tiempo y vida de Santa Teresa.* 2d ed. Madrid: BAC, 1977.

Egido Martínez, Teófanes. "Presencia de la religiosidad popular en Santa Teresa." In Teófanes Egido Martínez et al., eds., *CIT*, 1: 197–227.

———. "Tratamiento historiográfico de Sta. Teresa." In Teófanes Egido

Martínez et al., eds., *Perfil histórico de Santa Teresa*, 13–31. Madrid: Espiritualidad, 1981.

———. "Santa Teresa y su circunstancia." In Teófanes Egido Martínez, ed., *Teresa de Jesús: Mujer, cristiana, maestra*, 9–27. Madrid: Espiritualidad, 1982.

Egido Martínez, Teófanes, Victor García de la Concha, and Olegario González de Cardenal, eds., *CIT*, 4–7 octubre 1982. 2 vols. Salamanca: Universidad de Salamanca, 1983.

Eliot, George. *Middlemarch: A Study of Provincial Life*. Introd. W. J. Harvey. Harmondsworth, England: Penguin, 1965.

Elliott, Alison Goddard. *Roads to Paradise: Reading the Lives of the Early Saints*. Hanover: University Press of New England, 1987.

Etchegoyen, Gaston. *L'amour divin: Essai sur les sources de Sainte Thérèse*. Paris: Féret, 1923.

Eymerich, Nicolau, and Francisco Peña. *Le manuel des inquisiteurs [Directorium Inquisitorum]*. Trans. and introd. Louis Sala-Molins. Paris: Mouton, 1973.

Ferrari, Leo Charles. "The Theme of the Prodigal Son in Augustine's *Confessions*." *Recherches Augustiniennes* 12 (1977): 105–118.

Foucault, Michel. *Discipline and Punish: The Birth of the Prison*. Trans. Alan Sheridan. 1975; New York: Random House, Vintage, 1979.

Franco, Jean. *Plotting Women: Gender and Representation in Mexico*. New York: Columbia University Press, 1989.

Freccero, John. *Dante: The Poetics of Conversion*. Ed. and introd. Rachel Jacoff. Cambridge: Harvard University Press, 1986.

———. "Autobiography and Narrative." In Thomas C. Heller, Morton Sosna, and David E. Wellbery, eds., *Reconstructing Individualism: Autonomy, Individuality, and the Self in Western Thought*, 16–29. Stanford: Stanford University Press, 1986.

Frye, Northrop. *The Great Code: The Bible and Literature*. New York: Harcourt Brace Jovanovich, 1982.

García Cárcel, Ricardo. *Herejía y sociedad en el siglo XVI: La Inquisición en Valencia, 1530–1609*. 2d ed. 1976; Barcelona: Península, 1980.

Gilson, Etienne. *Reason and Revelation in the Middle Ages*. New York: Scribner's, 1938.

Gómez-Moriana, Antonio. "Problemática de la confesión autobiográfica destinada al tribunal inquisitorial." In *L'Autobiographie en Espagne*, 69–94.

Greenspan, Kate. "The Autohagiographical Tradition in Medieval Women's Devotional Writing." *a/b:Auto/Biography* 6, no. 2 (Fall 1991): 157–168.

Grosz, Elizabeth. *Sexual Subversions: Three French Feminists*. Sydney: Allen & Unwin, 1989.

Guilhem, Claire. "L'Inquisition et la dévaluation des discours féminins." In Bartolomé Bennassar, ed., *L'Inquisition espagnole: XV–XIX siècle*, 197–240. Paris: Hachette, 1979.

Gutiérrez Nieto, Juan Ignacio. "El proceso de encastamiento social de la Castilla del siglo XVI: La respuesta conversa." In Teófanes Egido Martínez et al., eds. CIT, 1: 103–120.

Haliczer, Stephen, ed. and trans. Inquisition and Society in Early Modern Europe. Totowa: Barnes and Noble, 1987.

Haliczer, Stephen. "The First Holocaust: The Inquisition and the Converted Jews of Spain and Portugal." In Stephen Haliczer, ed. and trans., Inquisition and Society in Early Modern Europe, 7–18.

Hatzfeld, Helmut A. Santa Teresa de Avila. New York: Twayne, 1969.

Hawkes, Terence. Metaphor. London: Methuen, 1972.

Hawkins, Anne Hunsaker. Archetypes of Conversion: The Autobiographies of Augustine, Bunyan, and Merton. Lewisburg, Pa.: Bucknell University Press, 1985.

Henningsen, Gustav, and John Tedeschi with Charles Amiel, eds. The Inquisition in Early Modern Europe: Studies on Sources and Methods. Dekalb: Northern Illinois University Press, 1986.

Herrero, Javier. "The Knight and the Mystical Castle." Studies in Formative Spirituality 4 (1983): 393–407.

Honeyman, A. M. "Matthew V.18 and the Validity of the Law." New Testament Studies 1 (1954–1955): 142.

Hoornaert, Rodolphe. Saint Térèse écrivain: Son milieu, ses facultés, son oeuvre. Paris: Desclée de Brouwer, 1922.

Howe, Elizabeth Theresa. "The Mystical Kiss and the Canticle of Canticles: Three Interpretations." American Benedictine Review 33 (1982): 302–311.

Huxley, Aldous. The Perennial Philosophy. 1944; New York: Harper Colophon, 1970.

Irigaray, Luce. Ethique de la différence sexuelle. Paris: Minuit, 1984.

———. Speculum of the Other Woman. Trans. Gillian C. Gill. 1974; Ithaca: Cornell University Press, 1985.

———. This Sex Which Is Not One. Trans. Catherine Porter with Carolyn Burke. 1977; Ithaca: Cornell University Press, 1985.

Jacobus de Voragine. The Golden Legend. Trans. Granger Ryan and Helmut Ripperger. 2 vols. London: Longmans, Green, 1941.

James, William. The Varieties of Religious Experience: A Study in Human Nature. Introd. Reinhold Niebuhr. 1902; New York: Macmillan, Collier, 1961.

Jameson, Anna Burr. Legends of the Monastic Orders as Represented in the Fine Arts. 4th ed. London: Longmans, Green, 1867.

Jara, René, and Nicholas Spadaccini, eds. 1492–1992: Re/Discovering Colonial Writing. Hispanic Issues, no. 4. Minneapolis: Prisma, 1989.

John of the Cross. The Collected Works of St. John of the Cross. Trans. Kieran Kavanaugh and Otilio Rodríguez, introd. Kieran Kavanaugh. Washington, D.C.: Institute of Carmelite Studies, 1979.

Juan de Avila. Obras completas. Ed. Luis Sala Balust. 2 vols. Madrid: Editorial Católica, 1952.

Kamen, Henry. *Inquisition and Society in Spain in the Sixteenth and Seventeenth Centuries.* London: Weidenfeld and Nicolson, 1985.

Kristeva, Julia. *Black Sun: Depression and Melancholia.* Trans. Leon S. Roudiez. 1987; New York: Columbia University Press, 1989.

———. *In the Beginning Was Love: Psychoanalysis and Faith.* Trans. Arthur Goldhammer. 1985; New York: Columbia University Press, 1987.

———. *Revolution in Poetic Language.* Trans. Margaret Waller, introd. Leon S. Roudiez. 1974; New York: Columbia University Press, 1984.

Laguardia, Gari. "Santa Teresa and the Problem of Desire." *Hispania* 63 (Sept. 1980): 523–531.

Laredo, Bernardino de. *The Ascent of Mount Sion, being the third book of the treatise of that name.* Trans. and introd. E. Allison Peers. London: Faber and Faber, 1950.

Lázaro Carreter, Fernando. "Santa Teresa de Jesús, escritora (El 'Libro de la vida')." In Teófanes Egido Martínez et al., eds., *CIT*, 1: 11–27.

Lea, Henry Charles. *A History of the Inquisition of Spain.* 4 vols. 1906–1907; New York: American Scholar, 1966.

León, Luis de. *Obras completas.* Ed. Félix García. 2 vols. Madrid: BAC, 1944.

Lerner, Gerda. *The Creation of Feminist Consciousness: From the Middle Ages to 1870.* New York: Oxford University Press, 1993.

Lincoln, Victoria. *Teresa, A Woman: A Biography of Teresa of Avila.* Ed. Elias Rivers and Antonio T. de Nicolás. New York: Paragon, 1984.

Lubac, Henri de, S.J. *Exégèse médiévale: Les quatre sens de l'écriture.* 4 vols. in 3. Paris: Aubier, 1959.

———. *The Sources of Revelation.* Trans. Luke O'Neill. New York: Herder and Herder, 1968.

Llamas Martínez, Enrique. *Santa Teresa de Jesús y la Inquisición española.* Madrid: CSIC, 1972.

———. "Teresa de Jesús y los alumbrados: Hacia una revisión del 'alumbradismo' español del siglo XVI." In Teófanes Egido Martínez et al., eds. *CIT*, 1: 137–167.

Llorca, Bernardino. *La Inquisición española y los alumbrados, 1509–1667.* Salamanca: Universidad Pontífica, 1980.

Malvern, Marjorie M. *Venus in Sackcloth: The Magdalen's Origins and Metamorphoses.* Carbondale: Southern Illinois University Press, 1975.

Mancini, Guido. "Tradición y originalidad en el lenguaje coloquial teresiano." In Teófanes Egido Martínez et al., eds., *CIT*, 2: 479–493.

Mandel, Adrienne Schizzano. "Le procès Inquisitorial comme acte autobiographique: Le cas de Sor María de San Jerónimo." In *L'Autobiographie dans le monde hispanique,* 155–175.

Mandel, Barrett J. "Full of Life Now." In James Olney, ed., *Autobiography: Essays Theoretical and Critical,* 49–72.

Márquez, Antonio. *Literatura e Inquisición en España (1478–1834).* Madrid: Taurus, 1980.

———. *Los alumbrados: Orígenes y filosofía, 1525–1559.* Madrid: Taurus, 1972.

Márquez Villanueva, Francisco. "Santa Teresa y el linaje." In *Espirituali-dad y literatura en el siglo XVI*, 141–205. Madrid: Alfaguara, 1968.
———. "El símil del castillo interior: Sentido y génesis." In Teófanes Egido Martínez et al., eds., *CIT*, 2: 495–522.
Martín Velasco, Juan de Dios. "'Búscame en ti-búscate in mi': La corre-lación entre el descubrimiento del hombre y el descubrimiento de Dios en Santa Teresa." In Teófanes Egido Martínez et al., eds., *CIT*, 2: 809–834.
Martínez Millán, José. "Aportaciones a la formación del estado moderno y a la política española a través de la censura inquisitorial durante el período 1480–1559." In Joaquín Pérez Villanueva, ed., *La Inquisición es-pañola: Nueva visión, nuevos horizontes*, 537–578.
Mazzeo, Joseph A. "Allegorical Interpretation and History." *Comparative Literature* 30 (Winter 1978): 1–21.
Menéndez Pidal, Ramón. "El estilo de Santa Teresa." In *La lengua de Cristóbal Colón y otros estudios sobre el siglo XVI*, 119–142. 4th ed. Madrid: Espasa Calpe, 1958.
Mirollo, James V. "The Lives of Saints Teresa of Avila and Benvenuto of Florence." *Texas Studies in Literature and Language* 29 (1987): 54–73.
Mitchell, Juliet, and Jacqueline Rose, eds. *Feminine Sexuality: Jacques Lacan and the "école freudienne."* Trans. Jacqueline Rose. New York: Norton, 1982.
Morson, Gary Saul, and Caryl Emerson. *Mikhail Bakhtin: Creation of a Prosaics*. Stanford: Stanford University Press, 1990.
Nicolás, Antonio T. de. *Powers of Imagining: Ignatius de Loyola*. Albany: State University of New York Press, 1986.
Nock, Arthur Darby. *Conversion: The Old and the New Religion from Alexander the Great to Augustine of Hippo*. London: Oxford University Press, 1933.
Olney, James, ed. *Autobiography: Essays Theoretical and Critical*. Prince-ton: Princeton University Press, 1980.
O'Malley, I[da] B[eatrice]. *Florence Nightingale, 1820–1856: A Study of Her Life Down to the End of the Crimean War*. London: Thornton Butter-worth, 1931.
O'Meara, J. J. *The Young Augustine: The Growth of St. Augustine's Mind up to His Conversion*. London: Longmans, 1954.
Ong, Walter J., S.J. *Interfaces of the Word: Studies in the Evolution of Consciousness and Culture*. Ithaca: Cornell University Press, 1977.
Origen. *The Song of Songs: Commentary and Homilies*. Trans. R. P. Law-son. Ancient Christian Writers Series, no. 26. London: Longmans, 1957.
Orozco Díaz, Emilio. *Expresión, comunicación y estilo en la obra de Santa Teresa*. Granada: Bolsillo, 1984.
Ostriker, Alicia. "The Thieves of Language: Women Poets and Revisionary Mythmaking." In Elaine Showalter, ed., *The New Feminist Criticism: Essays on Women, Literature, and Theory*, 314–338. New York: Pan-theon, 1985.
Osuna, Francisco de. *Tercer abecedario espiritual*. Ed. Melquíades Andrés Martín. Madrid: BAC, 1972.

————. *The Third Spiritual Alphabet.* Trans. A Benedictine of Stanbrook. Westminster, Md.: Newman, 1948.

Pagden, Anthony, ed. and trans. *Hernán Cortés: Letters from Mexico.* New Haven: Yale University Press, 1986.

Pascal, Roy. *Design and Truth in Autobiography.* Cambridge: Harvard University Press, 1960.

Peers, E. Allison. "Saint Teresa's Style: A Tentative Appraisal." In *Saint Teresa of Jesus and Other Essays and Addresses,* 81–135. London: Faber and Faber, 1953.

Pérez Villanueva, Joaquín, ed. *La Inquisición española: Nueva visión, nuevos horizontes.* Papers presented at International Symposium on the Spanish Inquisition, Cuenca, 1978. Madrid: Siglo XXI, 1980.

Perry, Mary Elizabeth. *Gender and Disorder in Early Modern Seville.* Princeton: Princeton University Press, 1990.

Peters, Edward. *Inquisition.* 1988; Berkeley, Los Angeles, and London: University of California Press, 1989.

Peterson, Linda H. *Victorian Autobiography: The Tradition of Self-Interpretation.* New Haven: Yale University Press, 1986.

Pietro della Madre di Dio. "La sacra scrittura nelle opere di S. Teresa." *Rivista di vita spirituale* 18 (1964): 41–102.

Pinto Crespo, Virgilio. *Inquisición y control ideológico en la España del siglo XVI.* Introd. Joaquín Pérez Villanueva. Madrid: Taurus, 1983.

————. "Institucionalización inquisitorial y censura de libros." In Joaquín Pérez Villanueva and Bartolomé Escandell Bonet, eds., *La Inquisición española: Nueva visión, nuevos horizontes,* 513–536.

————. "Thought Control in Spain." In Stephen Haliczer, ed. and trans., *Inquisition and Society in Early Modern Europe,* 171–188. Totowa: Barnes and Noble, 1987.

Pizan, Christine de. *The Book of the City of Ladies.* Trans. Earl Jeffrey Richards. New York: Persea, 1982.

Pope, Marvin H., ed. *Song of Songs: A New Translation with Introduction and Commentary.* Anchor Bible. London: Sheed and Ward, 1946.

Pope, Randolph D. *La autobiografía española hasta Torres Villarroel.* Bern: Herbert Lang, 1974.

Porqueras Mayo, Alberto. *El prólogo en el renacimiento español.* Madrid: CSIC, 1965.

Preus, James Samuel. *From Shadow to Promise: Old Testament Interpretation from Augustine to the Young Luther.* Cambridge: Harvard University Press, 1969.

Quilligan, Maureen. *The Allegory of Female Authority: Christine de Pizan's "Cité des Dames."* Ithaca: Cornell University Press, 1991.

Rees, B. R. "The Conversion of Saint Augustine." *Trivium* 14 (1979): 1–17.

Renza, Louis A. "A Veto of the Imagination: A Theory of Autobiography." In James Olney, ed., *Autobiography: Essays Theoretical and Critical,* 268–295.

Ribera, Francisco de. *La Vida de la Madre Teresa de Jesús, fundadora de las Descalças y Descalços.* Ed. and introd. Jaime Pons. 1590; Barcelona: Gustavo Gili, 1908.

Ricard, Robert. "Notas y materiales para el estudio del 'socratismo cristiano' en Santa Teresa y en los espirituales españoles." In *Estudios de literatura religiosa española*, trans. Manuel Muñoz Cortés, 22–126. Madrid: Editorial Gredos, 1964.

Rico Verdú, José. *La retórica española de los siglos XVI y XVII*. Madrid: CSIC, 1973.

Rivers, Elías. "The Vernacular Mind of St. Teresa." In John Sullivan, ed., *Carmelite Studies: Centenary of St. Teresa*, 113–129. Washington, D.C.: Institute of Carmelite Studies, 1984.

Ros, Fidèle de. *Le Frère Bernardin de Laredo*. Paris: Librairie Philosophique, 1948.

Rothfield, Lawrence. "Autobiography and Perspective in *The Confessions* of St. Augustine." *Comparative Literature* 33 (Summer 1981): 209–223.

Rougemont, Denis de. *Love in the Western World*. Trans. Montgomery Belgion. 1940; New York: Schocken, 1983.

Said, Edward. *Beginnings: Intention and Method*. Baltimore: Johns Hopkins University Press, 1975.

Sala-Molins, Louis, trans. and ed. *Le Dictionnaire des inquisiteurs: Valence 1494* [*Repertorium inquisitorum haereticae pravitatis*]. Paris: Editions Galilée, 1981.

Sánchez-Barba, Mario Hernández. Introduction to *Hernán Cortés: Cartas y documentos*, ed. Mario Hernández Sánchez-Barba, ix–xxiii. Mexico: Porrúa, 1963.

Sangnieux, Joel. "Santa Teresa y los libros." In Teófanes Egido Martínez et al., eds., *CIT*, 2: 747–764.

Saxer, Victor. *Le Culte de Marie Madeleine en Occident des origines à la fin du moyen age*. Paris: Clavreuil, 1959.

Selke, Angela. "El iluminismo de los conversos y la Inquisición: Cristianismo interior de los alumbrados, resentimiento y sublimación." In Joaquín Pérez Villanueva and Bartolomé Escandell Bonet, eds., *La Inquisición española: Nueva visión, nuevos horizontes*, 617–636.

Senabre, Ricardo. "Sobre el género literario del *Libro de la vida*." In Teófanes Egido Martínez et al., eds., *CIT*, 2: 765–776.

Schiesari, Juliana. *The Gendering of Melancholia: Feminism, Psychoanalysis, and the Symbolics of Loss in Renaissance Literature*. Ithaca: Cornell University Press, 1992.

Shepard, Sanford. *Lost Lexicon: Secret Meanings in the Vocabulary of Spanish Literature During the Inquisition*. Miami: Ediciones Universal, 1982.

Shuger, Debora K. *Sacred Rhetoric: The Christian Grand Style in the English Renaissance*. Princeton: Princeton University Press, 1988.

Silverio de Santa Teresa. *Procesos de beatificación y canonización de Santa Teresa de Jesús*. 3 vols. Burgos: Monte Carmelo, 1934–1935.

Slade, Carole. "Alterity in Union: The Mystical Experience of Angela of Foligno and Margery Kempe." *Religion and Literature* 23 (Autumn 1991): 109–126.

———. "Saint Teresa's *Meditaciones sobre los Cantares*: The Hermeneutics of Humility and Enjoyment." *Religion and Literature* 18 (Spring 1986): 27–44.

Smith, Hilary Dansey. *Preaching in the Spanish Golden Age: A Study of Some Preachers of the Reign of Philip III.* Oxford: Oxford University Press, 1978.

Smith, Paul Julian. "Writing Women in Golden Age Spain: Saint Teresa and María de Zayas," *MLN* 102 (1978): 220–240.

Starobinski, Jean. "The Style of Autobiography." Trans. Seymour Chatman. In James Olney, ed., *Autobiography: Essays Theoretical and Critical*, 72–83. Originally published in Seymour Chatman, ed., *Literary Style: A Symposium.* Oxford: Oxford University Press, 1971.

Swietlicki, Catherine. "The Problematic Iconography of Teresa of Avila's *Interior Castle.*" *Studia Mystica* 11 (1988): 37–47.

———. *Spanish Christian Cabala: The Works of Luis de León, Santa Teresa de Jesús, and San Juan de la Cruz.* Columbia: University of Missouri Press, 1986.

———. "Writing 'Femystic' Space: In the Margins of Saint Teresa's *Castillo interior.*" *Journal of Hispanic Philology* 13 (1989 [1990]): 273–293.

Tambling, Jeremy. *Confession: Sexuality, Sin, and the Subject.* New York: St. Martin's Press, 1990.

Tentler, Thomas N. *Sin and Confession on the Eve of the Reformation.* Princeton: Princeton University Press, 1977.

Tillich, Paul. *Systematic Theology.* 3 vols. Chicago: University of Chicago Press, 1951.

Tylus, Jane. *Writing and Vulnerability in the Late Renaissance.* Stanford: Stanford University Press, 1993.

Villacèque, Sol. "Rhetorique et pragmatique: La transformation du code dans le *Libro de la vida* de Thérèse d'Avila." *Imprévue* 2 (1985): 7–27.

Villegas, Alfonso de. *Flos Sanctorum* [The Lives of the Saints]. Trans. W. and E. K[insman] B[rothers] from Italian. 4th ed. Rouen: J. Cousturier, 1636. University Microfilms HN434407.

Vilnet, Jean. *Bible et mystique chez Saint Jean de la Croix.* Belgium: Desclée de Brouwer, 1949.

Walzer, Michael. *Exodus and Revolution.* New York: Basic Books, 1985.

Warner, Marina. *Alone of All Her Sex: The Myth and the Cult of the Virgin Mary.* 1976; New York: Random House, Vintage, 1983.

Weber, Alison. *Teresa of Avila and the Rhetoric of Femininity.* Princeton: Princeton University Press, 1990.

Weintraub, Karl Joachim. *The Value of the Individual: Self and Circumstance in Autobiography.* Chicago: University of Chicago Press, 1978.

Wilson, E. M. "Spanish Versions." In S. L. Greenslade, ed., *The West from the Reformation to the Present Day*, 125–129. Vol. 3 of *The Cambridge History of the Bible: The West from the Reformation to the Present Day.* Cambridge: Cambridge University Press, 1963.

Yepes, Diego de. *Vida de Santa Teresa de Jesús.* Tesoro de escritores místicos españoles, vol. 1. Paris: Garnier, 1847.

INDEX

Designer: U.C. Press Staff
Compositor: Prestige Typography
Text: 10.5/12.5 Trump Mediaeval
Display: Trump Mediaeval
Printer: Braun-Brumfield, Inc.
Binder: Braun-Brumfield, Inc.